Chasing Bas

D0390271

ALSO BY DOROTHY JANE MILLS

*A Woman's Work: Writing Baseball History
with Harold Seymour* (McFarland, 2004)

Chasing Baseball

*Our Obsession with
Its History, Numbers,
People and Places*

DOROTHY SEYMOUR MILLS

Foreword by
Richard C. Crepeau

MECHANICS' INSTITUTE LIBRARY
57 Post Street
San Francisco, CA 94104
(415) 393-0101

McFarland & Company, Inc., Publishers
Jefferson, North Carolina, and London

LIBRARY OF CONGRESS CATALOGUING-IN-PUBLICATION DATA

Mills, Dorothy Seymour.
    Chasing baseball : our obsession with its history, numbers, people
and places / Dorothy Seymour Mills ; foreword by Richard C. Crepeau.
        p.   cm.
    Includes bibliographical references and index.

    ISBN 978-0-7864-4289-8
    softcover : 50# alkaline paper ∞

    1. Baseball — United States.   2. Baseball — Social aspects —
United States.   I. Title.
    GV863.A1M54   2010
    796.3570973 — dc22   2009049607

British Library cataloguing data are available

©2010 Dorothy Seymour Mills. All rights reserved

*No part of this book may be reproduced or transmitted in any form
or by any means, electronic or mechanical, including photocopying
or recording, or by any information storage and retrieval system,
without permission in writing from the publisher.*

On the cover: The Canal Fulton Mules, a vintage team;
background ©2010 Shutterstock

Manufactured in the United States of America

McFarland & Company, Inc., Publishers
Box 611, Jefferson, North Carolina 28640
www.mcfarlandpub.com

96,357
1657

FEB 2 5 2010

Contents

Foreword

by Richard C. Crepeau

Dorothy Seymour Mills has spent a good portion of her life researching, thinking about, and writing about baseball. It is clear that she has an obsession with "Our National Game" and is deeply immersed in its history as well as all of its current manifestations. This is her fifth book, not to mention countless articles, on the subject of baseball and baseball history, and this volume represents the accumulation of both her expansive knowledge and her deep interest in the game.

Unlike many historians who have confined themselves to the study of professional and organized baseball, Dorothy Mills has cast her vision across a wide expanse of the diamondscape. This difference became evident with the publication of *Baseball: The People's Game,* for which she was the principal researcher and author, and it is reaffirmed here.

Historians seem genetically predisposed to quote the great American historian Jacques Barzun's famous line from *God's Country and Mine*: "Whoever wants to know the heart and mind of America had better learn baseball, the rules and realities of the game...." What generally remains unquoted is the conclusion of that line: "and do it by watching first some high school or small-town teams."

What is clear to anyone familiar with Ms. Mills's work is that she has studied high school and small-town teams, women's teams, youth league teams, senior league teams, and baseball at all levels at which it is played, irrespective of national boundaries. Her passion for the game emanates not from an attachment to a favorite team but instead from an interest in all levels of the game and the great variety of people who play it.

It might be said that anyone who has so much experience with a myriad of types and kinds of baseball, anyone who has spent so much time and intellectual energy on baseball, should be under an obligation to share her accumulated knowledge, passion, and wisdom with those of us who merely love the game. Fortunately for us, Dorothy Seymour Mills has chosen to share her lifetime obsession with baseball and the accumulated knowledge of that lifetime of experience with us in *Chasing Baseball: Our Obsession with Its History, Numbers, People and Places.*

What lies ahead for all the readers of this volume is a series of chapters presented in two parts: "A Manly Pursuit" and "A Womanly Pursuit," followed by a Conclusion. It is an interesting subdivision, which in many ways is appropriate, although of course the first section, "A Manly Pursuit," goes beyond the male gender to encompass all baseball fans and practitioners.

Mills challenges those who think baseball is dying because the public is losing its enthusiasm for baseball. Since this notion is alien to Dorothy Mills, she spends some portion of nearly every chapter documenting the high enthusiasm for baseball in its many manifestations across the culture. She starts by exploring the rich landscape of historical work on baseball and the many facets of professional academic life devoted to the game, then goes on to examine the subject of sportsmanship and the amateur spirit as manifested in baseball, past and present. Mills finds that the enthusiasm for the game, the sportsmanship nurtured by the game, and the place that winning occupies in the game are rooted in the past and continuous in the present.

When speaking of baseball the conversation inevitably turns to heroes and heroic deeds, and for at least one generation of baseball fans Mickey Mantle was the quintessential hero. Mills delineates the qualities that people found heroic in Mantle and then extends the vision to others. What she finds is a working definition of a hero as well as a range of forms of hero worship. She includes a tribute to Bob Feller, "the shining light" that came to baseball near the end of the Great Depression.

Mills also explores the great range of museums, collections, and minor league parks that fans can visit, as well as the less-well-known Baseball Reliquary, a museum that includes an interesting collection of relics and the "Shrine of the Eternals." And she pays tribute to the SABRmetricians and their guru, Bill James, with his and their endless invention of new statistical measurements.

A diversion into the issues surrounding Americanism and baseball encompasses a discussion of Cuban baseball, both contemporary and historical, up to and including the World Baseball Classic. Mills points out that fan obsession with numbers has given rise to fantasy baseball, and she includes a look at the phenomenon of fantasy camps and vintage baseball or reenactment leagues.

Mills also asks if baseball is a religion and surveys the thoughts of theologians and sociologists on that question. Following from that line of inquiry, she reflects on the role that religion should or should not play in baseball. As well, she contemplates the marketing and sale of baseball logos on clothing and souvenirs, then moves inside the stadium to the growing diversity of food offered at the ballpark, and then on to he incredible proliferation of guides and other reference works on the game, as well as websites, television, radio, art works, photography, cartoons, and academic courses.

The final topic in this first section deals with cheating in baseball, drug issues, and issues of race and gender, including whether gays will be accepted within the game. Mills laments the destruction of a historical monument, Yankee Stadium, but is pleased by the continuing popularity of baseball cards — a small measure of the ongoing enthusiasm for the game.

The section called "A Womanly Pursuit" is a monumental survey of women in baseball, including their baseball play. It features a direct challenge to Major League Baseball and all levels of organized baseball to open up the game to everyone.

Mills traces the history of women in baseball across the United States and Europe from the eighteenth century to the present. She points out that the twentieth century presented expanded opportunities for women in baseball, and on a parallel track in softball, although there were barriers as well. American Legion baseball included no girls, with one exception, and Little League baseball erected a rule barring girls. The one exception in American Legion baseball, Margaret Gisolo, created a crisis in the Legion program when she participated in Legion baseball in the 1920s.

The All-American Girls Professional Baseball League is given much attention here, as are a number of women who defied the odds to enter baseball as players and umpires. Title IX facilitated a transformation in women's sport, with many legal challenges by women seeking to play baseball. The Women's Sports Foundation and the Women's Baseball Federation both played a significant role for women in sport.

Some readers will be surprised by the remarkable number of women's baseball leagues in the United States and Canada that are revealed here. Mills chastises "USA Baseball" for its utter failure to support baseball for women.

Mills takes us on a world tour of women's baseball and the many international competitions available for women. She wonders why Major League Baseball is not supporting women's baseball internationally while it is constantly expanding its reach around the world in search of men who might play the game at the professional level. The number and size of international baseball competitions will surprise many readers, as it surprised me. We have been kept in the dark by an American sports media that refuses to recognize the existence of women's baseball.

Part Two includes a survey of the various forms and levels of discrimination against women in baseball and the way this derives from and reinforces general social values. Following on this theme, Mills tells the story of the AAGPBL exhibition at the Baseball Hall of Fame in Cooperstown and the presentation of women's baseball in other smaller museums. A section on historical works about women's baseball and women baseball historians is instructive and comprehensive, and Mills offers an extensive and useful survey of the historical literature on the subject.

Finally, Dorothy Mills discusses her own role in researching and writing the three volumes published under the name of her late husband, Harold Seymour. She has asked Oxford University Press to list her as co-author on any new printings of the books so that the title pages would reflect the reality of her contribution, but Oxford has declined the request. In regard to the Society for American Baseball Research (SABR) Mills points out how the women in the organization have elevated the subject of women's baseball. The section ends with a call for a woman's major league and a women's baseball structure.

In her Conclusion Mills reiterates her view that baseball is not in decline and that the future for women in baseball is unlimited. She notes that baseball brings us joy and entertainment, and perhaps most important of all it offers an institution around which to build community. In *Chasing Baseball* she invites us all to join the community, recognize baseball's expansive nature, and experience the joy of the game as we share the enthusiasm of Dorothy Mills's lifelong obsession with baseball.

Richard C. Crepeau is a professor of history at the University of Central Florida, Orlando. He is the author of *Baseball: America's Diamond Mind* as well as articles and reviews in sport history and literature.

Preface

I began research for this book after reading many dire assertions warning that baseball was in decline. Analysts writing about our national game have for several years been telling us that because of disappointment with players and club owners, fewer fans were attending games. Supposedly, fans' attention had wandered to other sports and even other types of entertainment. One writer, declaring that baseball was "in crisis," wrote that the game faced "an uncertain future."

Is our national game in danger of dying out? From evidence I've gathered and presented in this book, I'm convinced that love of baseball remains as strong as it ever was. In fact, innovative baseball activities have sprung up that reinforce and broaden fans' interest in the game they love. These activities, most of which are pursued outside organized baseball's parks, constantly confirm fans' pleasure in playing the game as well as in watching it being played. So although the way we celebrate baseball has changed somewhat, our continued fascination with the game keeps it in focus as a permanent thread in American culture.

This book reveals the surprising variety of ways in which baseball fans demonstrate their serious and abiding interest in the national game. At times the interest of our citizens in baseball borders on addiction. But so far that addiction remains benevolent. Nobody has yet been arrested for spending hours every day enjoying fantasy baseball, participating in vintage games, competing in board-and-dice games, blogging about baseball, buying and collecting souvenirs, or dressing up like ballplayers. In fact, such activities benefit not only our psyches but also our economy, for business in general as well as organized baseball gains financially whenever a fan so much as buys a Yankees baseball cap.

In researching this book I discovered a lot more about what it means to be a baseball fan than I ever thought there was to know. The depth of interest in the national game, expressed through many types of baseball activities, surprised me and may surprise you. Learning about all these activities has helped me to better understand the varieties of baseball experience in American life.

The first section of the book, "A Manly Pursuit," reflects the way Americans of both genders have long viewed their national game: as an activity for boys and men to play and for both sexes to watch. Some women, I learned during my research, have also begun to engage in the same outside-the-park baseball activities that men enjoy.

But for other girls and women, their pursuit of the game goes beyond such activities as traveling to baseball museums or watching men play. They want equal opportunity to take part on the field. So the second part of this book, "A Womanly Pursuit," describes women's experiences with baseball that differ from men's. Despite a century and a half of running into obstacles that keep them from full participation in the national game, girls and women have gradually been moving toward a pursuit of baseball that is much like men's. Over the years they have bravely continued to conquer barriers to playing the game themselves. In so doing, they have developed their skill far beyond what most Americans realize. Because of their efforts, baseball is finally beginning to approach its early promise as a game for all Americans.

Some of the ideas in this book were originally touched on in issues of the *HSC Baseball History Newsletter* that I published electronically over the years 1998–2008 for four hundred subscribers. Terminating the writing and publishing of that newsletter gave me the time and inspiration for this book.

What I write here is based upon my own opinions; I describe baseball as I see it. Some Americans who believe that organized baseball, its practitioners, and its offshoots represent the embodiment, even the apex, of heroic endeavor may be a bit taken aback by some of my thoughts. I maintain that there is much more to American baseball than organized baseball alone.

After sixty years of researching and writing baseball history, I believe it's time to share my opinions about the game. I hope readers will find my ideas refreshing as well as based securely on facts.

Contributing to my work on this book are the many replies I received to queries I sent to fans, players, and other writers about their baseball experiences. In preparing this book I have credited, in the text or the bibliography or both, the many persons who so kindly shared information with me. I am very grateful for their cooperation and generosity. I alone, however, take responsibility for any factual errors that may have crept into the book.

Readers may notice that I have begun signing my work in baseball history by using my late husband's last name as my middle name. This usage, which I have copied from members of the Society for American Baseball Research, appears to help long-time fans recall that it is my status as the late Harold Seymour's colleague that enabled me to become a baseball historian. Never having been the fan that he was, I developed views of the game not exactly parallel with his but perhaps of some value nonetheless.

Dorothy Seymour Mills • Naples, Florida • January 2010

PART ONE.
A MANLY PURSUIT

1

Our National Game

Baseball, the quintessential American game!

It's our game, isn't it? Even Walt Whitman knew that. Having played and watched it for so long and so enthusiastically, we show it off proudly to foreigners as embodying the strong, driving, masculine expression of American life.

Because of our devotion to the game, baseball players have become heroes worshipped at our Mount Olympus, named Cooperstown, where the Hall of Fame houses their likenesses and records of their accomplishments and where fans thrill to visit. "I get goose bumps whenever I think of it," says fan Bern Connolly, who roots for the Chicago Cubs and is looking forward to his first visit to Cooperstown.

Americans are devoted to baseball and show their passion in many ways. Children and adults collect, trade, and sell the heroes' autographs, read about the details of their lives in countless books and articles, and watch their exploits over and over on film and television. Actors portray strong, athletic baseball players in popular American stage plays and movies. Their performances on the field inspire works in music, art, and poetry: we all know "Take Me Out to the Ball Game" and "Casey at the Bat." Children imitate the athletes, and adults discuss them and their performances endlessly.

Baseball players are American "heroes" embodying what we perceive as distinctly American characteristics like speed, power, drive, and winning over others. We celebrate baseball because of its uniquely American features, and we pursue baseball partly because it's ours. The chairman of a global business service organization, Ernst & Young, stated that "baseball's values ... are the hallmark of the American experience." Already in the 1850s, publications were calling baseball "Our National Game." In 2003 the chairman of the Hall of Fame said that the game "symbolizes the fabric of our society."

What are baseball's values? According to the Ernst & Young chairman, they are "leadership, teamwork, diversity, innovation, opportunity, and performance excellence." Wow. If we play baseball, will we develop these values? How do they fit in with the admiration we have for speed, power, drive, and winning? Leadership and teamwork, as valuable as they are, seem secondary in baseball to the all-out push to win, the dominating characteristic of the American game. Winning, not the development of teamwork, is the ultimate objective, and because it is, sportsmanship considerations sometimes slide away. But that's American, too.

Is it possible that baseball could have been invented by anyone but Americans, with American goal-oriented views, American delight in speed and action, American respect for strength and power?

Yes, it's possible. In fact, it's certain. Europeans were playing baseball even before we were. To us it may sound preposterous, but it's true. David Block, who pursues baseball's origins relentlessly, has discovered proof that the game of "base ball" (written as two words) was being played in England in 1755. In fact, it must have been played there even earlier, because scholars have found references to "base ball" play by English children and adults in English books published in the 1740s.

How early was it played in the United States? The earliest evidence we have of baseball play in the States is from the 1790s, evidence provided by researchers Thomas Altherr and John Thorn, although an English book describing how "base ball" was played came into print in the States in 1740. So Americans could have, and probably did, know of it, and maybe even played it, in the 1740s. Obviously, however, the English must have known of it first.

The discovery of early baseball in England has startled scholars of the game. The most striking evidence arrived when researcher David Block found an Englishwoman who owned the diary of a man named William Bray. This man told of playing ball in 1755. His diary is no *Remembrance of Things Past,* no dredging of the memory for wisps of early events like those of Abner Graves about his friend Abner Doubleday, a Civil War general whom Graves named as the 1839 inventor of the game in Cooperstown, New York. Bray, an English diarist, wrote in his journal about his enjoyment of a game of "base ball" on the very day he played it; so Bray's record is what historians term a primary source. You can't get any better source than that.

The game of base ball that Bray played in Surrey with local friends, four other men and six women, on March 31, 1755, doubtless looked different from the game played today by sweaty male athletes striving for victory by hitting the ball as hard as they can, running as fast as they can, and pushing their bodies to the limit. That's because in England in the 1750s, base ball was a social activity like cards, lawn bowling, and dancing. It was played for enjoyment not by hired specialists but by groups of young men and women gathering to have fun. I think of it as resembling a polite game of croquet on the front lawn, indulged in by young folks as part of enjoying each others' company.

Although we know that the English were playing "base ball" in the 1750s, we cannot be sure it was they who created the game, since for centuries people around the world have engaged in games uncannily similar to it. The Germans, the Russians, and the Finns, for example, can all show records of games played in almost the same way by similar rules on similar fields. Evidence of even older stick-and-ball games survives through simple sketches showing ancient Mayans, Greeks, and Egyptians playing their versions of this game.

Furthermore, games like baseball, hopscotch, and others played on a field designed for running counter-clockwise in a circular path may boast an even more ancient origin, one that is prehistoric rather than historic. Scholars speculate that such prehistoric games might stem from religious rites or fertility practices celebrated in the ancient pattern called a labyrinth. To use a labyrinth, people walked through it on a circular path laid out on the ground in order to meditate on life or spiritual matters. Or they ran through the path to apprehend a sexual partner as part of spring fertility rites. Both practices, for religious reasons or to encourage the harvest, were designed to honor ancient gods and goddesses. Activities like bat-and-ball games could easily have been created on the path of a labyrinth or in a pattern copied from a labyrinth, with the runner starting from home (the one opening of a labyrinth) and ending up there after successfully negotiating the path.

So the modern game of baseball that we Americans like to consider our own creation might have primitive ancestors in prehistoric spiritual or religious rites involving sex. It could have evolved from there into the polite social game played in eighteenth century England.

But that's not what we think of today when we see baseball headlines on the sports page, which mostly celebrate professionals receiving huge salaries to entertain us with their skill at playing the game. Neither do we realize that black Americans, only fifty years ago allowed for the first time in the top professional ranks of the game, played baseball about as early as whites. In the United States, according to the research of Thomas Altherr as well as my own research, slaves played ball games resembling baseball in this country as early as the 1700s, which is the earliest century for which we have evidence that white colonists were playing the game on this continent. In other words, blacks were pursuing baseball about as early as whites were, as I discovered when doing research for *Baseball: The People's Game*. I found evidence of their delight in the game particularly when I studied the Federal Writers' Project of the 1930s, which recorded more than two thousand oral interviews where ex-slaves described their activities while they were owned by others.

Yes, these records of slave life represent memories, not "primary source" diaries written on the day the games were played — it was illegal for slaves to read and write — but the intensity of their descriptions is impressive. Moreover, before the Civil War of the 1860s, freed and never-enslaved blacks in northeastern cities like New York and Philadelphia had already developed an educated and relatively wealthy middle class that formed its own clubs, including baseball clubs. That's when white Americans were forming baseball clubs, too.

Fans at current American baseball games seldom stop to think of "their game" as having roots in the distant past, long before the coming of the major leagues. But we should realize that ancient people as well as settlers in colonial America desired fun, too. Organizing a game by means of some simple rules made it easy to share it with others as part of their social lives.

Early New York City proved to be a hotbed of baseball play by young men. Many fans know of the existence in the 1840s of the New York Knickerbockers, a group of business and professional men whose organization came to be admired by other local clubs. They played by rules requiring honor, fairness, and politeness; the rules even forbade them to question the decisions of the umpire.

For a long time baseball writers believed that the Knickerbockers — particularly a prominent member, Alexander Cartwright — established the basic rules of the New York style of play, a style that is close to the way the game is played today. Alex began to be called "the father of the game." Now the research of Monica Nucciarone has shown that Alex probably had no more effect on the shaping of the game than any other team member. So much for another long-held assumption about our game.

Moreover, the Knickerbockers were not even the first American club to play the game: researcher John Thorn has found newspaper evidence of a well-organized group called the New York Magnolia Ball Club playing in 1843, before the Knickerbockers recorded their famous organization. Researchers like Peter Mancuso have established that organized clubs were playing bat-and-ball games surprisingly like baseball decades before the Knickerbockers even organized. The Knickerbockers are evidently not as important as researchers once thought.

So if Americans didn't invent the American national game, if Abner Doubleday didn't create it one afternoon in Cooperstown in 1839, if the Knickerbockers weren't the fellows who organized the first baseball club, if Alexander Cartwright didn't set down the modern rules — if, in fact, not one of our beloved American baseball myths is true, then whose game is it?

You know the answer: it's ours. We've imbued it with our spirit. It's still ours, if we want it to be. And we obviously do. Just as soccer has become the European game, baseball has become ours. Even though the game may no longer top others in attendance, it has not lost the devotion of its millions of fans. Maybe Gene Budig, former American League president, is right when he says baseball is "part of our national being." I agree with the comment of researcher Peter Morris: "Perhaps it's better just to feel that baseball is the national game and not to reason why." We'll continue to pursue it, despite our possible dismay over learning of its real origins and our disappointments over what has happened to it since. It's ours now. For better — *and* for worse.

We Americans have always been so proud of our national game that we assume other countries need it, too, just as we assume they need democracy. We have been trying to export both for at least a century and a half. Our efforts to convert the world to baseball have worked better when we weren't trying to do it deliberately, as they worked in Meiji-era Japan, when the Japanese saw railroad workers, missionaries, and teachers playing the game in the 1860s and learned it from them, and as they worked during foreign wars, when Europeans saw American soldiers playing baseball and learned it from doughboys and G.I.s. In China, at about the same time the Japanese were learning baseball from American residents, Chinese students sent to America were picking it up from their college classmates and then bringing the game home.

Many of us see baseball as the cornerstone of that strange word "Americanism," the other three corners being hot dogs, Mom, and apple pie. Since we seldom hear such terms as Germanism, Italianism, or Frenchism, there must be something about America that enables its style of life, or system of beliefs, or attitude, or geography, or all of the above to be characterized as peculiarly distinct and so entitles it to attach the "-ism" suffix to its name. Baseball may be that peculiarity, for many commentators throughout our history have declared that it expresses the American spirit more than anything else does.

What is that American spirit? Analysts claim that virtues like honesty, resourcefulness, adaptability, fairness, consideration for others in need, patriotism, and the desire to improve and succeed, all comprise the American spirit.

Most of these characteristics can be found in the playing of amateur baseball, although not always in professional baseball. Of course, as Google reveals, "American Spirit" is also the name of a rifle, a cigarette, and the magazine published by the D.A.R., the Daughters of the American Revolution; these products may characterize Americans as much as baseball does.

Those who have long pursued baseball often appreciate knowing more about its history. In addition to watching players' performances, they enjoy reading about the exploits of baseball's heroes, whether present or past. After all, present-day heroes are avatars of those who came before them, like Babe Ruth and Lou Gehrig. If present stars are heroes, past heroes deserve veneration, too.

Devotion to the stars of the game can lead fans to appreciate its past on a higher level than simple admiration. Aside from reading the reports and feature stories by newspaper reporters, fans may graduate to meatier fare: biographies, club histories, league histories, journals of a season's events, reviews of pennant races and World Series. Baseball has inspired the publication of all sorts of books, magazines, journals, and pamphlets for fans who want to really get into the subject.

Sports Illustrated even publishes a magazine called *Sports Illustrated for Kids,* but despite its name this magazine generally features adults. I've never seen any article in it covering children's baseball — and certainly not girls' baseball, although it once printed a picture card of a girl softball player. That's as close as the children's magazine gets to celebrating children's accomplishments, preferring to specialize in adult basketball, football, and other sports, in the assumption that children want to read about adult accomplishments. Perhaps children care little for the sporting exploits of other kids. Instead, the editors include comics and reviews of video games. "Will the Shaman's family get away from Arazul and his pack of evil baboons?" hardly relates to sports.

Adult baseball publications help provide fodder for discussions about momentous events of baseball's past, for special moments in baseball are, says Bruce Weber of the *New York Times,* "relished, lamented, argued and revisited with the kind of what-if? passion that absolutely defines fandom." For example: Did Ruth really make that called shot in 1932, or did fans and newsmen remember the whole thing wrong? Should umpires have access to instant replay technology, or should we go along with the way baseball has always been handled on the field — accepting umpires' errors as simply human and moving on from there? Arguments over questions like these are emblems of true fandom.

What's really amazing is fan devotion to baseball trivia, which sometimes becomes too trivial. A systems analyst, annoyed by insufferable bores challenging him with meaningless details like "What was the highest fielding average ever achieved by a third baseman using a Wilson glove?" devised a Trivia Sting created mathematically to prevent trivia bores from succeeding in challenging any of their chosen contestants. It's not clear if the bores were stung hard enough.

The world of fandom is not the only circle where baseball finds itself under observation. Scholars, too, as revealed by the research on early baseball they have been producing in recent decades, have become deeply interested in the subject, so much so that almost forty years ago they formed an association to study baseball. Americans, although highly individual, prefer to advance any cause by forming a group of like-minded people to discuss it.

The association of baseball scholars came into being in 1971 at the suggestion of Robert "Bob" Davids, a government employee whose avocation for the previous twenty years had been writing articles about baseball, primarily about the statistics of the game. He invited forty other statisticians (he thought of them as "statistorians") to join a group that would study baseball. Sixteen of them met in Cooperstown, New York, to form the Society for American Baseball Research, now known as SABR, to foster the study of baseball, stimulate interest in the game (did it really need stimulating?), and disseminate baseball information.

SABR has grown over the years from the original group of sixteen American researchers to almost seven thousand members worldwide, some of them researchers and writers, the others zealous fans, who meet at a four-day convention in a different city each year.

Typically, about seven hundred people show up for these conventions. There they present the results of scholarly studies, listen to the presentations of others, attend baseball games together, and — probably most important — chat endlessly in the hotel hallways and public rooms about baseball events, exchanging information that could help in each other's research. They also mill around the vendors' room to examine and purchase baseball publications as well as to meet and talk to the authors who have come to autograph their new books. They enjoy special events like judging posters, watching films, trying to beat others at trivia contests, taking part in receptions, attending luncheons with nationally known speakers, touring the facilities of elaborate stadiums, and working with fellow committee members on joint projects.

For SABR now boasts two dozen committees that study, report on, and publish information about such topics as scouting, umpires, Asian baseball, spring training, and Armed Forces baseball. In addition to having formed these committees, SABR has also organized itself into fifty-five regional chapters — one of them named for Bob Davids — where members continue baseball discussions with enthusiasts in their geographical area, in a sort of continuous hot-stove league.

For members of SABR, baseball is, according to the organization's membership booklet, "a passion. An event of complex possibilities. The quintessential pastime. It is life itself played out in the course of nine carefully metered innings, invented by brilliant minds — now long gone, but not forgotten." Wording like that reveals a depth of devotion seldom encountered elsewhere.

Of course, nobody knows for sure whose "brilliant minds" created baseball, but that difficulty doesn't keep researchers like David Block from trying to find out. And meanwhile, fans can, as the booklet states, enjoy hobnobbing with others united by "a common ardor for baseball history, personalities, statistics, literature, and the joy of sharing their passion."

SABR publications help feed that ardor. Frequent bulletins keep members informed of baseball events and SABR news, and an annual journal publishes articles based on new research findings. A complex web site offers moderated discussions, research resources, announcements, and lists of members, chapters, and committees — groups that have themselves begun to go forth and multiply by publishing newsletters and building web sites.

Historians and statisticians comprise most of the scholarly side of SABR's membership, but it includes other specialists like those studying baseball literature, baseball language, and baseball in art and music. Many baseball scholars are professors, for baseball courses have infiltrated the curriculum, especially the discipline of American History.

The first person to begin studying baseball formally on a scholarly level was Harold Seymour of New York, who in the 1940s convinced his Ph.D. committee at Cornell University that baseball was worth historical attention. His residence requirements completed in 1942, he left to teach and write his dissertation, with interruptions for health reasons and the war emergency. The supervisor of his work, Professor Paul W. Gates, registered Seymour's proposed study in the June 1947 *List of Doctoral Dissertations in History Now in Progress at Universities in the United States* on the basis of preliminary research. Further delays, however, kept Seymour from completing the dissertation until 1956, when he received his degree for a study called "The Rise of Major League Baseball to 1891." Originally a two-volume thesis, it is now available through University Microfilms at Ann Arbor as a single, but very fat, 625-page paper-covered volume.

The Seymour dissertation covered the beginnings of baseball, so far as they were known at the time, revealing that General Abner Doubleday's so-called invention of the game in 1839 was apocryphal, taken as gospel only as a result of nationalistic fervor and then used as the basis for the establishment a hundred years later of the Hall of Fame in Cooperstown. The dissertation presented a great deal of evidence of early ball play by amateurs in various walks of life, showed how the professional game arose, and covered the business and labor relations in the professional leagues and teams through the nineteenth century, not neglecting the excitement of the game as played on the field. Heavily documented, it showed evidence of extensive research in early newspapers like *Sporting Life*, guidebooks like *Beadle's* and *Spalding's*, early league constitutions, law cases, government hearings, scrapbooks, diaries, and sheet music. All this was accomplished with my enthusiastic help, because becoming his wife meant also that I had become his colleague.

Although a few scholars had begun to study sports in general, nothing like a detailed study of baseball history had ever been done by a scholar before. Up until then, all baseball histories had been written by untrained journalists and so had no academic standing.

The Seymour dissertation attracted a publisher that in those days most scholars only dreamt of: Oxford University Press, which in 1960 published it in revised and expanded form as *Baseball: The Early Years,* and in 1971, the year when SABR started, published *Baseball: The Golden Age* as the second volume of a planned three-volume chronological series on baseball and its impact on American life. In 1990 came the final volume, *Baseball: The People's Game,* which told the early history of amateur ball in America. This book won four prizes.

Viewing Dr. Seymour's innovative foray into baseball and his success with it emboldened other scholars, who picked up on many of the topics mentioned in the Seymour books and began researching and writing articles and books exploring baseball's relationship to economics, the law, sociology, biography, linguistics, literature, memoirs, business, and history. Other respected scholarly publishers joined Oxford in handling their work, and even journalistic books on baseball began improving in quality. Seymour joined SABR in the early seventies, and so began the era of cross-fertilization with others studying the national game. SABR now awards several prizes for superior work in the field as well as financial grants for specialized projects.

Other academic organizations also pay attention to baseball. The scholarly *Journal of Sport History* and similar publications often present serious baseball research articles. The Cooperstown Symposium on Baseball and American Culture publishes the heavily footnoted papers of serious scholars who meet in Cooperstown annually to share their ideas and research. Scholars contribute to *NINE: A Journal of Baseball History and Culture* as well as to *Base Ball: A Journal of the Early Game* and to the *Elysian Fields Quarterly: The Baseball Review,* which is largely literary in content. The North American Society for Sport History often features baseball scholarship in its publications and meetings, as does the International Association for the Philosophy of Sport. Since the Seymour dissertation's acceptance through the farsightedness of Cornell's history department and Oxford University Press's innovative decision to publish in this field, baseball studies have gradually been made welcome in the rarefied atmosphere of university scholarship and are no longer confined to the box labeled "popular culture." Seymour's idea to study baseball on a scholarly level altered the field of history as we understand it today, making it much broader and more inclusive.

Before Seymour, there was no such thing as a baseball historian. The academic establishment, initially skeptical of the value of baseball studies, has gradually come around. And now a new generation has grown up to think of sports history as part of history. I myself have received many queries like "How did you become a baseball historian?" and "How can I best become one?" By far, the question asked most often is typically American: "How much money can I make as a baseball historian?"

The best way to become a baseball historian, of course, is first to become a historian; getting a thorough grounding in American history before specializing is always the right tactic. Then one needs to study under a baseball historian who is currently teaching and who knows the field. I always recommend those whose books and articles I admire.

As to the last question, about money, the answer, of course, is that historians don't go into teaching and researching for the sake of money. Students fail to realize that research in libraries and other institutions around the country takes a heavy expenditure of personal funds, since even those with university connections cannot expect their employers to support all the necessary travel. In order to pursue baseball history, prospective historians need to have a passion for research and writing as well as for the subject.

Most people don't grasp that becoming a best-selling author in any field of writing is unusual. I like the story in which an author was asked which type of writing made the most money; his accurate response was "ransom notes." It certainly isn't baseball history. And for me personally, the answer is the one I've read on commercial T-shirts:

> I started out with nothing.
> I have most of it left.

Although many fans remain unaware of all this scholarly activity, research and what it can contribute to our understanding of baseball has become an important offshoot of our national game. Scholarly study has become a way for some fans to pursue their passion for baseball.

As I pointed out to SABR in a presentation before the 2008 convention, "Research" is not just SABR's middle name, it's SABR's family name — the organization's basic reason for being. Baseball research is now on a level with every other kind of research. Because of the attentions of scholars, baseball has developed from a simple way to have fun with bat and ball to the subject of serious study revealing the foibles of Americans as they pursue their passion for their beloved baseball.

The national game, first in the hearts of American sports fans, inspired a song published in 1869. Despite the quaint wording of its refrain, we might sing it today:

Hurrah for our game, our National Game,
There's health in its every bound.
A thrill of delight in its very name,
A joy in its simple sound.
It lends new strength to our hardy race,
And its pleasures are never tame.
Then, here's to the bat, the ball and the base:
Hurrah for our National Game.

MECHANICS' INSTITUTE LIBRARY
57 Post Street
San Francisco, CA 94104
(415) 393-0101

2

The Amateur Spirit

When grownups began playing baseball in America, they played it as a game, a light diversion, an amusement. Notions of fair play and honor guided the actions of the fellows who pursued baseball in the 1840s in the New York area. The Knickerbockers and their contemporaries, if we are to believe their club rules, tried to act in gentlemanly fashion. Umpires watched to ensure that players acted honorably. That meant no cheating. Playing honorably, which was considered a manly virtue, was more important than winning.

Penalties for deviating from the code of honor underlined its importance. For the relatively light infractions of using a swear word or disputing an umpire's decision, a Knickerbocker player paid a fine. Anything the club members deemed "improper conduct" called for suspension or expulsion from the club.

Enforcing punishments for devious or illegal behavior lasted a relatively short time in baseball history, however. Within ten years, the intense rivalry that had built up between teams and among their fans caused unruliness in the stands and often on the field. Police sometimes had to take charge. Once in Rochester, when the umpire called a close play against the Rochester Live Oaks, the captain threw the ball in the air, and the whole team walked off the field. Clubs of the 1840s and 1850s would hardly have accepted that kind of behavior.

Betting by fans heightened tensions in the 1870s. Why betting? Because winning had become more important than honorable play. Pitchers threw illegal pitches without being called on their infractions; they wanted to win above all. Umpires sometimes proved incompetent and raised suspicions that they might be crooked. Fans ignored rules against betting, and rumors that dishonest players had planned a game's outcome in advance became common. The era of pure amateurism was collapsing almost as soon as it began. Fans and players were effectively saying to the world, "Nix on the Knickerbocker ethic."

When Charles W. Eliot, president of Harvard University, called for a Harvard "aristocracy which excels in manly sports," he was thinking of "gentlemanly sport" as a supplement to a gentleman's education, but he opened a Pandora's Box that never closed. By the end of 1910 it was clear even to Eliot that the emphasis in college sports had switched from gentlemanly play to "winning above all else."

Yet these negative developments failed to weaken American ardor for the game and probably increased it. Winning has little to do with sportsmanship, and the new focus on winning permeated baseball. It was winning that made professionalism supreme. Professional baseball thus represented the first main offshoot of the early amateur bat-and-ball games.

The swift movement to professionalism caused a change in focus, principally in hiring players to do our playing for us. That change alone elevates winning to the main goal, so some of the players will be impelled to do most anything to achieve that success. After all, winners, not losers, receive fan tributes.

Let's step back for a moment and consider: is winning really desirable? That sounds like a strange question, but it's strange only because we're conditioned by our culture to try to win. Not all social groups consider winning to be the best outcome. According to anthropologist Colin Turnbull, in one society, the Mbuti, in order to "foster harmony," the members engage in "teaching cooperation, not competition. It is unacceptable to win, for winning isolates the winner and saddens losers. Those who excel at something encourage and help others." This society therefore sees and considers the negative side of winning.

The ancient Greeks went to the opposite extreme. In the time before the Common Era, men of Athens were trained to be highly competitive. One scholar tells us that nothing had meaning to the ancient Greeks if it failed to involve defeating someone. At the early Olympic Games, only the one person who beat everyone else in a competition counted for anything. Winners received wreaths on their heads, were showered with flower petals and carried around on the shoulders of their friends, were feted in great banquets, had statues made of them, and won a great deal of money. Those who came in second, third, or any place else, according to scholar Tony Perrottet, earned only "shame, embarrassment, and public mockery." The historian Pindar said these humiliated athletes slipped away from Olympia quietly, skulked home to their mothers via back roads, and tried to hide from everyone.

To our culture, winning is important, almost vital, but even those who attain second or third place in a race or tournament receive some recognition for their accomplishment. After all, they almost won.

In the States, the emphasis on winning seemed to arise from the ethic of striving to build a new country. That ethic soon engendered a desire to win by any means. Although the new ethic gradually infiltrated baseball, the older ethic of "honesty and fairness first" remained as a tradition among sporting nonprofessionals. In the early twentieth century, "Yours in sport" was still the correct way for the leader of an amateur team to sign letters challenging another team to a game. Accepting victory or defeat graciously, as in old-time tennis, remained the ideal, even if it had eroded somewhat. In these amateur games, if any fans were present, they might protest pitchers' sneaky attempts to use a foreign substance on the ball or runners' efforts to avoid touching every base. They were likely to applaud good plays on the part of either team, even the opposition, as cricket fans do.

That kind of sportsmanship has worn away. Even Olympic performers occasionally protest decisions that prevent them from obtaining gold medals; once in 2008 a wrestler angrily discarded his bronze medal in disgust during the awards ceremony and received a reprimand from the International Committee. So did a taekwondo practitioner who deliberately kicked a referee in the face.

Olympians' actions interpreted as political are treated variously. Many sports fans recall that in 1968 two runners combined a salute to Black Power with their recognition of the national anthem during the ceremony. Although their act did not reflect disappointment with the awards they received, Avery Brundage, head of the International Olympic Committee, insisted they be summarily ejected from the Olympics; he saw their salute as a political protest. On the other hand, Brundage failed to object to the Nazi salute performed in 1936 by German athletes during the medal awards ceremony, so to him that gesture was acceptable.

Neither the 1968 nor the 1936 actions really reflected lack of sportsmanship, but they engendered comment nonetheless, showing that fans at the games expect exemplary behavior typical of amateur performers — behavior like that of the swimmer adjudged electronically to have come in second behind Michael Phelps by the length of a fingernail in the Beijing Olympics of 2008: "I'm taking what I got and I'm happy," he said. Fans expect this even though the Olympic Games have evolved into what a letter to the editor of the *New York Times* termed "a gigantic celebrity show in which companies invest heavily for publicity and television rights," thus detracting from the sports competitions on which the show is based.

True amateur players express a certain joy in play that cannot be entirely dissipated by their desire to win. Those who play for fun have no need of an audience and feel no necessity for an unnatural advantage like drugs to help them win, because although they plan on winning, having fun playing the game they love is at least as important. Their delight comes from engaging in the game itself. A visitor to the Elysian Fields in Hoboken, New Jersey, saw that joy expressed in 1853 when he wrote in an 1854 book: "The centre of the lawn has been marked out into a magnificent ball ground, and two parties of rollicking, joyous young men are engaged in that excellent and health-imparting sport, base ball." Amateurs of today could be considered the descendents of those rollicking, joyous young men.

Although professionalism came to dominate baseball as the preferred way to pursue the game, during the nineteenth and early twentieth century amateur play survived, in the form of children's pickup games in city streets and cow pastures, school children's practice on playgrounds, factory workers' play on company fields, servicemen's games both in the States and abroad, college students' play on campuses around the country, "muny" (municipal) league participation loosely organized by big-city governments, town games supported by small business and local citizens, prisoners' play in penitentiaries and reformatories, American Indians' play in restrictive boarding schools, and black men's play on plantations and in their own clubs. These groups provided the underlay for the more intense, straining, driven professionals, and it was these groups who kept the amateur spirit alive.

Most fans today know that for a lot of baseball's history, excellent black amateurs and professionals were unwelcome among their white peers. The few fine black players who made it to the majors in the 1880s were soon forced out by racists with the increase in general racial prejudice after the Civil War. So much for baseball's vaunted reputation as an example of democracy in action; actually, baseball reflects the culture of its time, which in the 1890s remained profoundly racist. With the continuation of segregated neighborhoods, black children and white children were getting fewer chances to play ball together, so that when the American Legion formed a league for boys in 1925 and the Little League did the same in 1939, boys who wanted to join played for the most part on all-black or all-white teams.

Now that amateur play is much less well-known than professional, not everyone remembers it as a possibility. Fay Vincent, a recent commissioner of baseball, was quoted in the *New York Times* as saying, "I'm intrigued by the concept of people playing baseball for fun." This comment sounds as though he thinks playing ball just for the joy of it represents an unlikely dream. His mind-set is the spectacle called "professional baseball for money," not enjoyment through participation in play whether the outcome is "I win" or "you win." When we forget the amateur spirit, we lose something valuable. By the late twentieth century nostalgia for this spirit engendered new ways of playing baseball.

I've often wondered why American baseball failed to take the route of

Canadian curling, in which the best players still remain resolutely non-professional. Canadian curlers, instead of being organized into professional leagues, form club-type organizations and play from September to June on ice rinks in their spare time or during time off from work.

The way Canadians engage in curling doesn't apply to Canadian hockey, which many consider the national game of our northern neighbors. That game epitomizes the same killer instincts as American professional baseball. But Canadian curling, originally a Scottish sport, seems to me to more closely characterize the Canadian view of life.

When you watch Canadian curling, although you know the curlers want to win, you sense the same attitude as in amateur baseball. When amateurs try to win, they are doing it not because their entire future and millions of dollars are at stake but simply because winning is satisfying. Canadian curlers display delight and pleasure in the game, and their entire demeanor shows that they could not cheat at the game they love. If they lose, instead of collapsing in despair, they shake the hands of their opponents.

I knew nothing about curling when I was asked to write an article on the history of women's curling for an encyclopedia of women and sports — nothing beyond having seen a few televised games when I lived in Canada during the late nineties. I found watching those games intriguing, observing not only the skill and intensity of the players but also their sporting attitude. Respect for one's opponent lies at the heart of that attitude.

While performing the necessary research for my article, I was struck with the similarity of curling's early development to that of early American baseball — and its dissimilarity with present-day professional baseball. I asked my husband, Roy, to take me to a local curling match so that I could observe the game first-hand. He had been a champion curler in the Royal Canadian Air Force and proved to be an invaluable resource for my article. Seeing the game played close up not only informed me about the style of play, it gave me a sense of the players' pleasure. I could see that their approach to curling differed from the way professional baseball players viewed their sport.

The reason for the respectful attitude maintained in curling appears to be the participants' rejection of professionalism. The game has remained what we might call semipro. Even the very best players and clubs pay their own way to bonspiels (tournaments), which do get some commercial backing but are not professional in the same sense as the American professional leagues. Because the clubs are made up of people who work at jobs or professions, participants don't have to wonder what they will do when they can no longer engage in the sport they love. As a result, curlers are likely to be well-rounded people with other interests in their lives besides their favorite sport, people not as focused as ballplayers on achieving stardom and making a great deal of money. They need not cut corners in order to win. Sportsmanship rules their games: players who inadvertently touch another player's rock report it immediately as a foul. Can you imagine anything like this happening in professional baseball?

Moreover, curling is a highly social game. Club members socialize between and after games and bonspiels because socializing with their colleagues is an important part of playing. Professional baseball players, by contrast, appear to escape from the baseball park as soon as possible in order to avoid colleagues who seem to be as much rivals as they are fellow team members.

How has the erosion of the amateur spirit affected baseball players? Baseball films and novels often depict professional players as torn between greed for monetary success and their joy in playing the game. The plots develop in a way to show that the players, tempted as they might be to play unethically (cheat, take bribes, fall in with crooks), instead find their way back to their love of baseball in time to avoid ruining their lives with greed. Those films, like the early silent movies that featured baseball, lack realism. I think professionalism draws players inexorably along the route of playing for as much money as they can get and thus leaving themselves vulnerable to corruption. When professionals do exhibit joy and delight in the game, as Pete Rose did, reporters notice it as different and comment on it. Rose played exuberantly, much the way children do. Yet Rose, too, left himself open to improbity by betting on baseball. After all, he was a professional.

We tend to think of amateurism as continuing as it was in the past, in the form of children's happy play. But, as the *New York Times* has reported, "sandlot baseball, a slice of American life enjoyed for decades for youngsters from coast to coast, appears on the verge of extinction." Young players no longer develop on the sandlots, for where are the sandlots? Fewer inner-city kids choose to play unorganized, spontaneous baseball and other pickup games, while urban and suburban children, who spend a lot of time on video games, join structured, organized groups set up by adults and are delivered by parents to already-constructed baseball parks. Writer Mark Hyman calls this parent intrusion a "hostile takeover" of children's sports.

How different today's behavior is from the way boys pursued baseball before the advent in 1939 of Little League! Children found empty spaces, cleared them of rubble or overgrowth, chose up sides, and played with whatever equipment they could devise. This kind of play is so unusual now that when in 2008 some children in Greenwich, Connecticut, cleaned up a vacant lot to play a form of baseball called Wiffle ball, the town government objected. Concerned citizens — at least, those who didn't live nearby — defended the children in letters to the editor of the *New York Times* applauding their ini-

tiative, creativity, and energy. But the lot that the teenagers cleared turned
out to be worth more than a million dollars and had been set aside for
drainage; besides, it was in the backyards of people who wanted peace and
quiet, not the forty teenagers who turned up for the Wiffle ball game. The
initiative that the children displayed in creating their own play space went to
waste.

I'm afraid the days are over when children can easily find a vacant lot
that nobody cares about. As a result, baseball is losing its status as a way for
children to exercise initiative and learn cooperation, fair play, and negotia-
tion as preparation for practicing their physical skills, as David Ogden pointed
out in an article in *NINE*. (Ogden was commenting on African American children, but his remarks apply generally.) The different initiation of boys' baseball means the onset of what could be called an early stage of professionalism.

In the 1920s, teenager Harold Seymour and his friends found and cleared
fields in what was then suburban Brooklyn. They learned to choose sides
fairly and get along with others of different ethnicities in order to pursue the
game they loved with honor and efficiency. Now adults arrange children's
play spots in spaces that are convenient to them and contact organizations
that set up leagues, teams, and schedules for the children. How can children
gradually develop enterprise and organizational skills if we do it all for them?
I think the possibilities for children to show initiative are eroding right along
with the amateur spirit. What is growing instead is a sort of herd instinct.

Another place the amateur spirit once flourished was in "muny ball"—
municipal baseball, set up by the great city amateur associations of the twenties and thirties. During the Depression, major cities like Chicago, New York,
Cleveland, Indianapolis, Detroit, Buffalo, Pittsburgh, and Portland, Oregon,
as well as many smaller cities, took pity on the hundreds of teams of youngsters that congregated at city parks trying to scrounge a spot to play ball. Federal funds helped the city governments lay out baseball diamonds, and city
recreation departments set up amateur leagues that children's teams could
join. The cities' recreation departments often scheduled the games and furnished the umpires, and some provided dressing rooms and took care of
injuries, covering expenses with small entrance fees, forfeit fees, and protest
fees, and by occasionally charging admission to important games. Sometimes
the local big-league club recognized and encouraged these amateur associations by offering a medal to a season's winning team. Muny ball thus provided a minimal amount of organization and appeared to be more conducive
to amateurism than do today's Little League and the commercial leagues set
up for men.

Muny ball, as a way of pursuing baseball that was infused with the amateur spirit, became wildly popular. In an era when free and cheap entertain-

ment was greatly sought after, the amateur game as promoted by municipalities offered simple, homey fun for adults as well as loosely organized local activities for youth.

Most muny ballplayers played as amateurs. They received no recognition, of course, beyond the attention of local fans and occasional newspaper mention. Cities also acknowledged muny achievements in annual guidebooks listing the teams and leagues and mentioning the winners in different age classifications.

These muny ball leagues have been forgotten. Proof is that one day a baseball fan wrote me from Chicago for help in identifying a baseball medal he owned. He said it was awarded by the Chicago White Sox in 1938 to an all-star team that played in something called the Chicago Baseball Federation. Trying to identify this federation, the fan had written without success to the front office of the White Sox Baseball Club and to the Hall of Fame in Cooperstown, neither of which had ever heard of the Chicago Baseball Federation and both of whom thought it might be a minor league. The fan contacted the minors, too, but he found nobody who could identify this organization.

This fan's medal was of course an award given by a federation of amateur clubs in Chicago that was well-known during the era of muny baseball. I even mentioned it in *Baseball: The People's Game.* I recommended that he research it by checking the 1938 issues of the *Chicago Tribune*, which the Chicago Historical Society keeps on microfilm. I was confident he would find activities of the federation mentioned there, and maybe a mention of the tournament in which it was awarded. The Cleveland papers of the era often printed news of the similarly named Cleveland Baseball Federation. I told this fan that when he found a newspaper reference to his medal, he would be able to educate the Chicago White Sox, the Hall of Fame, and the minor leagues about the popularity of muny ball in the thirties.

Similar groups in the thirties that helped carry on the amateur spirit were the semipro tournaments for adults — not really complete amateurs, but not members of organized baseball, either. Adult leagues like the Ban Johnson League sprang up in the Midwest. Some clubs like the famous Bushwicks of Brooklyn and the Bismarck team of North Dakota, which hired well-known black professionals, called themselves semipro but paid their players salaries and remained independent of any leagues. Many were touring teams, like the House of David teams. Most players on these teams never reached major league status but joined the touring pro and semipro clubs because they could make a living of sorts by pursuing the game they loved.

The National Baseball Federation grew out of the more localized city amateur federations, and so did the American Baseball Congress, which included some muny associations in its setup. In response to demand, similar groups called the National Baseball Congress and the Denver Post Tournament formed in the same era. In the thirties, these were prominent semipro baseball organizations that grew out of the amateurs.

Players in these groups were part-timers, generally paid by the companies that employed them, so those clubs were essentially playing "industrial ball" instead of professional ball. Winning clubs earned publicity for their companies. How curiously American it is that companies moved all the way from forbidding their employees from playing baseball in the 1850s to actually recruiting players less than thirty years later! Company leaders, like colleges and universities, gradually recognized the publicity value of baseball to their institutions; they stopped banning it and began to recruit players as employees so that they could use baseball for their own profit.

Sponsorship by their companies, local groups, or national groups meant that many young men of the 1930s could pursue baseball on at least a part-time basis even while holding down a job. In that sense, they resembled the members of curling clubs. Among them, the joy of playing remained supreme.

Refusal of most white Americans to recognize the professional-level skill developed by black players, who formed their own separate clubs and leagues, led to their being classified as "amateur" or "semipro," even in the published indexes to newspapers like the *Cleveland Plain Dealer*. Was there anything amateur or semipro about Satchel Paige? Yet those who actually saw the black clubs playing reported their use of their own special style of play, one characterized by shows of exhilaration and pleasure at engaging in their chosen sport. I look upon this style as a remnant of the amateur spirit.

Incarcerated men certainly have to be classified as amateur baseball players, and the material some of them sent me about covering prison ball in the 1920s and 1930s when I was researching *Baseball: The People's Game* startled me with its upbeat tone. They appeared to organize and conduct their games with unexpected good humor and great pleasure. In their published newsletters I found no hint of resentment, anger, or bad behavior; in fact, the sports writers whose stories appeared in these newsletters strongly recommended honorable conduct. Could it be that these imprisoned men had somehow absorbed the idea that engaging in baseball required fair play? The game reports in their newsletters gave me the impression that these men accepted their imprisonment because of having broken society's rules, decided to make the best of it, and were determined to get what fun they could out of the situation. They sometimes behaved so well that the warden felt able to permit them to play a game outside the prison walls with a rival team in the area.

Another unexpected haven for the amateur spirit is the relocation centers for Japanese Americans set up in 1941 in places like Wyoming when the government feared that Japanese-born citizens might be spies. "One of the first things we did when we arrived was to set up baseball leagues," remembers an internee interviewed for Ken Burns's documentary *The War.* "There was a baseball game played nearly every evening." The young men who played internment camp baseball exhibited "a deep and passionate enthusiasm for organized baseball," which "kept them connected to the American ideal," according to William Rhoden of the *New York Times,* who interviewed players in the internment camp leagues.

Where has that spirit gone today? Although some of it has been redirected into parabaseball activities like Vintage Ball, I think much of it has flown abroad. South American children pursue *beisbol* with a passion; Samuel Regalado, who studies Hispanic players, believe they possess a "special hunger" for the game. But baseball has also been picked up on the European continent: the Germans boast leagues for both adults and children. Hundreds of teams play all over Austria. Even Poland, Slovakia, and the Czech Republic have developed teams. Nova Scotians in Canada have been playing baseball since at least 1841. And the Cubans have for many years dominated international play. In Japan, professional players are expected to follow several rules including behaving like a gentleman on the field and like a good Japanese off the field; these rules reflect the requirements of religions that dominate baseball-playing Asia. If you draw a Venn diagram, designating one circle "amateur spirit" and the other "Japanese rules for ballplayers," the overlap would be considerable.

Even more improbably, in Baghdad you can attend the enthusiastic games of the Northern Regional Junior Baseball Tournament, founded in 2003 by a young fellow named Ismael Khali Ismael, who as a child saw American workers playing baseball when his father worked with an American contracting company that was building a dam. Ismael found out about baseball much the way the Japanese did back in the nineteenth century. He could use some help in the way of baseball equipment, but instead the United States has sent 2,000 skateboards to something called the "Baghdad Zoo and Entertainment Experience."

International baseball is exciting baseball. When the American amateur team was beaten in 2006 by teams from Mexico, Korea, and Canada, a *New York Times* writer commented, "There is nothing like being beaten at your own game to focus the mind." But the mind of American players was already focused: on earning money in the big leagues, not on representing the United States in baseball. The professional ethic has put the kibosh on amateur play and deeply undermined the amateur spirit.

In 2004 the Olympics shocked the American sports world by eliminating baseball from the games. Although the 2008 games in Beijing included baseball and the 2012 Olympics will, too, its future beyond that remains iffy, partly because MLB has been slow to adopt effective drug testing but also because few of America's best players have participated; the best have all turned professional. What could confirm more clearly that amateur baseball means nothing in America any more? The Olympic Games represent the standard-bearers of the amateur spirit, if not the reality. American amateur baseball players can't cut it internationally any longer, so some players under contract to teams in organized baseball competed in the Olympics as members of Team U.S.A. Baseball. Harvey Schiller, president of the International Baseball Federation, believes the federation's best hope of returning to the Olympics is its attempt to bring baseball's best players to the competition — and that means persuading MLB to send more professionals to an event originally created for amateurs.

The entire Olympic Games have themselves become less amateur. It became clear to close observers in the late twentieth century that most performers sponsored by their countries had become full-time performers and that those part-time players with little national support came to the games at a great disadvantage. After Avery Brundage left the presidency of the International Olympic Committee, the I.O.C. dropped requirements for complete amateurism and left such matters as pay and rewards to the individual federations controlling each sport. In the case of baseball, that's the International Baseball Federation, which is campaigning for baseball's return to the 2016 Olympics.

The decision by the I.O.C. to let the sports federations decide whether to pay or support athletes opened the way for Olympic players to accept training expenses and sponsorship at the games from their federations or their nations. As a result, many countries now set up elaborate national training centers, where top athletes can live and train at no cost to themselves as they prepare, under the guidance of free coaching, for the Olympic Games. That free training can be expensive; MSNBC.com estimates that each gold medal earned in the Olympics costs a country thirty-seven thousand dollars in training costs.

In the United States, Olympic contestants receive training stipends, medal bonuses, and health insurance, although the Paralympic contestants receive less than the Olympians do despite suing to end this discriminatory treatment. So even if the competitors present themselves as amateurs earning no money, they are still accepting a lot of support from the sports committees or the citizens of their countries. And after their Olympic performance is over, performers can exploit their Olympic achievements by hiring themselves out to endorse products while still remaining eligible for future Olympic competitions!

Although not professionals in the same sense as major league baseball players (since they receive no salaries), Olympic performers today are therefore not strictly amateurs, either. They can even play for countries other than their own if they can show some good reason for doing so, like possessing dual citizenship. Their situation is pretty far removed from the one that obtained just following the 1912 Olympics, when the I.O.C. took away the medals from the great athlete Jim Thorpe after the revelation that back in his college days he had received money for playing summer baseball.

The gradual but drastic loosening of the rules governing amateurism has penalized Olympic players of the past, who made their records under different, stricter conditions. Should this liberalizing of the rules mean that the record books ought to print asterisks after the names of today's Olympic athletes? Hardly. All of us must accept with good grace such changes in our status as occur with time. As the world changes and the I.O.C. recognizes those changes, athletes and their federations cannot fairly be criticized for accepting and taking advantage of new operating conditions.

Although organized baseball is now the source of many if not all players on Team U.S.A. Baseball, it refuses to shut down for a couple of weeks every four years to send its best players to the Olympics. Therefore Team U.S.A., although it includes professionals, does not consist of the best baseball players in this country, as, for example, Cuba's formidable team does.

So with some players representing their countries' top practitioners and others not, is Olympic competition equalized? Is it fair for some players to change the countries they represent, or to receive free training and support while others get none or next to none? No, competition is not truly equalized, but the world may still be too big and diverse for us to be able to standardize Olympic opportunity for all prospective competitors. Perhaps we are just lucky to have achieved the level of equality we've managed so far. When the members of many nations march proudly around the Olympic arena in national costumes waving their national flags, their smiles seem to indicate that they have forgotten, at least temporarily, about whatever disadvantages they might be under in comparison with others. Their obvious pride in representing their nations and in their acceptance by other participants appears to overwhelm any feelings of envy of the support that others have had. How amateur they are, if at all, seems less relevant to the chance they have earned of participating in world competition.

If Olympics can no longer feature true amateur play, where do we find it? In the baseball game played during the company picnic, in pickup games some kids manage to play on vacant fields, and in the "fun games" held by members of clubs that engage in Vintage Baseball. That's where you can see pure amateurism in action. That's where you find the infectious jollity, the smiles and laughter, that are the trademarks of amateurism.

A resurgence in amateur play through what I call the pay-to-play leagues has enabled men, including those who live otherwise sedentary lives, to recapture their youthful pleasure in playing ball by joining weekend baseball leagues. Those who do this find it more challenging than hooking on with softball leagues. These pay-to-play leagues, being strictly commercial enterprises and operating in several parts of the country, vary in quality of offerings, but the best of them inspire enthusiastic comments from players about re-connecting with other men through baseball and thus show once more that players consider baseball a manly game.

Perhaps an unexpected place for amateur baseball to thrive is among war amputees. After World War II the National Amputee baseball teams flourished for a while, playing exhibition games against other amateurs, although wheelchair basketball appeared to overtake it in popularity. The team names that players chose, the Broken Wings and the Flat Tires, indicated the parts of their bodies that were missing, as well as their admirably good-humored acceptance of their physical condition.

The real joy of amateur baseball came home to me during the final scenes of the film *Good Morning Viet Nam*, in a scene showing the soldiers teaching some locals how to play the game with a stick and a grapefruit. The merry group of actor-players was obviously having such fun that it became difficult, when viewing the scene, to keep in mind the tense situation in Vietnam at the time. Although fictional, this scene seemed to epitomize what is happening to baseball: others around the world will carry the amateur spirit for us. Although professionalism has spread to some countries, feeder teams of young amateurs abound.

The powerhouse international baseball teams have long been the ones representing Cuba and Japan, but they can hardly be considered amateur, either. In 2008 South Korea's team took the Beijing gold medal in a surprise upset of the Cubans, despite the best wishes of Fidel Castro sent "to the glorious Cuban athletes." The team from Chinese Taipei—the name used by the Republic of China (Taiwan) for competing in international sporting events—like those from Canada, China, and the Netherlands, placed low in the 2008 Olympic standings. The United States team, made up largely of players from professional baseball's farm teams, lost to Japan.

Some European countries boast good teams, with Netherlands long the standout. England has four leagues, with each team supported by a local business. But the center of baseball energy seems to have moved from Europe to Asia, with Latin America furnishing a lot of the youthful interest that American scouts look for. Caribbean baseball is now affiliated with Major League Baseball's Winter League and includes Puerto Rican and Dominican baseball as well as the Mexican League, which is composed of sixteen teams in two leagues, with an annual playoff. Caribbean play is sparked by the eight-team Venezuelan League. Australia and New Zealand feature club baseball, in which each club fields more than one team. The Australians have state and national leagues and engage in international competition; they relish their 1999 defeat of the powerful Cuban team in competition for the Intercontinental Cup. New Zealanders like to recall that their country hosted one of the first baseball games played in the Southern Hemisphere when Albert Spalding and his tour group played a game at Auckland in 1888, but not until about a hundred years later did baseball really catch on there. American baseball enthusiasts are often involved in promoting and forwarding baseball in these and other countries. Only those involved can tell whether to consider them pro or amateur.

So practically the whole world knows baseball today, with an estimated one hundred countries supporting teams and more than twelve million players engaging in the sport. Some countries aspire to field professional teams; some do not.

What shall we make of this mixture of professionals, semiprofessionals, amateurs, and what-have-yous? Who has the amateur spirit, and is that even important? It's important to us as fans only if players are one thing and claim to be another. It's important to the players only if they lose the spontaneous joy in playing that amateurism can engender.

3

Our Heroes

"When most people thought about getting their first black-and-white TV in 1950, '51, all of a sudden there's the biggest sports hero in the country, Mickey Mantle. He was the idol of every man, woman, little girl, little boy. They watched the World Series with Mickey Mantle. You know, the clean-cut — everything. I couldn't believe he could be a real person."

That's Richie Scheinblum speaking, a major leaguer of the seventies, remembering the childhood thrill of recognizing and idolizing a baseball star of the fifties. His worshipful feeling about the baseball star of his era, and his belief that everyone in the country felt the same way as he did, could be echoed by thousands of fans who pursue baseball tenaciously.

Unquestionably, Mantle cut a manly figure at the plate. Excellence in sport has long been linked with masculinity, and in the nineteenth century, baseball was called "a manly pursuit." Mantle, with his thick neck and muscular body, looked like the epitome of masculinity. But scholars who analyze sport point out that sports are gender-stereotyped — that is, when we watch sports played by men we assume that one must be a man in order to succeed in that sport. This assumption is what scholars call a "social construct": we've associated a sport like baseball with men for so long that we believe only men can succeed in it. This belief leads us to create gender stereotypes. We link women with more aesthetically graceful sports like synchronized swimming, and we link men with sports like baseball, which we view as requiring much more courage, strength, and endurance. Actually, of course, both men and women succeed at every sport, including baseball and synchronized swimming. But actuality fails to affect our assumptions. Because men dominate professional sports, baseball remains inflexibly linked with maleness.

An expression we commonly use at the start of a competition, "May the best man win!" supposedly implies a wish that the person who deserves to win will come out on top. But we don't use the word *person*; we use the word *man*. That phrase illustrates our assumption that the competitors in any game or sport will be men. The "social construct" has permeated every aspect of sports, including its language.

Sports writers build baseball players into heroes. From the beginning (explain two scholars who have studied the subject), sports journalists wrote about players' "amazing feats" and omitted mention of any character flaws. Not until after World War II did journalists begin writing of our heroes more critically and cynically. The writers' long cover-up of ballplayers' character weaknesses is deliberate. For many years, at least into the 1950s, ball clubs paid all expenses of the newspapermen who traveled with the players — trains, hotels, and food. In that way they made friends of the writers. Joe Trimble, a friend of Harold Seymour's from the days of their Brooklyn boyhood, told us that his employer, the *New York Daily News,* did not have to advance him a cent for travel expenses, because Joe traveled with the players as if he were one of them — hardly a situation that helped him remain objective in his writing.

Reporters' feelings about the players seem not to have changed much even after newspapers took over the funding of their employees' travel. William Falk, an editorial writer for *The Week* magazine, told me in an email that in his experience with baseball reporting, journalists often see the players as friends, or as people whose privacy and stardom they need to protect, so writers don't always write what they know about a player. In a piece he wrote for *The Week,* Falk was a little more analytical: "Famous athletes," he said, "are our society's last remaining gods, and sportswriters know that it's their job to stoke the myth-making machine. In return for their complicity, the writers get to shine with the stars' reflected glory. Why spoil the illusion?"

This protection for players granted by those who report on them can give fans a skewed version of players' character that surely helps build them into falsely unblemished figures. They become bobbleheads worthy only of fan veneration, their shortcomings kept hidden. Nobody except some teammates may be aware that a certain player was, for example, what Falk learned was called "a family man with a road wife," a phrase meaning that a woman companion traveled to the player's road-trip cities and lived with him there. Reporters kept the story from their readers, thus preventing the player's devoted supporters from learning about the "road wife" and letting the fans believe only the "family man" aspect of the player's life.

When player-writers like Jim Brosnan in the '60s and Jim Bouton in the '70s revealed what some of their heavy drinking-and-carousing teammates were really like, fans were scandalized — temporarily. Some fans mourned "the old days" when "real heroes trod the base paths, heroes who played hard, lived hard and gave us everything they had on and off the field." Were there ever such days? We think we remember them, but how about the great Babe Ruth? He's long been known to have been as voracious while womanizing as he was when eating. A recent biographer calls him "a bombastic sloppy hero," sadly portraying his tendency toward excess as overshadowing and ultimately eclipsing his genius on the field.

Sports journalists' exposure of players' personal shortcomings came about sooner than other journalists' exposure of presidential "escapades," as Helen Thomas, long-time political correspondent, called them. She revealed in her book that she and other reporters censored themselves in order to honor the "gentleman's agreement" not to reveal President Kennedy's sexual adventures but that by the time of the Clinton presidency, the press was no longer extending that kind of protection. As public entertainers, major league baseball players fell a little more quickly than presidents into the category of "fair game."

Revelations of players' weaknesses never seriously affected fans' pursuit of baseball. They were able to take it all in stride and seem to have decided that players' questionable private lives faded in importance compared with their on-the-field accomplishments. Players' failings were explained away. But, to be fair to the players, can you imagine what a strain it places on a person to live up to the idea of being considered a hero? Trying to project a false image is living falsely. "It's an unreal life," commented player John Roseboro, "and when you leave it, you're lost. You can't deal with reality." Perhaps that's why so many Hollywood stars experience unsuccessful private lives.

In 2008 the *New York Times* advertised a forthcoming exhibition of professional players' pictures by headlining the story "Sports Heroes." Perhaps I shouldn't have been surprised that a respected newspaper would characterize as "heroes" the men who make their living by playing a game to entertain us. *The Times* is hardly the first to fall victim to its own puffed-up rhetoric. But why is such nonsense continued? Probably because it sells newspapers.

So what is a real hero? Someone who helps others who need help, often at great risk to himself or herself. Heroes reputedly have "nobility of purpose." Winning a game, or having a large part in winning a game, is an exciting goal, but nobility (something lofty and exalted) hardly enters into it. The only ballplayer I can think of who fits the bill is Roberto Clemente, who lost his life while trying to help others. There's a heroic man. In attempting to personally relieve suffering, he showed nobility of purpose. Although those who followed his career said that he lacked a perfect character, I think his final act of generosity counts for a lot.

In searching for a hero, some writers and fans have focused on a player who demonstrated exemplary behavior: Cal Ripken. Columnist Thomas

Boswell believes Ripken "epitomizes essential human values, like fidelity to a code of duty and honor ... a decent guy who showed up for work every day, signed a lot of autographs, and didn't cheat ... a hometown guy who understood responsibility and an adult who grasped that players simply were custodians of a game owned by its fan." Ripken is thus Boswell's nomination to the level of hero, but even Boswell admits that these qualifications erect "a very low hurdle for sainthood." Low indeed. Ripken, because he eschewed illegal drugs while other players were rightly suspected of using them, made himself look good. He demonstrated adherence to commendably high standards, but where is it written that a person who follows the rules is automatically a hero? Shouldn't fans have the right to expect this behavior of every player?

Some observers believe that Danny Gardella and Curt Flood qualify as heroes because they sacrificed their careers to undermine the reserve clause, which from 1879 until 1975 kept a player tied to a club that bought him, even if he wanted to leave, until the owner didn't want him any more. The free agency status that eventually resulted from the actions of Gardella and Flood limited a club's control and gave players the right to hire on with another club after a certain period of service. Gardella and Flood, by putting themselves on the line for an idea, ruined their own careers by taking those actions, but the men who entered baseball after them were helped immensely: they could operate more like film stars, whose period of service with a particular studio is limited by contract. And players could negotiate salaries that were several times what they had been before: by 2007 the *average* major leaguer earned close to three million dollars a year. Current players should probably think of Gardella and Flood as heroes.

But it's fans, not players, who usually engage in hero-worship. At its extreme, hero-worship can cause mayhem. When the local major league team wins the league pennant or the World Series, the town goes mad with joy, as Cleveland did in 1948 when the Indians won the Series for the first time since 1920. Non-fans like me were startled at the intensity of the street celebrations and the loud noise. Police tried to be tolerant of the wildness, for, after all, they were fans, too. When the Detroit Tigers thrilled citizens by winning the pennant and then the World Series in 1968, a year after the city had been torn by terrible riots, observers saw barriers between the races break down as Detroit erupted not with fighting but with joy: citizens forgot their problems to celebrate downtown.

After the Phillies won the 2008 World Series, more than a million fans packed the route of the parading players. Celebrants knocked down traffic signals, sprayed beer everywhere, shot off fireworks, and generally engaged in vandalism — overturning cars and street-side planters, damaging bus shelters, smashing store windows, upsetting garbage bins, and leaving broken bottles all over the streets. Said the police commissioner, "It's okay. It's all right. People are having fun." Well, it's not okay to destroy property and endanger other people. What he meant was, "It's understandable."

Even presidents show their baseball partisanship by wearing the team jackets or caps that identify them with their preferred teams. They may do this to demonstrate that they are "regular guys," like the rest of the country — loyal fans who root for their own particular teams. Representing oneself as a fan is as important for gaining public office in the United States as declaring publicly that one believes in God. Avoiding presenting oneself as a fan of the national game might be as politically unwise as avoiding showing affiliation with a religion.

Of course, when a fan's favorite team wins, the fan feels like a winner, too. Peter Beinart, writing in *Time* magazine, says he's uncovered research proving that some male fans gained so much surety from the glory reflected off their winning team that they grew more confident of getting dates with women.

When the team to which a fan is devoted loses the pennant, the opposite happens. Fans wallow in self-pity. (Perhaps they even despair of attracting a woman.) One devotee of a losing team described himself as suffering "anguish," "misery," humiliation," and "bitter disappointment." This distress seems like an overreaction. Just because your favorite team was defeated, must you feel vanquished, too? Yes. If you are a real fan, you feel the same pain as the team does. You love the team as you do your child or your mother or your country. Each player on your team represents the beloved.

But when a fan's favorite team sells a favorite player to another team, that player morphs immediately from hero into enemy. The beloved has suddenly become the foe. Are fans crazy? No, just quirky. We all have our quirks, our aberrations from logic. No doubt psychologists will some day be able to explain these oddities, but we may not want to know the reason for them.

One way fans demonstrate their devotion to individual players is to collect their autographs. For generations children and adults have relentlessly pursued players to ask for their signatures. At first these autographs were collected simply to look at and share with others, as proof that the collector had actually seen the hero close up and exchanged a word or two with him. But it wasn't long before the monetary value of autographs changed the way fans viewed those scribbled signatures.

When Harold Seymour became batboy for the Brooklyn Dodgers in the late 1920s, it was easy for him to collect names of the players on teams that came to Ebbets Field. He did nothing with these autographs beyond showing them to friends. But late in life he finally realized that they no longer meant much to him and sold them to someone who already owned a huge collection and wanted more. Once as an adult Seymour attended an Old-Timers' game at Yankee Stadium as the guest of George "Specs" Toporcer, a former big-league player and manager, and as they emerged from the VIP exit, some boys asked for their autographs. Seymour, who had red hair, obliged by signing the name "Red Schoendienst." So somewhere in the world is a collector with a fake Schoendienst autograph.

No doubt other fake autographs exist. Catherine Petroski, who researched and wrote about the career of her grandfather, player Bob Groom, is sure that an autograph of Groom published in a SABR guide called *Deadball Stars of the American League* isn't his, since she knows his signature well. Cindy Thomson, author of *Three-Finger*, a biography of pitcher Mordecai Brown, disputes the authenticity of the Brown signature in the same publication. Petroski, after talking to dealers about the authenticity of autographs, believes that this field leaves "much room for chicanery." So does any field where thousands participate. Believable assertions of fakery include claims that players sometimes hire clubhouse employees to do their autographing for them.

Such claims of fakery have reached the point where collectors hire auditors to authenticate signatures on objects they consider buying. In 1999 the Federal Bureau of Investigation successfully prosecuted a California forgery group that flooded the internet, baseball card shows, and retail shops in every state with thousands of fake signatures, many of them still in circulation in 2008. The reason for the group's success, according to a book on this scam, was that the public, obsessed with celebrity, "is desperate for the pseudo-intimacy that autographed collectibles provide." It seems that when their idols become less accessible than they were in the past, fans pursue any putative evidence of their presence ("My hero once touched this paper") and so make themselves easy marks for criminals.

Not every player was polite to every autograph hunter in the early days of collecting. Players, like other prominent people, have things on their minds besides scribbling their names a dozen times in a row. And when the idea of selling these autographs became widespread, players were brought up short, realizing that fans were making money on them. Autographs, especially those of deceased players, brought high prices. When fans began pestering players mercilessly to sign their names, some players started charging for the service, for if the fans were going to make money on signatures, the players wanted a piece of it. After all, this is a monetary society. I doubt that the necessity for paying players for their signatures has discouraged resolute autograph-hunters, although I've heard them grumble about paying.

Now autograph-seekers in New York have another gripe: the new Yankee Stadium has placed so many barriers shutting fans off from the players at every former access point that the club has, according to reporters, further widened the huge gulf between those who make millions playing the game and their supporting fans. A businessman known as A.J. Romeo points out that he is stepping into the breach to offer Yankee fans an opportunity to get an autographed baseball — for prices that range from $50 to $2,500. But buying an autographed ball is hardly the same experience as standing next to one's idol while he is signing his name and perhaps even saying hello.

Fans collect other objects associated with their heroes — but they do not always savor those objects forever. The fan who caught the ball with which Mark McGwire set a home-run record sold it for more than three million dollars and changed his style of life to suit his new status. A memorabilia dealer estimated that the last ball hit out of Yankee Stadium, which two fans both claim to have caught, is worth between $25,000 and $50,000. But who owns it? What these two fans claim is called a "fugitive baseball," and legal historian Paul Finkelman, a professor at Albany Law School, has written a scholarly article examining the law behind this kind of dispute. Two statistical-minded fans have even studied where in several stadiums fans should sit in order to greatly increase their chances of catching baseballs, because "clearly, in America, this is a question of basic importance." Tongue in cheek or not, the analytical comments of these two fans made a serious journal article.

Private collections of baseball memorabilia, especially baseballs and bats, can rival those in public museums. Don Gunther of Naples, Florida, owns 350 signed balls and 300 signed bats, including a ball signed by Babe Ruth. In 2007, during the annual Naples Winter Wine Festival, Gunther opened his collection to some ballplayers and ex-players who were in town for the occasion. When Harmon Killebrew saw Gunther's acquisitions, he said, "I haven't seen such a collection. He has everything." Hank Aaron remarked, "I'm just amazed. There's more stuff in here than they have in Cooperstown."

Some collectors specialize in rather narrow groups of items. George DeMaio, host of a radio show in Bridgeport, Connecticut, claims to have the largest collection of minor league baseball bats anywhere. *Minor* league. Bob Bailey, editor of a newsletter for SABR's Nineteenth Century Committee, collects graves — that is, for twenty-five years he has been collecting photos of dead professional players' gravestones and now owns "a few hundred."

At least one movie star is a collector of baseball objects. Charlie Sheen, who has played ball since he was a child and who portrayed Happy Felsch in the film *Eight Men Out,* found that one can become a "slave" to a collection "because if you care, you want to display it properly." Between trying to fiberoptically light it for heat and humidity control and avoid damaging objects that had survived a century, Sheen declares, "it's a full-time job."

Collectors like those I described can be viewed merely as acquisitive people whose passion is to own items of value, but they also do historians a service. If we all gain an understanding and appreciation of memorabilia and begin saving and annotating interesting objects from our culture, archival collections everywhere can become richer and more evocative of the era from which they came and therefore of more use to historians. We do well to save that old scorecard from a memorable ball game. "Objects," says Sarah Henry, deputy director of the Museum of the City of New York, "are the eyewitnesses of the past, and they're more than that. They're emissaries from the past."

University representatives, like sports fans, grasp the symbolic value of a sports object. In 1922 Cornell inaugurated a new baseball field, naming it after the university registrar and bench coach, David Fletcher Hoy, who was also an alumnus of the class of 1891. After throwing out the first pitch, Hoy preserved the baseball he had used, sealing it in a handmade bag and locking it in the family's home safe. Eighty-six years later, in a formal ceremony, Hoy's grandson presented the beloved baseball to the university archivist, Elaine Engst, expressing his pleasure in knowing that now the ball "can be properly taken care of." Having been handled by the university's early sports heroes, this object has become precious.

The Smithsonian Institution has not been left by the wayside in the urge to own objects related to the game. It houses a collection of autographed baseballs signed by many noted players, some purchased from memorabilia dealers and others obtained from the collections of fans. The Smithsonian has singled out 350 valuable baseball items from twenty-one private collectors and published their descriptions in a pamphlet. In a separate catalog of items offered for sale, the Smithsonian plays up its holdings by featuring a silk "Autographed Baseballs Tie" picturing many of its signed balls, including one bearing a copy of Babe Ruth's autograph. This item of haberdashery will set you back thirty-five dollars.

Photos, too, can become valuable collections. Bonnie Crosby, daughter of Barney Stein, the official photographer of the Brooklyn club from 1937 to 1957, has published a book of her father's baseball photos. A collection of DiMaggio's baseball belongings sold in 2006 grossed nearly five million dollars, and in 2008 the family of catcher Thurman Munson decided to auction off about 150 items related to his baseball life: World Series rings, uniforms, even his custom-designed Mercedes Benz convertible. One of Munson's rings is valued at about $50,000. No doubt some fans will pay these prices just to be able to boast of owning something that their hero touched. The large sports auctions handled by Sotheby's have reportedly brought in huge sums for collectors who want to dispose of their holdings. A Honus Wagner card advertising Piedmont Cigarettes went for more than a million and a half dollars in

2008. The fan who bought it, John Rogers of North Little Rock, Arkansas, declared this card "the holy grail of baseball cards" and admitted that he had "hoped and dreamed" to own it since he was eight years old.

Less-wealthy fans prize commercially published cards bearing players' pictures, statistics, and copies of their signatures. Fans can buy a Ty Cobb card for ten dollars on eBay, or pick up a boxful of Topp cards covering the players of one year, 1956, for $140 plus shipping. Thus do small pieces of cardboard without intrinsic value take on worth when imprinted with the image of the hero.

The baseball card is a descendant of the *carte de visite*, a small card with a person's photo pasted on it, which persons generally sent to friends or family members back in the nineteenth century. The similar baseball cards developed as innovative sales promotions because photos or sketches of prominent players helped sell bubblegum and cigarettes. At first merely ephemera, baseball cards became collectors' items and then souvenirs so desirable that fans were soon saving, trading, and selling them. By the 1950s the Topps Chewing Gum Company had reportedly changed a childhood diversion into "a highly profitable facet of American culture." In 1991, when the gum became less important than the baseball cards, Topps stopped bothering to put the gum in the packages.

Once a pair of collectors found, in a box of antiques they had purchased, what may be the oldest baseball card still extant: one picturing the Cincinnati Red Stockings of 1869. Expert evaluators claim this card may be worth as much as a hundred thousand dollars. Dramatic evidence of baseball souvenirs' high value to their owners, as well as their link to religion, is the habit in Cuba of depositing sports memorabilia at the shrine of the Virgin el Cobre, located about fifteen miles from Santiago de Cuba. These offerings include "signed baseballs thanking the virgin for some clutch home run or essential out, as well as Olympic medals offered by athletes who believe their victory came about because of her intervention." Cubans devoted to Roman Catholic saints habitually dedicate to them whatever is of most value to the believers, so the piles of baseballs at the Virgin's altar lie among stacks of other gifts like diplomas, snapshots, and jewelry.

Casual collectors of souvenirs "just for fun" can buy a package of twenty-four samples of "genuine big league baseball mud," the clay from the Delaware River that home-plate umpires use for rubbing new baseballs to remove their gloss. And now those who want to step on the grass trodden by famous players can purchase "Yankees Grass," strips of sod grown for Yankee Stadium (although not actually taken from the Stadium): the grower of "Yankees Grass" holds an MLB license to sell his turf, and the seed with which it is grown, under that name. Or they can buy a beautiful four-color National Baseball

Hall of Fame calendar bearing photos of many Hall of Fame displays and facts about ballplayers.

But serious collectors dominate the field of baseball souvenir trading. Psychologists' studies of collectors describe them as "hoarders" who display an "unruly passion" for self-assertion born of "a need to control." According to studies, these obsessed persons substitute their collected items for human intimacy: they collect things instead of developing relationships with others. This seems like a harsh judgment pronounced on persons engaged in a harmless hobby. For some, collecting becomes not a hobby but a business. One "sports marketing guru," Brandon Steiner, who maintains more than 10,000 collectibles in his inventory, runs a fifty-million-dollar enterprise, selling to more than five thousand regular clients.

Fans' desire to possess anything related to professional baseball can get way out of hand. Some collectors go so far as to steal baseball objects. In 2000 the Hall of Fame in Cooperstown revealed that over a couple of decades it has lost through thievery many valuable baseball objects and documents. The FBI has been tracing, locating, and returning some of these. Since at least 2009 the FBI has also been investigating the robberies of priceless historical baseball documents from the New York Public Library, the Boston Public Library, and the Library of Congress, many of these items having been offered openly through auction houses, where they are eagerly bought by thoughtless fans.

It seems that in our pursuit of baseball, we reveal our weaknesses and peccadilloes — the extremes of our innermost desires and the odd ups and downs of our devotions. I think what we really want, in admiring our heroes, is to *be* our heroes, and since that isn't possible, we find other ways of identifying ourselves with them. Being heroic must fulfill a deep yearning within us.

Perhaps in Jackie Robinson's brave agreement to offer himself as the sacrificial lamb in Branch Rickey's bold experiment we can see heroism in action. In paving the way for blacks to return to organized baseball, a place they had occupied back in the 1880s, Robinson vindicated those who had long pointed to blacks' exclusion as a huge, illogical, and cruel gap in our vaunted democratic system. Subjected to extreme vilification and even physical danger, Robinson toughed it out in a way that Ripken did not need to. Could the rest of us have mustered as much courage as Robinson did? Knowing that we might not have been able to handle it as well as he did makes us admire him more.

But Robinson is not what most fans have in mind when they speak of baseball heroes. Instead, they mean players who hit in the pinch, who manage to make the big run that wins the game, and who attain "good numbers." If these players also avoid fights, try to play regularly despite injuries, get along with teammates, and maintain good humor in the face of adversity, fans think of them as even more heroic. Admirable as these traits are, they fail to add up to heroism. Perhaps what fans have in mind when they think of these players is not heroism but success, which is defined either as achieving something desired or as attaining fame and prosperity. Both definitions can be applied to admirable players. Calling them heroes is more than exaggeration, it's being inexact. Editors reading written statements calling successful players "heroes" find that their blue pencils twitch; they long to place the letters "W W" ("wrong word") on that term.

Fans cannot seem to keep in mind that ballplayers, like everyone else, come in all types: educated men like Moe Berg, complex personalities like Joe DiMaggio, players who don a threatening persona like Sal Maglie, cheerful charmers like Yogi Berra, tragic figures like Tony Conigliaro, silent Sams like Ted Williams, ferocious meanies like Ty Cobb, and humorists like Rabbit Maranville. Are these all heroes? No, but they're all successful players.

Ballplayers sometimes become "heroes" because they fill a perceptible need at a certain moment in history. Here is one who did just that, according to biographer Mark Stang:

> At the height of the Depression, the nation was hungry for heroes and the sudden arrival of Bob Feller provided instant headlines for the nation's newspapers. Feller struck out 15 Browns in his first major league start. Three weeks later, he matched Dizzy Dean's major league record of 17 strikeouts. The press dubbed him "Rapid Robert" because of his blazing speed.
>
> Feller was an instant celebrity. Attendance soared as fans flocked to ballparks to catch a look at the young phenom. He was flooded with endorsement offers. He finished the 1936 season with five wins in eight starts and struck out 76 batters in 62 innings. That fall, Feller returned to Iowa and began his senior year of high school. He was still just 17.

Such a dramatic story made news, so America immediately turned Bob Feller into a hero. Feller is still a beloved figure in Cleveland, where he completed a successful career and then decided to make his home. Still admired for a lifetime of records, he plies the rubber-chicken circuit. And why not? With all this adulation, he can take advantage of his status as a hero.

Fans often reward player-heroes with money and gifts, even though the players may be far wealthier than the fans are. In 1912 Napoleon Lajoie received from his "adoring fans" a monstrosity of a floral horseshoe nine feet high, inset with more than a thousand silver dollars. At that time the money in the horseshoe represented the average pay of a working person for a year.

Fans also show up to worship at spring training games, taking time off from work or using their vacation days to fill the stands in the small parks of

Florida, where they can watch Grapefruit League games, and of Arizona, for Cactus League games. In these intimate settings they can view their heroes at close range, call out encouragement, and cheer them on. On returning home they can boast that they saw close up, and even exchanged a few words with, their idols.

Players have learned to expect tributes and accolades as if they were true heroes. As the saying goes, they start to "believe their clippings." Like Hollywood actors, as a result they sometimes succumb to arrogance. If they manage to maintain a balanced view of themselves and their careers, they deserve our admiration.

Fans can show their passion for the national game in weird ways. Once journalist Rob Neyer and author Bill Nowlin, a Red Sox authority, decided to spend the night at Fenway Park, just to see what it felt like. They experienced the noise and actions of the cleanup crew and the scurrying of rats, but that's about all. Nowlin soon realized, as he wrote later, that "there is really nothing happening." Yet boasting to fellow fans later about their adventure, they found the common reaction to be "Wow! I wish I'd done that!"

4

The Pantheon

No group is more straightforward in its unabashed reverence for the national game than an organization called the Baseball Reliquary. What is a reliquary? When I first heard of the group, I had to refresh my memory by checking the definition of its name, and I learned that a reliquary generally turns out to be a receptacle, like a coffer or shrine, for keeping or displaying relics. And a relic? It's an object of veneration, usually religious veneration. Remember the custom, dating from the Middle Ages, of venerating the bones of people that the Roman Catholic Church selected as saints? The bones were known as relics.

The Baseball Reliquary, an organization built by folklorist Terry Cannon, takes a different view of baseball than does the Cooperstown Hall of Fame. Instead of emphasizing statistics and achievements, it features the legends and traditions of the game. Although the Reliquary has not yet revealed its ownership of any players' bones, it has collected some baseball souvenirs not many people will admit to desire viewing, like a piece of skin from the thigh of Abner Doubleday, the man who didn't invent baseball; a jockstrap that belonged to Eddie Gaedel, the little person that Bill Veeck once sent up to the plate to hit for the Indians; Veeck's wooden leg; Dock Ellis's hair curlers; a clump of dirt from the Elysian Fields in Hoboken, where the Knickerbockers and other early teams played; and a hot dog partly eaten by Babe Ruth.

These items have a certain cachet; the *New York Times* has described them as reflecting "an irreverent sort of reverence." Cannon considers them art related to social history, and he views his collection as "sort of a sporting version of the Museum of Jurassic Technology," another California gathering of items that can best be described as bizarre, since the Jurassic Age ended millennia ago and lacked any technology.

Besides collecting baseball curiosities, the Reliquary elects baseball people to an honor roll called the Shrine of the Eternals, a sort of alternative Hall of Fame. Members nominate anyone, including owners or umpires or fans, who they believe affected baseball in a way unreflected in the record books. Fictional characters like Charlie Brown are sometimes nominated.

To its credit, the museum has selected Curt Flood as an Eternal, for his work as a pioneer in obtaining economic rights for players. Marvin Miller, the players' representative who did so much for them, is also recognized by the Reliquary (although not by the Cooperstown Hall of Fame — to its everlasting shame, believes Fay Vincent, former MLB commissioner). Roberto Clemente, too, is honored by the Reliquary. And Lester Rodney, the sports writer who worked hard to get black players into the majors, is on the Reliquary's list of baseball people recognized for their significant contribution to baseball.

The Baseball Reliquary pays attention to various branches of the sport, including fans. In keeping with its religious motif, the Reliquary's annual induction ceremony opens with the ringing of a bell, not a church bell but any bell, in honor of Hilda Chester, the late Brooklyn Dodgers fan, who always brought a cowbell to games and rang it joyfully and often. In Hilda's honor, the Reliquary awards an annual prize to a fan for his or her "extraordinary passion for and dedication to baseball." In 2008 that honor went to a lifelong Cleveland Indians fan named John Adams, then celebrating his thirty-fifth year of emphasizing his pursuit of baseball by pounding his drum in the bleachers at all Indians games.

Donning a different baseball cap, the Reliquary also sponsors scholarly conferences with well-qualified speakers, as well as exhibits held in the Pasadena Central Library and the Pomona Library, since the organization has no permanent home except for Terry Cannon's (and I will keep his address secret in case robbers take a fancy to that rotten hot dog or the used wooden leg).

Cannon disdains the Hall of Fame at Cooperstown as a static collection of artifacts; he sees the story behind each relic as at least as important as the object itself. At the Shrine of the Eternals, Terry Cannon is pursuing baseball in his own quirky way.

Most Americans know of the more mainstream baseball museum in the charming town of Cooperstown, New York, where a long-ago citizen named Abner Graves declared that his friend, Abner Doubleday, invented baseball in 1839. For years Cooperstown was thought of as the place where baseball was born. Cooperstown even celebrated baseball's so-called centennial in 1939 with the dedication of the Baseball Hall of Fame and Museum, and the official program of the occasion is labeled "The Birthplace of Baseball." For a time, the town's baseball park boasted a street sign reading "Doubleday Field, Where

Baseball Was Invented and First Played in 1839." Struck with the surprising confidence this sign expressed, I published its image in my autobiography, *A Woman's Work*. Cooperstown realtors that Harold Seymour and I talked to became irritated when we pointed out that the sign commemorated an apocryphal story; no doubt they could charge more for homes when Cooperstown was considered the site of baseball's origin. Nowadays, the Hall of Fame's chairman words his reference to the town more carefully and accurately, calling it "the institutional and spiritual home of the game." The museum's promotional material avoids claiming the invention of baseball for Cooperstown, instead labeling the museum "the home of baseball" and keeping track of the number of fans who "make the pilgrimage" to "baseball's hometown." Americans and others recognize its drawing power to the tune of 350,000 visitors a year.

Museum spokesmen admit that baseball artifacts collected over the years range from valuable to not-so-worthy. When Harold Seymour heard that ballplayers' belongings would be on display in Cooperstown, he remarked, "Who would want to come and see Babe Ruth's old jock strap?" As it turns out, many people no doubt would, if it could be found. Exhibits attract thousands each year, even though admission prices are high. The central feature is the Hall of Fame Gallery, where plaques celebrating the nearly 300 elected members line the walls. Most inductees are star players, but some are prominent officials.

Promotion material for Cooperstown's Hall of Fame and Museum describes it accurately as "one of the country's most popular destinations" and "surely the best-known sports shrine in the world" as well as "the definitive repository of the game's treasures" and "a symbol of the most profound individual honor bestowed on an athlete." With its many special exhibits, programs, and events, the organization is certainly fulfilling its stated mission: "to preserve [baseball] history, honor excellence, and connect generations."

No baseball collection can compete in thoroughness with the one in Cooperstown. For the veneration of the baseball-pursuing public, it boasts holdings like 130,000 baseball cards along with 33,000 bats, balls, uniforms, gloves, and similar pieces of equipment. Many artifacts, like players' old jerseys and sweaty caps, are not even on display and remain in boxes in a vault. For scholars, Cooperstown has three million research files, 500,000 photos, and 12,000 hours of recorded media programs. No wonder the official brochure describes the Hall of Fame and Museum as "Baseball's Mecca."

To those who study the game on an academic level, the most important section of this institution is the Hall of Fame Library, housing many cabinets full of carefully filed documents and a superb photo collection. Those engaged in serious research projects may visit the Giamatti Research Center, named after A. Bartlett Giamatti, who was not a baseball researcher but a former professor of Renaissance literature and president of Yale University; he loved the game and for one year held the post of commissioner of baseball.

It came as a surprise, as well as a mild disappointment, when I learned that the research center was named not for the first major baseball researcher but for someone who admired and respected baseball research. It's well-known among baseball researchers that the scholar who epitomizes baseball research and devoted his life to developing baseball history was Dr. Harold Seymour. Nobody pursued baseball more persistently than he did. With my full assistance, he opened the field of baseball history to other serious researchers and made baseball research an acceptable field for scholars to enter. It was Seymour who had the innovative idea to study baseball on a formal basis and write a doctoral dissertation on the subject. His pursuit of baseball on an entirely new level helped to change the Hall of Fame's library from a room with a few books and boxes of manuscripts to a huge building with a valuable repository of materials that became a magnet for scholars.

A director of the Hall of Fame's library, Thomas R. Heitz, grasped this when he said in 1992, the last year of Seymour's life, "Dr. Seymour is without question the prototype and ultimate role model for baseball history practitioners." When Professor Charles C. Alexander won SABR's Seymour Medal in 2003 for a book on the history of baseball in the Depression era, he remarked in his acceptance speech, "None of us would be in this room today without Harold Seymour's work." William M. Simons, a history professor at the State University of New York, put it this way in a paper given at the Cooperstown Symposium:

> The writing of history, like the past it chronicles, is marked by defining benchmarks. For U.S. historians, the presentation of Frederick Jackson Turner's seminal paper, "The Significance of the Frontier in American History," at the 1893 meeting of the American Historical Association, redirected examination of the nation's past to new sources and new themes. For baseball historians, the 1960 publication of Harold Seymour's *Baseball: The Early Years* by Oxford University Press initiated the process that ultimately granted respectability to scholarship about the national pastime.

By putting Seymour's contribution to historiography on the same level as that of Turner, Simon made clear Seymour's unique status in baseball history.

In 2002 Dr. Steven Riess of Northwestern Illinois University devoted an entire scholarly article to an explanation of Seymour's contribution to history, calling him "the father of modern baseball history" and "The Lead-off Batter" in the field. Riess points out that Seymour's work "created the essential narrative for the history of baseball" and that he was "the real pioneer in the history of sport.... He paved the way to intellectual respectability for all of us."

Giamatti himself recognized Seymour's contribution to baseball by using his work (and mine) in his 1985 lecture at the Boston Public Library on "Baseball and the Public Character." Quoting from our work, he called it Seymour's "excellent history of baseball, to which I am [for this presentation] throughout indebted."

Although the Cooperstown museum remains the prime destination for both fans and scholars who pursue the national game, many other groups besides Cooperstown have established baseball museums. Their major purpose appears to be straightforward promotion of baseball and its practitioners. That purpose is clearest among those museums set up inside major league ball parks. The Cardinals and the Texas Rangers, for example, have established sections for viewing player photos and artifacts. The Rangers, through the club's "Legends of the Game Museum," even give fans a chance to feel what it's like to catch a Nolan Ryan fastball. The Cardinals set up autographing sessions with players and photographing sessions with the World Series Trophy as well as innovative activities like learning to create rubbings from the Cardinals logo.

One museum inside a park is devoted to the star hitter Ted Williams, although other hitters are recognized. Tina and Dave McCarthy operate their museum as a tribute to the "Greatest Hitter Who Ever Lived," as they call Williams, inside Tropicana Field in St. Petersburg, home of the Tampa Bay Rays, and on game days fans are admitted free to the museum. This arrangement attracts about a thousand visitors each day and two hundred at night during the Rays' home games. "I don't think we would have those numbers," admits McCarthy, "if it was in an ordinary building." Fans attending Rays games can also view another exhibit: thirty live rays (the fish) swimming in a huge tank behind the right center field fence.

Fans enjoy visiting the Babe Ruth Birthplace Museum, which features the life and times of the man called "the greatest baseball player ever," his prowess demonstrated through objects displayed at his childhood home in Baltimore. In a play on the common phrase about George Washington, the museum's web site says about its building, "Babe Batted Here." Nearby is the Sports Legends Museum, which occupies two floors of Camden Station, next to Orioles Park; it includes Ruth mementos as well as those from other Baltimore sports professionals, notably the city's Negro League baseball teams.

The remarks of museum curator Shawn Herne show understanding of the significance of sports and the way they affect fans. He points out that the two museums he directs, the Babe Ruth Birthplace and the Sports Legends Museum, deal not only in sentimental significance but also historic and cultural value. "Sports," he opines, "transcend the boundary of age.... People [young and old] build a common identity around the games and the athletes who play them." That's because entire families often visit these places and find that the experience gives them a closer bond.

More directly related to economics is a Pittsburgh entrepreneur's idea to turn a former player's home into public sleeping accommodations. Stanley Klos bought the home of Honus Wagner for $15,000 and planned to convert it into a bed-and-breakfast site as well as a museum. What could be more apt? He could claim, "Honus slept here."

Like most museums dedicated to one person, the Ty Cobb Museum is up-front about its purpose, which is to collect artifacts relating to Cobb, preserve and exhibit the collection, and enhance appreciation of Cobb's accomplishments. Recently, a collector named Karen Shemonsky contributed a new piece of Cobb memorabilia to the museum: his dentures. She bought them at an auction for more than eight thousand dollars. Cobb's more significant legacy is the establishment, with his initial contribution of $100,000, of the Ty Cobb Healthcare System, which includes a hospital, a convalescent center, and a health care center, all of it self-supporting. The people of Georgia doubtless appreciate this at least as much as they do the opportunity to review Cobb's accomplishments as displayed at the Cobb Museum.

The Ripken Museum, too, centers on the accomplishments of the player, particularly his record streak of games played. It has been located in Cal Ripken's home town of Aberdeen, Maryland, but is seeking a new location.

Bob Feller, although he makes his home nowadays in Cleveland, created the Bob Feller Museum in Van Meter, Iowa, his original home town, and even publishes a newsletter describing its special events and new displays. Feller's museum naturally emphasizes pitching. Besides giving fans the chance to relive the life and career of the famous pitcher through examining reminders of his work, the museum offers recognition of excellent Iowa pitchers by giving awards to high school seniors who excel at their sport. Feller himself often shows up at his museum.

The museum devoted to Roger Maris may be the most highly accessible of all: it has been mounted on the walls of an inner corridor at a shopping center in Fargo, North Dakota, where even fans not expecting them will come across the exhibits devoted to his exploits without paying an admission charge.

Some museums have been created not around individual baseball stars but around baseball subject matter. The Negro Leagues Baseball Museum devotes its displays and programs to the history of African American baseball, using artifacts dating from the late 1800s through the 1960s. Established in the section of Kansas City that is the historic area for black life and culture, the museum sees itself as a community center. Through its programs it strives to explain to visitors the historical significance of the black leagues, a subject discovered relatively recently by scholars. Its staff has even prepared an elaborate teachers' guide to help school children learn about their baseball heritage.

The Baseball Heritage Museum in downtown Cleveland also emphasizes the history of the black players in the Negro Leagues, with its rich collection of artifacts, photos, and printed materials, but its owner, Bob Zimmer, searches and finds other types of baseball materials and hosts visits from fans of all ages, including busloads of schoolchildren.

Other museums consider themselves primarily educational and research centers. The Yogi Berra Museum and Learning Center in Montclair, New Jersey, is actually on the site of Montclair State University. Its promotion material indicates that its activities have been arranged especially for children, although it presents "topical programs for all ages." The Learning Center's stated mission, "to preserve and promote the values of respect, sportsmanship, social justice, and excellence," sounds less related to either standard educational goals or even the promotion of baseball history than to the promotion of ethics. In fact, several of the Learning Center programs have been designed specifically to promote leadership, character-building, and personal discipline, although some historical and sports medicine courses are also available. Is it possible that we finally have an institution that recalls and tries to advance the amateur baseball ethic?

Canadian baseball might be a subject for a museum that Americans don't expect, but it offers more than fans think. Inspired by the discovery of an 1886 newspaper reference to a baseball game played in Beachville, Ontario, in 1838, interested Canadians helped set up a museum in nearby St. Marys. Besides a Hall of Fame for star Canadian players and a display of Canadian baseball exhibits, the museum, located about a half-hour from London, Ontario, offers baseball camps where Canadian boys and girls can improve their baseball skills under the instruction of baseball coaches. The museum doesn't neglect baseball artifacts; it houses an exclusive collection on the life of Ferguson Jenkins, a black player from Ontario, who overcame racial barriers to become a star major league pitcher. Another unusual exhibit is one devoted to the "inspiring and heart-wrenching tale" of a team of Japanese Canadians, the Vancouver Asahi, who won five Pacific Northwest Championships before being interned during World War II; like the Japanese Americans sent to Wyoming, the club continued playing while interned. Now, that's devotion.

Like the Negro Leagues Museum, the Canadian Baseball Hall of Fame and Museum also has big plans for the future. It is in the midst of constructing several ball fields, an education center, and even a dormitory for the summer campers as well for as the Canadian Olympic Baseball team. It aims to make its organization an important center for the pursuit of many aspects of baseball. So for this museum, fan devotion provided the impetus for something much larger.

Amateur baseball players, like the professionals, are celebrated in museums. Fans of South Dakota baseball can visit the state's Hall of Fame at Lake Norden, where a pictorial history of amateur ball in South Dakota is displayed along with used equipment and other memorabilia. Since the state's baseball-minded citizens have participated in various levels of baseball — high school, college, American Legion, and town team — their exploits are recognized at the museum.

Another amateur association, the National Baseball Congress, one of those popular from the Depression days of the thirties, established the National Baseball Congress Hall of Fame so that NBC participants who eventually made the majors could be honored. Actually, of course, many NBC participants were less amateur than they were semipro. Like the Negro Leagues Museum, the NBC Hall of Fame honors Satchel Paige as one of the first selected, since he, backed by a team from Bismarck, North Dakota, won the first NBC national title with 60 strikeouts in one tournament.

Even the Little League has a museum. Its building in Williamsport, Pennsylvania, looks strikingly like the Hall of Fame in Cooperstown: a graceful one-story red brick building, its entrance formed from a porch with three arched openings, known now as a portico in Palladian style, and surmounted by a long white stone eyebrow. Janice Ogurcak, director of the Little League Museum, confirms that the resemblance is intentional. Little Leaguers, after all, want to be big leaguers.

Commercial aspects of baseball can also be pursued via the route of a museum. One of the most famous pieces of baseball equipment is the bat called the Louisville Slugger. The building that celebrates its creation can't be missed, even at a distance, because a construction called the World's Biggest Baseball Bat towers over the Louisville Slugger Museum and Factory, seemingly leaning casually against it as if left there by a Bunyanesque batter who has just walked away. Inside, fans learn the history of the company and watch the bats being made.

The Louisville Slugger bat owes its fame to an amateur baseball player whose father owned a wood-turning shop in the 1880s. When professional players began ordering bats from the company, and then amateur players learned they could order the same model their favorite big-league players used, the company's business took off. Like the Yogi Berra Center and similar baseball organizations, the Louisville Slugger Museum and Factory offers educational tours.

Some baseball museums have even combined with others into an organization called the Sports Museum of America, headquartered in lower Manhattan and representing more than fifty North American sports museums (although not the Cooperstown museum). A *New Yorker* writer who attended its opening cocktail party in 2008 and viewed the baseball collection commented wryly that "there were no syringes or asterisks to be found." While it lasted, the organization's members provided exhibits displayed in a sleek and modern exhibition hall, but in 2009 the museum declared bankruptcy

Perhaps the most affecting museum is the one devoted to Shoeless Joe Jackson, whom Judge Kenesaw M. Landis banished from organized baseball after the 1919 Black Sox Scandal, even though Jackson's guilt was never proved and a court of law exonerated him. Unlike most baseball museums, with their modern buildings, the Shoeless Joe Jackson Museum and Library is housed in Jackson's cozy home, a building hardly larger than a cottage, which was moved to a site across from the ballpark in his home town, Greenville, South Carolina, and set up as a monument to Jackson.

Shoeless Joe Jackson Museum

The former home of the ballplayer Shoeless Joe Jackson, Greenville, South Carolina, is now the home of the Shoeless Joe Jackson Museum and Baseball Library, where Arlene Marsley is the curator. Jackson was suspected of cheating in the 1919 "Black Sox" World Series, so Commissioner Kenesaw M. Landis banned him from playing, along with others on his team (courtesy of the Shoeless Joe Jackson Museum and Baseball Library).

Gene Carney, the late historian who wrote much about Jackson and the Black Sox Scandal, took part in the opening ceremony at the Jackson Museum in June of 2008 and said the house, although it includes displays showing Jackson's accomplishments, is not over-loaded with posters and artifacts, and those few on display blend in with the period architecture of the home. Instead of being a beginning of a new campaign to clear Jackson's name, as some journalists interpreted the museum's opening, it was, Carney believed, a way to honor Jackson despite organized baseball's refusal to recognize him and his stellar playing career.

Many organizations unrelated directly to sports mount temporary baseball exhibits. Institutions from the great Metropolitan Museum of Art in New York City to small historical societies put on baseball displays that attract fans as visitors. The Iroquois Indian Museum in Howes Cave, New York, has presented an exhibit called "Native Americans in Baseball" to celebrate famous Indian baseball players like Moses Yellowhorse. The Elliott Museum of Stuart, Florida, is opening a new baseball exhibit that includes not only the thousands of baseball cards but something less expected: a Ty Cobb diary. Those nostalgic for the days when radio announcers were the main source of game events enjoyed a "Media Day" exhibit in 2008 at the Baseball Heritage Museum in Cleveland, featuring the announcers themselves, complete with their broadcast booths and studios. And in Allentown, Pennsylvania, the Lehigh Valley Heritage Museum mounted a 2008 exhibit presenting stories and artifacts relating to local baseball heroes and combining those with historical material from the national game's stars, including Babe Ruth's cap and Mike Schmidt's 1980 World Series uniform.

Curators are certainly trying hard to find innovative baseball exhibits. The George Bush Presidential Library and Museum arranged an exhibit called "Born to Play," featuring not Bush family players but fifty well-known professionals, five chosen from each position. Cities like Schenectady, New York, and states like Minnesota have presented exhibits to celebrate local baseball. Schenectady's exhibit, "Covering the Bases: The Science of Baseball," is designed to "merge the science of baseball with all the wonderful history of the sport we have here in the area," explained the museum's archivist, Chris Hunter.

New York City has an especially rich baseball history to celebrate. "The Glory Days: New York Baseball, 1947–1957," at the Museum of the City of New York on Fifth Avenue, presents memorabilia, film footage, and photos to take fans back to the days of the intracity Yankee-Dodger rivalry.

The Metropolitan Museum of Art, on the other hand, features baseball cards from the Burdick Collection. Jefferson Burdick collected a great many objects, including 30,000 baseball cards, and among them is one of the rare

Honus Wagner cards that has changed hands for more than two million dollars. A boy who looked briefly at some of the Burdick cards displayed at the Met commented that they were "cool." An adult fan collector named George Vrechek, looking them over, discovered a carefully posed "action picture" on a card showing Connie Mack "with hands at his side [as he] stares at a ball on a string moments before it would have hit his midsection had it actually been moving." The ball-on-a-string card, assuming anyone would like to buy it, is valued at $15,000.

Several museums have prepared traveling exhibits: The Negro Leagues Baseball Museum in Kansas City sent out its "Discover Greatness" exhibition to the Historical Society of Washington, D.C. The Anacostia Community Museum in D.C. showed a related exhibit cleverly named "Separate and Unequaled." Early black players also get attention at Mesa, Arizona, because the director of the Mesa Historical Museum, Lisa Anderson, found that Mesa was "one of the few places that would allow African-American players to play" before organized baseball would hire them. She declared that although the beginning of the Cactus League as a spring training venue came in 1947, evidence showed that barnstorming major league teams visited Mesa as early as 1909. Robert Brinton, president of Mesa's Convention and Visitors Bureau, hopes to expand the museum in order to "document and celebrate baseball in Arizona."

The North Carolina Baseball Museum at Wilson showcases major league and Negro League players born in its state, featuring those selected as "the Magnificent Seven," but its web site consistently misspells Luke Appling's name.

"Baseball As America," a richly detailed traveling exhibit prepared by the Hall of Fame in Cooperstown, has entertained and enlightened fans from New York to Houston and from Philadelphia to Los Angeles. When I saw it in Cleveland at the Great Lakes Science Museum in 2007, I was struck with its balance and comprehensiveness. With more than 500 valuable and well-explained historical artifacts, the exhibit is the best all-around visual presentation of baseball that I have ever experienced.

If fans prefer to travel in order to pursue their passion for baseball, they can see a lot of it on their summer vacations with the family. Those looking for suggestions can find several books on the subject, such as *101 Baseball Places to See Before You Strike Out*. More ideas for baseball-related venues and events are easily found by checking a site called Magical Baseball, where Morris Eckhouse, past president of the Society for American Baseball Research, offers his own list of a hundred and one destinations, including college baseball sites, along with places to experience baseball events, not just games but special baseball celebrations, as well as other places simply to visit, like baseball museums, stadiums, famous players' birthplaces, and the gravesites of various baseball personages. Eckhouse also helps fans plan their baseball trips. With Bob Becker, a film producer, Eckhouse has prepared an audio walking tour of downtown Cleveland places that connect with local baseball history — something like the Heritage Trail in Boston, which tourists follow in order to see the historic places in town.

Fans can receive travel tips about many baseball attractions, especially those in major league cities, through the *Fan Guide; Your Major League Baseball Travel Resource,* a perk received when joining MLB's new Insiders Club. Pursuing the trail of baseball heroes all around the country is one way of immersing ourselves in baseball for an extended period. Writer Tim Kurkjian met one thrilled family that visited all thirty major league ballparks in one summer, capping off the tour with a visit to Cooperstown. Said the father of the family, an Alabama preacher: "It was the trip of a lifetime."

For fans who love minor league baseball, Bob Carson of Strongsville, Ohio, began publishing in 1989 a lively multi-page newsletter featuring minor league parks, suggesting places to visit and providing room for fans to report on their favorite trips. With more than four thousand subscribers to a sixteen-page newsletter, each paying ten dollars a year, he can present a lot of information about topics like places to stay, reviews of ballparks, club news, and even trivia, book reviews, and fiction. And because Carson can list 214 minor league teams operating in the United States and Canada, he finds himself with an almost endless supply of ballparks to visit and describe, with much of the description furnished by his subscribers. New York alone boasts 16 minor league teams, California 17, and Florida 14.

Carson enhances his service business with spinoffs like filming one team's adventures in Chillicothe, Ohio, and selling the DVD made of that film; writing pieces for magazines like *Trailer Life,* whose readers make up a natural audience for travel to minor league parks; and holding writers' contests to reward the best contributors to the newsletter. Now that's a variety of baseball experience.

What do travelers to minor league parks get out of the experience? They find friendly, small-town staff members whose schedule seems light enough to enable them to spend lots of time with visitors, even giving them unscheduled tours of the facilities on non-play days. Visitors traveling to minor league towns find "light traffic, little danger, friendly people, and a slow pace," as one fan put it, and they "return refreshed." The newsletter, which arrives in the off-season, whets fans' appetite for baseball and gives them "the best cure for the winter doldrums," so receiving *Minor Trips* and the seed catalog "is what makes January and February bearable" for these fans.

Some companies actually escort fans on cross-country baseball tours, which offer surprising diversity. Tom Broach of North Carolina quit his insurance business to form Broach Sports Tours, a company that offers sports tours but specializes in baseball bus trips, and his list has grown to 200 different tours, some of them featuring spring training trips. Tours often include visits for games at several stadiums and a tour of at least one city plus admission to museums and meals at restaurants operated by former players (more contacts with heroes available). Broach's company is hardly a one-man outfit: it has grown to include 28 employees. When he began offering these tours, Broach anticipated a male audience, but he found that forty percent of those who take the tours are women. Some clients are repeat tourists who call themselves "fanatics" and who say they love the "excitement" of it all.

Jay Smith of Massachusetts garners rave reviews from the clients who enjoy his itineraries for a company called Sports Travel and Tours. Testimonials for S.T.A.T. trips use words like "joyful" to describe their experiences. Smith caters to many fans whose goal in life is to see every ballpark in the nation. Baseball obviously plays a major part in the lives of fans who want to spend their travel time seeing firsthand what every ballpark looks like.

Jay Buckley of Wisconsin operates a similar tour company. This one bills itself as the largest baseball tour company, because it handles no other sports. Since 1982 Buckley has been giving tours featuring extensive spring training trips that include several parks either in the Cactus League of Arizona or the Grapefruit League of Florida, where fans can see their big-league heroes close up. Or they can take a regular-season trip, like the one starting in Los Angeles and continuing to San Diego and Oakland, then up to Portland and Seattle, and back down to San Francisco and Los Angeles, ending up in Arizona. This trip can cost nearly three thousand dollars; it includes eleven games with sixteen teams in eight ballparks. Buckley fans believe he offers good value for the money; one satisfied fan noted that he learned not only about baseball "but about our grand land." Others also mention the educational aspects of his trips, for both Buckley and Broach hire knowledgeable tour guides to accompany the tourists.

For baseball fans who want something different, Kit Krieger, a former Pacific Coast League pitcher, offers "CubaBall: Tours for the Baseball Aficionado." He has been visiting the island since 1997 and has made many friends and contacts there. Each year he takes groups of fans on trips to see the excellent games of the Cuban National Series, meet ranking Cuban baseball officials, and explore Cuba's rich baseball past through visiting various parks as well as, in the evenings, enjoying local musical events. Fans do more than "see the sights"; discovering that teams and players are deeply connected with their communities, they begin to understand how baseball fits into the Cuban culture.

"What Kit is doing to get American fans down there is great ... he has exposed a lot of new people to Cuban baseball," comments Peter Bjarkman, the historian of Cuban ball, who has himself made many trips to the island and developed close contacts with Cuban baseball figures. It seems clear that people like Krieger have education in mind with his trips to see how others live, play, and approach their problems as well as their pastimes.

Despite the political stalemate between Cuba and the United States, Krieger finds no difficulty arranging these tours through Prime Travel of West Vancouver in British Columbia, which specializes in sport tours, and he points out that interested Americans are always welcomed warmly in Cuba. Krieger's customers find his tours highly stimulating; they represent, as he says, "a window into a culture not easily assessed any other way." Some point out that American baseball is so highly commercialized that in order to find the kind of baseball they used to love, they must go abroad. Participants in these tours find them "eye-opening," "a pilgrimage," "life-changing," "magical," "terrific," and "incredible," since their experiences in Cuba are so different from any other tour they have taken.

Many tourists who visit Cuba with Krieger have been stimulated creatively. Byron Motley, a Los Angeles filmmaker, was inspired by his trip with Krieger to write a book-length manuscript about Cuba and to design an exhibit to be shown in Havana. Stephen Cummings, a clinical psychologist, wrote a newspaper report of his experience, and Eli Gorn, who traveled on Krieger's very first tour, produced a film about that adventure called "Cubaball: The Lure and the Legend of Cuban Baseball." Reporter Tom Hawthorn, who writes a weekly column for the *Toronto Globe and Mail*, wrote a richly detailed summary of his trip. Alexa Van Sickle, who traveled from England to Miami to join Krieger's tour, came in order to perform research on Cuban baseball for her doctoral dissertation in anthropology. Oscar Soule, a professor at Evergreen State College, used the experience as part of an interdisciplinary college course he taught with a sports writer friend who took the Cuban trip with him. People like Soule and Van Sickle pursue baseball at an intellectual level. Some baseball aficionados travel to Cuba independently; Mike Ross, founder and chairman of the United Kingdom's chapter of the Society for American Baseball Research, was inspired by his own trip to Cuba to write an article about his discoveries there for SABR-UK's baseball journal, *The Examiner.*

Young people can pursue baseball in Cuba, too. Peter Bjarkman's travel colleague, Bob Weinstein, has arranged legal trips for youth groups to Cuba through an international organization called the World Amateur Athletic Congress. Under the auspices of WAAC, the young American ballplayers raise the money for their own trips, and then, accompanied by coaches and par-

Children still play ball in the streets, but not as much in the United States as in
Havana, Cuba. Mike Ross of London, England, snapped this photo in the Buena Vista
area of Havana when he traveled to Cuba to observe Cuban baseball (courtesy of Mike
Ross).

ents, they compete against Cuban youth teams in Havana and other Cuban
cities. The highlight of the trip, Weinstein says, is the last game, in which
Cubans and Americans play on the same team. Quite an experience for young
people!

Most baseball tours are, however, confined to the continental United
States. In addition to working people, retired folks also pursue baseball
through travel. Elderhostel, whose purpose is "lifelong learning," sometimes
features baseball games and other events at spring training sites. I have myself
spoken twice on baseball history before Elderhostel gatherings at Vero Beach,
where the Dodgers were training and where the groups met under the sponsorship of Stetson University. I found a lively interest in baseball history
among the tourists — who were, as found in the Broach tours, nearly half
female.

As a result of this resolute dedication to the game on the part of fans,
baseball players have become different from the rest of us. By building players into larger-than-life heroes, we have diminished their humanity and made
them into the surreal figures that Richie Scheinblum thought Mantle was
when he first saw the star switch-hitter on television. Even after sports writ-

ers broke their tacit agreement not to reveal players' personal failings, many fans discounted the writers' revelations and continued to idolize their heroes. Today, years after Mantle's shortcomings became known, fans enthusiastically buy a seven-inch "action figure" of "the Mick," a tiny statue of him, for fifteen dollars. Since Americans have revived the ancient Asian activity of constructing household shrines, I wonder if, when walking into a friend's living room some day, I will see players' action figures standing in a little nook, complete with votive candles.

Perhaps we have some psychological need to think of ballplayers as heroic. Sports writer Robert Lipsyte believes that baseball heroes, "through their courage and personal sacrifice, give us a glimpse of the potential for heroism that every one of us, with or without a mitt, is born with."

5

Go Figure

American fans love to pursue baseball by using statistics to study, compare, and pronounce upon the abilities of favorite players. Guidebooks full of numbers have been published, and now online sites like *baseball-reference.com* and several others furnish fans with the figures for every professional player, team, and league in all of baseball history, including their batting, field, running, pitching, and catching numbers — and sometimes different numbers depending on whether they were playing at home or away. As Casey Stengel reportedly remarked, you could look it up, "it" being any baseball record you want. And after researchers look it up, they analyze it. David Zavagno, a devoted baseball researcher who spoke at a recent SABR convention about the balls used in major league games, explained his interest in the game's statistics by stating that baseball "is played at a speed that allows us to analyze and overanalyze."

The big name in statistics is Bill James, whose obsession with baseball statistics brought him to the attention of manager William Lamar "Billy" Beane of the Oakland A's and then to a job with the Boston Red Sox. A biography of James portrays him as growing up a social misfit and suffering an unhappy childhood until he discovered the world of statistics as it applies to baseball.

To look at James, an extremely tall man with considerable presence, one can hardly help believing that he must know what he is talking about as he dissects baseball performances in what seems to non-nerds like arcane ways. Many members of the Society for Baseball Research (SABR) who devote themselves to understanding players' skill through the numeric interpretation of their accomplishments are Bill James followers. A recent review of a book on fantasy baseball calls him "Dalai Lama Bill James." Once known as "figure filberts" or even "statheads," SABR members who study baseball stats call themselves Sabermetricians, and they represent a separate breed of baseball historians.

Knowledge and use of baseball statistics can help produce winners. The careful application of statistical analysis by baseball club owners has put better teams on the field for lower costs. Beane, along with John Kerry, senator from Massachusetts, and Newt Gingrich, former speaker of the House, have proposed that the government apply a similar approach to the American health care system and reward decision-makers who deliver care that is based soundly on results proven by statistics. So baseball statistics are useful not only for baseball.

The social historians and other scholars from the liberal arts field seem unable to communicate easily with the statisticians, and vice versa, so they have agreed to work in the same organization but separately. (Kindergarten teachers used to call this sort of activity "engaging in parallel play.") At the annual SABR meetings, a statistician like Alan Nathan, a professor of physics specializing in nuclear/particle physics, might present a paper called "What Can We Learn from PITCHf/x?" about using a set of data available on Major League Baseball's web site, while David Bohmer, who directs a media program at DePauw University, gives a presentation called "Marvin Miller and Free Agency: The Importance of 1969." These two radically different kinds of researchers pursue baseball in their own entirely different ways.

SABR has also established a Baseball Records Committee, dedicated to both researching and clarifying (and maybe altering) records that players have attained from the beginnings of professional baseball through the present. Are these records definitive? Hardly. A small sign just outside the gallery of great players at the National Baseball Hall of Fame in Cooperstown tells viewers that the numbers on each plaque came from sources "believed to be reliable and accurate at the time [they were] written," thus warning viewers that maybe errors have crept in, as they did with Walter Johnson's plaque. Numbers on Major League Baseball's own web site occasionally differ from those in other statistical guides, and the web site's representative, Rich Levin, explains, "There's no official record book" and therefore no official numbers. This situation fails to curb the constant number-crunching among those who pursue statistical baseball.

In addition to the scholars are the many everyday fans who find themselves fascinated by the statistical evaluation of their favorite players. They argue the players' relative accomplishments endlessly. What seem to others like small permutations in records loom large to them. Shall we talk about those hitters who made 40 home runs in a season? No, it has to be those who both made 40 homers *and* fewer than a hundred runs batted in during the season. Shall we consider the ten pitchers who won the most games in a season? No, make it pitchers with the most wins *and* who were members of teams with more than 110 losses in a season. Sabermetricians also rely on statistics like WHIP (walks and hits per inning pitched) and VORP (value over replacement player). After a while, those of us who shrink from rating players by means of whips and vorps begin to picture the proverbial angels dancing on the head of a pin. What about the excitement generated among fans when a favorite hitter steps up to the plate in a tight situation? That's what fans want. Steve Shymanik, a corporate manager, tries to put statistics into perspective when he uses this figure of speech: "Numbers on a page can no more capture the spirit of a game than sheet music can capture the power and grace and beauty of a live performance." Or, as Toby Harrah, a professional player of the seventies, reputedly put it, "Baseball statistics are like a girl in a bikini. They show a lot, but not everything." Statistics, as Billy Beane has shown, do contribute a great deal of useful information. And, according to baseball writer Leonard Koppett, "it is entirely possible that more American boys have mastered long division by dealing with batting averages than in any other way."

Not an everyday fan but a math whiz, Nate Silver, used his skill polished in fantasy baseball to win national fame in 2008 by analyzing political polls and picking Barack Obama as winner well before the television networks did. For baseball he had built a well-known predictive system that used some unusual factors like pitchers' height to foretell successfully what teams would rise to the top. It worked for politics, too.

Some fans analyze baseball players' accomplishments compulsively because they interpret players' deeds as typifying the masculine in our culture. It's a guy thing: baseball heroes are seen as masculine heroes, men whose skills and accomplishments appear to fans to be typical of healthy American males. That's one reason baseball rides the tailcoat of nationalism, as did the highly successful American Legion Junior Baseball program for boys, established in the 1920s. The Legion still promotes both nationalism and the masculine ideal.

When in the twenties observers thought boys' baseball showed a decline, the Legion started baseball leagues and tournaments for them, not in conjunction with community work but as part of its "Americanism program." The plan was to "teach Americanism ... through playing the game," and its end purpose was "the training of soldiers for future wars and the rearing of citizens who will accept the status quo without criticism or objection." Somehow, the ideas of "training soldiers" and promoting "unquestioning acceptance" got tacked on there.

The Legion's definition of "Americanism," which the organization's leaders thought could be developed by boys' baseball leagues, bound masculinity and nationalism with baseball. "Nationalism and masculinity converged," says Jacob Bustad of Kansas University, commenting on the Legion's program, "through the playing of baseball by young American males." The Legion's view of Americanism evidently failed to include black children, for college coaches looking for young recruits find that fewer black than white youths are involved in baseball because of lack of opportunity: the inner city, where many black boys live, offers few baseball diamonds and fewer sponsors for clubs. "American Legion is where blacks get shelved," says Lyle Mouton, father of the only black player on Louisiana State's team. Those who do not get to play Legion ball are unlikely to play college baseball, and college is where players can be seen by organized baseball's scouts. And if a scout signs a college player considered to be a hot prospect, the player can expect a signing bonus above two million dollars. Not playing Legion ball means the boy is more likely to stay poor.

The Legion's idea of Americanism appears to be similar to that of the Public School Athletic League formed early in the last century. The PSAL's founder, George Wingate, saw to it that schoolboys participating in the PSAL saluted the flag and marched in review at athletic meets; he declared that competitive athletics developed "the robust, manly qualities of courage, nerve and hardihood" that our country needed. Around the same time, a leader of another nation voiced a similar belief in combining physical development, masculinity, and nationalism:

> Only when a nation is healthy in all its members, in body and soul, can every
> man's joy in belonging to it [women's joy isn't mentioned] rightfully be
> magnified to that high sentiment which we designate as national pride. And this
> highest pride will only be felt by the man who knows the greatness of his
> nation.

This is Adolf Hitler speaking. The "high pride" in his nation that he planned to develop in male citizens is something we now identify as chauvinism, that militant glorification of one's nation often reaching the heights of fanaticism.

When it came to the boys who swarmed into the program set up by the American Legion, however, the young fellows weren't thinking of national pride; they merely wanted to play ball. As it happened, so did some girls, so the design of the Legion's program went slightly askew. But that's another story.

Meanwhile, among the thousands of boys who have played American Legion ball since it began in 1926, many honed their skills well enough to reach the major leagues. In fact, more than fifty Legion graduates have been inducted into the National Baseball Hall of Fame in Cooperstown. That includes Ted Williams, Roy Campanella, Bob Feller, and Stan Musial.

The Legion's program for boys therefore probably affected nationalism less and professional baseball more, since Legion ball prepared and developed many professional players for the major leagues, who in turn paid the Legion for its services.

As for nationalism, it suffered during eras like the sixties, although not in baseball. As historian Ron Briley pointed out in a presentation before the Cooperstown Symposium, during the Vietnam era baseball officials embraced the war, and although dissent "permeated" our culture, "the sport was less tolerant of those who questioned authority or military policy." Reportedly, the government kept ballplayers out of the draft, and few of them spoke out against the Vietnam War (were these two facts related?). Major league baseball also sent groups of players to Vietnam on good-will tours. Afterwards, some players admitted to feeling some guilt about holding back their opinions. Tom Seaver, who arose from the Legion's "Americanism" training, which called upon boys to accept national policy, did make a few remarks about the war, but they were judicious, and they attracted little attention.

Not until 2004 did one player, Carlos Delgado, publicly show his feelings about government actions when he refused to stand during the seventh-inning stretch while "God Bless America" was being played at Commissioner Bud Selig's direction. Delgados, raised in Puerto Rico, might have been deprived of the American Legion Junior Baseball "Americanism" instruction, but according to a former manager, Jim Fregosi, he was also sophisticated, intelligent, and "wise beyond his years"; Mets manager Willie Randolph said he respected Delgados for being a man of conviction and being unafraid to speak his mind.

Delgados had grown up in Puerto Rico, where he and many islanders became resentful that the island of Vieques, expropriated by the American Navy, had for more than 60 years been used, and largely destroyed, by the Navy as a weapons testing ground. Active local protests escalated in 1999 when an American bomb killed a Puerto Rican employee of the Navy; they intensified until in 2003 the Navy finally left. In 2004 Delgado, as a protest against the Iraq war, disappeared into the clubhouse when the national anthem was played and drew some criticism for his action. But the protest didn't last, and matters were smoothed over; Delgado went on to pursue a satisfying career, his patriotism unquestioned.

Major league baseball's effort to link itself with "Americanism" could be said to have begun with the spring of 1889, when Albert Spalding's Chicago club returned from a world tour promoting what he called "the American National Game." The event took place at Delmonico's restaurant in New York City, where celebrities had gathered to praise the returned ballplayers. At this celebration, Abraham G. Mills, chairman of the National Commission (and no relation of mine!), a man appropriately known in some quarters as Awful

Gall Mills, declared that baseball was American in origin. Cheers greeted this claim. From then on, few would venture to risk tarnishing their patriotism by pointing out that baseball actually came from England.

During World War One, major league baseball's patriotic activities in selling war bonds and directing players to march around the park like soldiers, drilling with their bats, were part of the owners' push to keep professional ball going despite the government's imposition of the draft. Patriotism, or the appearance of it, was good for business. It always has been. Professional players were drafted and served in both world wars, and fans cheered their appearance on Movietone News.

When in 2003 Dale Petroskey, president of the Hall of Fame in Cooperstown, suddenly cancelled the Hall's showing of the popular baseball movie *Bull Durham* because two of its stars who opposed the Iraq War, Tim Robbins and Susan Sarandon, were to appear there in person, many fans protested. Petroskey finally recognized that he had made a mistake in asserting that these two actors were unpatriotic and that their appearance might endanger U.S. soldiers fighting in the war.

To Petroskey — and apparently to the American Legion — patriotism demands agreement with the president's decisions. All of them. Nothing could have made clearer the Hall of Fame's position solidly in the cement of the establishment than Petroskey's attempt to muzzle two movie stars. Petroskey, a friend of the president's brother Marvin, had once presented U.S. president George W. Bush with a lifetime pass to the museum when Bush visited Cooperstown, so it was natural for him to place himself squarely in the president's camp in the matter of the Iraq War.

Probably, Petroskey's action in canceling the Robbins and Sarandon appearances can be ascribed to his personal embarrassment when he found that he had invited to a public baseball occasion two prominent artists who had been open about their disagreement with the president of the United States. Just their appearance at the event might remind the audience that not everyone approved of all the president's actions.

Criticism by public figures over his apparent attempt to undermine free speech made Petroskey realize that his decision to cancel the stars' appearance was misguided, and he apologized. As it happens, both Tim Robbins and Susan Sarandon knew that a mention of their political views on such an occasion would have been inappropriate.

What would have happened if the two stars had been allowed to appear? And what if they had even taken the opportunity to mention their disagreement with the president on the Iraq War? Petroskey might have been fired sooner than he was — in March of 2008, for "failure to exercise proper fiduciary responsibility."

In rescinding the invitation to Robbins and Sarandon, Petroskey obviously thought he was defending America, but actually he was defending an unpopular decision of the president, and he was undermining the American right to free speech. Thus do baseball institutions like the American Legion and the National Baseball Hall of Fame try, and fail, to promote their versions of Americanism. They do better when they stick to their original purposes: the Legion to defend the rights of veterans, and the Hall of Fame to collect and support the preservation of baseball records.

President George W. Bush nearly fell into a similar error when his administration denied the application of Cuba, which has long boasted a superior national team, to play in the World Baseball Classic of 2006 with fifteen other teams. He based his decision on the ground that the players would take the money they would earn back to Cuba, where it would benefit the communist regime. Bush never considered, I believe, that the players might spend it to better their lives. Cuban players have no unions or agents; their pay is low, and their playing assignments are controlled by the state's sports bureaucracy.

Bush's decision received support from at least one baseball historian. Roberto González Echevarría, the author of *The Pride of Havana: A History of Cuban Baseball,* declared that because Cuban players have no freedom to bargain and play for a different club, "those who want Cuba to participate are asking to be entertained by a team of slaves." González Echevarría forgot that for nearly a hundred years, 1879–1972, when club owners controlled American players with the reserve clause, professional ballplayers in the United States stood in that same position. They lacked the right to play for any team other than the one with which they had initially signed, or one that their owner sold them to. Those who "jumped" to another league were banned from returning; the Cubans who leave are banned for only five years. Not until 1972 did an arbiter grant free agency to two American players on the basis of groundwork laid by earlier players Danny Gardella and Curt Flood, thus opening the way to improve players' position. Until then, sports writers sometimes referred to American professionals as "well-paid slaves."

After threats of cancellation by the International Baseball Federation, and after Cuba declared that any profits made from the team's appearance in the World Baseball Classic would be donated to victims of Hurricane Katrina, President Bush relented. Cuba then participated, but its team was beaten by Japan. Lincoln Diaz-Balart, a member of the United States House of Representatives, who is a Cuban-American, commented, "I hope that the Cuban players will use this opportunity to escape totalitarianism and reach freedom in the U.S." Only one defected.

Like the American Legion's Junior Baseball Program, and like Petroskey at the Hall of Fame, President Bush would have done better to keep his eye on his main responsibility, which in his case was seeing that America helped promote peaceful international relations instead of hindering them. Baseball could become a better vehicle for friendly international contacts, and fans around the world would benefit.

The Little League and other youth leagues as well as college leagues have avoided falling into the trap of emphasizing nationalism over play. Adult leagues, too, make enjoyable play central to their purpose. Men in their thirties, forties, and fifties who love to pursue baseball join these weekend leagues for a fee, either individually or in teams, in order to enjoy play at whatever level they can manage it. The Roy Hobbs League (named after the hero of the novel and film *The Natural*), operated by Tom Giffen of Ohio; the Boston Men's Baseball League; and the American Amateur Baseball Congress, among others, offer play for a fee at various age and ability levels. Men who join these groups want to "enjoy the game, aches, pains, and pleasures of playing hardball" because playing enables them to recapture their youthful dreams: "When I walk onto the field in my uniform," said a Toledo, Ohio, player, "I'm in high school again." A New Jersey fellow commented, "It's a great way to spend a Sunday afternoon!" A third remarked, "I feel like a kid again being out on the baseball diamond."

Other baseball activities that have grown up alongside these play-for-a-fee leagues help to keep baseball central to the American spirit. Two of the most important are fantasy baseball and vintage baseball. Records and statistics dominate the lives of those who pursue the national game through the hugely popular format of fantasy baseball, or Rotisserie baseball, the latter name deriving from a restaurant where early practitioners met to devise their version of this activity.

Fantasy baseball is a game played almost exclusively by male fans; it's primarily a guy thing. To play it they select some of today's players for their teams and keep track of how these players perform during the season. Each team takes part in a virtual league, and all sorts of statistics are used and kept by the fans to learn who wins at the end of the season. An early fantasy league rejoiced in the clever name "the Pacific Ghost League"; one of its founding members was Jules Tygiel, a baseball historian.

When I learned about fantasy baseball, I thought it was copied from the idea of Robert Coover, the author who wrote the best baseball novel I ever read: *The Universal Baseball Association, Inc., J. Henry Waugh, Prop.* Coover made his protagonist's pretense of owning and operating a league full of players seem realistic and possible. I never dreamed that in the decades following publication of this novel, fans other than Coover would begin inventing their own teams to compete in pretend leagues made up of clubs created by other fans, or that the fad to take part in these competitions would, in the words of a critic, become "a game that unites thousands of American men in a time-wasting exercise of epic proportion." This phenomenon might be classified by a term that the CEO of a Chinese toy company has dubbed "kidult."

Focused on what was actually transpiring on the playing field and in front offices, I failed for a long time to realize that the greatest desire of many fans beginning in childhood was to become their own favorite big-leaguers, and if that were impossible, then to direct their own teams and leagues of big-leaguers. That's why boys used to get together and say "I'm Ty Cobb!" "I'm George Sisler!" and then act like these players. Like Walter Matthau, who says he wanted to be Hank Greenberg, they wanted to be their heroes, and this was the closest they could come to jumping inside those players' skins. Many fans of today want to be not their heroes but their heroes' owners.

Who invented fantasy baseball? The standard explanation is that the writer Daniel Okrent persuaded friends to join him in his Rotisserie League at a New York restaurant in 1979, but others had tried out the fantasy league idea earlier. Probably the most famous early player of fantasy baseball was Jack Kerouac, the literary voice of the Beat Generation. As early as the 1930s he played his own creative versions of the game with cards, broadsheets, and boxes he designed for his play, and he continued to make diagrams and cards and to invent players, teams, and on-the-field action into the 1950s. Now fantasy baseball is a huge business.

Perhaps it's significant that while the popularity of baseball among sports fans in general is, according to a study called *Baseball in Crisis*, actually in decline, the popularity of fantasy baseball has swelled. Fantasy, or Rotisserie, baseball represents a way for fans to control their game, a method of allowing them to slip into Coover's version of Neverland. No wonder fantasy baseball players have been termed "fanatics" and members of "baseball's lunatic fringe."

Statistics dominate fantasy baseball, so if statistics leave you cold, this game isn't for you. Using a variety of statistical measurements, those who pursue this game gain a grasp of a player's strengths on an entirely different level from that learned through simple observation. These measurements permit them to more readily compare a player's abilities to those of others, perhaps even predicting each player's performance under certain conditions and circumstances. Textbook authors use fantasy baseball to help teachers and parents use this game to teach mathematics — to children as young as grade five.

Fans who indulge in fantasy baseball pursue issues like player rankings, projections, scouting reports, strategy advice, and depth charts. They act like clubowners and managers, assembling their teams through a draft, making trades, and picking up free agents. The success of the "owners" in their fantasy leagues is calculated by points awarded when the teams they have assembled succeed; and at the end of the season the owner with the most points wins the game.

At least a dozen web sites offer these virtual clubowners assistance, advice, referees for trades, handbooks on how to play, and leagues to join, some of which cost money — especially those that offer prizes for winners. Some men make their living by telling others how to win at fantasy baseball through subscription websites or by lecturing or writing on the subject. Others make money winning at the game. Some admit that it interferes with the rest of their lives; one said rather sheepishly, "I have to get out more."

Both ESPN.com and MLB.com offer web sites to guide fantasy baseball players. But MLB (Major League Baseball) isn't thrilled with the existence of virtual baseball, taking the view that the baseball players are the property of the leagues and that their names and records cannot legally be used by web sites, handbook writers, or virtual leagues without the permission of the players' owners. By the mid-nineties fantasy baseball had become a big industry, conducted largely by means of the internet. To get a piece of the action, the club owners and the baseball players got together and formed a group called Major League Baseball Advanced Media, which signed licensing deals with some of the companies offering fantasy league formats but ended deals it had agreed to make with others. One of the rejected companies sued and won on the basis of free speech.

Disagreement over this issue went all the way to the Supreme Court, which ruled against Major League Baseball on the grounds that famous players are so well known to the public that their names and numbers ought to be freely used without having to pay a fee. So baseball players and their accomplishments are in the public domain, part of our heritage as Americans, who can pursue their passion for fantasy baseball without owing money to organized baseball.

Critics sometimes decry the shift of fans' attention away from baseball on big-league fields to baseball competition created in men's minds. Richard Crepeau, a baseball historian, was at first appalled to discover that a fellow SABR member, Jules Tygiel, played this game and "vowed I would never succumb to this evil that had befallen the delusional Tygiel," but Crepeau, too, surrendered to the game's allure and has passed his fifteenth year of playing fantasy baseball. Kent Oliver, director of the Stark County Library in Ohio and a devoted George Brett fan, plays the game every year. Sports writer George Vecsey claims that fantasy leagues are "a sure sign somebody has way too much spare time." That could include players like former governor Mario Cuomo of New York and former governor John G. Rowland of Connecticut, who are both avid players. But Vecsey also points out that, on the other hand, if fantasy league players "did get a life, maybe Major League Baseball would be out of business."

Vecsey has a point; fantasy baseball may be an improvement on real baseball as played in our big stadiums. John Benson, who publishes a forecasting annual for fantasy aficionados and is known as the "high priest of fantasy baseball," claims that fans "see owners threatening to leave their cities and players demanding outrageous sums of money.... The players are crazy and so are the owners.... In Rotisserie league baseball, the game is returned to the fan." Benson seems to be saying that fans turn to this mental and intellectual baseball activity as a reaction to the flaws and vagaries of real baseball as it is played on major league fields and that they prefer the invented competition to the reality. Thus might fantasy baseball be thought of as a withdrawal symptom.

But surely fantasy baseball also stimulates interest in the game on the field. After all, isn't mental baseball the ultimate Hot Stove League? It keeps fans' interest in the real game glowing even when snow piles high on stadiums. Mel Poplock, a certified public accountant who also chairs a Florida chapter of the Society for American Baseball Research, has been playing fantasy ball for twenty years and maintains his interest in Major League Baseball as well.

When he first began playing in 1988, Poplock explains, the points won by players were calculated by hand weekly, from statistics found in the publication called *USA Today*. Now computers calculate them instantly. Mel's twelve-member league uses CBS-Sportsline.com for statistics and advice. Poplock admits to often staying at his computer "until the wee hours" to learn how "his players" on the West Coast did that day, but why not? He points out that many people pursue their hobbies as diligently as fantasy players do.

Perhaps the ultimate in fantasy games is Sony's MLB.09 The Show, designed for the PlayStation 3, a video game that reviewer Seth Schiesel rated as "utterly gripping" and even "sublime." With this game you can act as one of the players or be a manager — even a general manager, if you prefer. Because of the superlative videos, MLB 09 evidently far surpasses the Wii experience.

Baseball inspired board games early in its history. In the 1930s a fan named Dick Seitz created a board game with team cards and involving a throw of the dice. He introduced his creation to friends under the name "American Professional Baseball Association," which quickly became "APBA" and is now pronounced "Ap-bah." Yes, the APBA game, simpler than the more elaborate Rotisserie but still based on player statistics, has lasted three quarters of a century, and the APBA company has sold more than half a million sets. Most buyers play at home, with friends or family. APBA president

Marc Rinaldi states that fans from seven continents have bought APBA sets but that New Englanders, Midwesterners, and residents of the Mid-Atlantic states in particular love the game. Famous aficionados of APBA include comic Danny Kaye, former president George Bush and sons, former New York mayor Ed Koch, and players Joe Torre, Curt Schilling, and Harmon Killebrew, along with manager Frank Lucchesi. Baseball researcher Gene Carney told me he has been playing the APBA game for fifty years: "I've been hooked on APBA since 1958." He several times replayed the 1919 World Series with a group of friends fascinated with the Black Sox Scandal, and "the Sox have not lost a series yet." Carney warned, "APBA baseball can be addictive."

Perhaps the best fantasy, however, is a fantasy that comes true. What do baseball fans fantasize about most? Being able to play ball with their heroes in the flesh. And if they have the money, they can do it. That's what fantasy baseball camps are for: to enable fans who can afford it to realize their wildest and most fantastic dreams.

At a fantasy camp, fans pay between three thousand and five thousand dollars for the chance to practice and play baseball for a week with a group of ex-professionals at a major league spring training camp, wear the team uniform, obtain playing instruction from the ex-players, and just hang out with their heroes. Fantasy camps, as one ad puts it, "allow for Middle Aged Jocks to put on the uniform and become a kid again," for most of the participants are in their forties or fifties; some are in their nineties! The median age of participants in Randy Hundley's fantasy camp is 42.

A baseball fantasy camp, says one ad, is the perfect gift for "Father's Day, corporate recognition, graduation, 40th birthday; 50th birthday; retirement." Participants need not be good players, because, as the web sites point out, "skill is not a requirement" and "your playing level doesn't matter as much as your desire to have a good time." Michael Goldsmith, a New York sports fan who has played in his thirties with an amateur league, attended an Orioles fantasy camp in 2008 despite suffering from the beginning stages of A.L.S., known as Lou Gehrig's disease. Praising his coaches — former Orioles players — Goldsmith reported that they pushed him to do his best and "never let me get maudlin."

Each year fans can choose from as many as thirty fantasy camps to attend. The company or club sponsoring the camp structures the week to include games with and against the professionals as well as some meals with them, including a final awards banquet. Participants receive souvenirs like their own baseball cards, signed baseballs, photos of themselves with the stars, and videos of "the Big Game with the Pros." Many camps take place in luxurious quarters and offer good meals as well as cocktail parties and other camp activities. Games may be held in front of thousands of fans in fine minor league parks.

The ultimate fantasy camp experience, according to highly experienced camper Dennis McCroskey, is the luxury-level camp held at Dodgertown in Vero Beach, Florida, which until recently represented "the camp by which all the other camps are judged." Until it was closed, at Dodgertown men could experience the thrill of a lifetime by hobnobbing with their heroes. Imagine spending a week with people named Duke Snider, Carl Erskine, Ralph Branca, Preacher Roe, Don Zimmer, Tommy Lasorda, Carl Furillo, Roy Campanella, Don Drysdale, Pee Wee Reese — especially if you were a Brooklyn fan. As many as a hundred men attended Dodgertown sessions at one time. Some men enjoy the experience so much that they repeat it more than once. Dennis McCroskey specializes in this activity and has attended forty-one camps!

Fantasy camp participants exult in these experiences. McCroskey declares, "When we put on the uniform, we all become little boys again, and only the baseball matters." Comments from other men who attended these camps include statements showing that the experience was a revelation: "Now I am hooked! It is the best week of my year, hands down!" said one. "I've just got to figure out how to pay for this again!" commented another. "Three times now; this is an unbelievable amount of fun," declared a third.

One camper, Mark "Stoney" Stone, mounted on the internet a journal of his thrilling experience at Dodgertown. Readers can deduce from his ruminations that Stone felt a little guilty about spending the family vacation money on something that only he could enjoy, but fulfilling the lifetime dream of playing ball with his heroes meant so much to him that the thrill outweighed the guilt. Looking back over the experience, he said:

> I ... can only say that I feel truly lucky to have been given the opportunity to participate in this experience. It is true that this is, generally speaking, not the "vacation of the lifetime" that the whole family might enjoy. I know my wife would definitely prefer a trip to Europe, the Middle or Far East, or even a cruise of the Caribbean. But in listening to the others talk about their childhood dreams and memories, previous camp experiences, whether here or at other pro camps, there was no doubt that this experience, from a baseball lover's point of view, was one that has no equal and will never be forgotten. The guys who attended came from all parts of the country, though most were either from California or New York, and represented a variety of professions. We had our lawyers and doctors, investment consultants and insurance types, contractors and cops. We had guys who could play, former college or minor league players, and guys who could barely swing a bat. But we all had one thing in common, the love of baseball and the love of the Dodgers. I can only hope that I get the opportunity to return again someday.

Those are truly passionate fans reaching their goal in life.

Another way fans can pursue their devotion to baseball is to join a vintage baseball club. Analysts like writer Alexa Van Sickle point out that nostalgia plays a powerful part in the enjoyment of baseball; fans can express this nostalgia for baseball's past, as well as their own past in baseball, by indulging in the game as it used to be played. They do this by dressing in old-time uniforms and playing games according to the rules of the nineteenth century, as do the New York Mutuals of Old Bethpage, New York, who since 1980 have been playing 1864-style vintage games at the Old Bethpage Village Restoration.

In playing these vintage games the Mutuals stick with the early rules of the game: they pitch underhand, they wear no gloves, and they can make an out by catching the ball on one bound. They dress and act like old-time players, too: they wear uniforms modeled after the real New York Mutuals of the 1870s, grow facial hair, and use the game terminology of the time (a batter is a "striker," a run is an "ace," ground balls are "daisy cutters"). Other clubs follow the rules of the 1850s, 1860s, or 1880s.

Doing this takes historical research. In the case of the Mutuals, the necessary historical information, including the phrases to be used in talking

The Canal Fulton Mules of Canal Fulton, Ohio, a "vintage baseball" team, play other teams in the Akron-Canton area. This photo shows them in 2006 at the Ohio Cup Vintage Base Ball Festival, Columbus, Ohio. The captain, Ed Shuman, stands third from right (courtesy of the photographer, Michelle Phillips).

together and the manners expected from each member, is available in a booklet provided by the club, but sometimes it is furnished by the association that the club belongs to.

Yes, an association binds these clubs together, for naturally, fellows who play on vintage teams have followed American custom and formed a Vintage Base Ball Association. It opened in 1996 and now boasts more than a hundred and fifty members, mostly in the Northeast and Midwest — Michigan and Ohio lead in numbers of clubs — although clubs operate in Texas, Florida, California, and Canada as well. Clubs can use the association's web site to contact others and arrange games.

The Canal Fultons of the Akron-Canton area in Ohio exemplify the true vintage spirit. They travel to play other vintage teams an hour away and sometimes farther. When visiting clubs arrive, the Canal Fultons take them for a canal boat ride and explain the history of the club's name, then treat them to a picnic. The New York Mutuals sometimes bring two teams to a town's festival and put on a game as entertainment, or else one team of Mutual players will arrive carrying a set of old-time uniforms for a town's team to wear in competition with the Mutuals.

Vintage players promote and enjoy the amateur ethic. Players in the five-team Bay Area Vintage Base Ball League from San Mateo County, California, consider themselves to be gentlemen. The umpires wear top hats and tails, and they must be addressed as "sir." The New York Mutuals, too, stick to the amateur ideal. "Though the games are competitive and we do want to win," says Tom Fesolowich of the Mutuals, "we have fun, and it is a 'gentleman's game'.... The rest of the players on the Mutuals are not just my teammates but my best friends." For Ed Shuman, captain of the Canal Fulton Mules, the social aspect of vintage play remains paramount, and even the club's frequent rivals, the Akron Black Stockings, are his best friends, as close as his team members, and they often travel together to play for another town. For umpire Harry Higham of the Mutuals, as with Tom Fesolowich, the camaraderie with other like-minded fellows provided by vintage play supplies a great deal of the enjoyment in participation.

To the non-fan, all this may sound like esoteric and even weird play-acting, but for vintage teams, adhering to the amateur ethic in every way is paramount. The Mutuals, Tom declared, "discourage" from joining their team those who are "selfish and overly competitive." I can't think of any professional player who could play for the Mutuals, who sound as though they operate much as Canadian curlers do. The Vintage Base Ball Association in fact states that it expects its members to "conduct all matches, meetings, and other activities — both on and off the field — according to the highest standards of sportsmanship, gentlemanly behavior, courtesy, and respect for others which characterized the Knickerbocker Base Ball Club, established September 23, 1845." So playing vintage ball is a way of continuing nostalgia for the amateur ethic on which the national game was founded. Vintage players are really slipping into the past.

How do men become interested in vintage play? Ed Shuman, who works as a computer-assisted graphic designer, explains that for him the attraction lay in the opportunity to combine his interest in history with baseball. For Fesolowich, his work as a history teacher provided the impetus, since vintage baseball requires knowledge of the way something was done at a particular time in history. "I'm a big history fan," says Steve Gazay of San Mateo's vintage league; "I just like the roots of the game." Jason Conyers of the Canal Fultons, another teacher, has a strong interest in Civil War history.

One aspect of vintage baseball is the common use of nicknames, like "Buttons," "Pappy," or "Beefy," derived from a player's characteristics or situation. Jim Walbeck of the Santa Clara Stogies points out that because of the use of nicknames, "you don't go by your real names anymore; you become a new person." Or perhaps a person of the past.

For Harry Higham, a Mutuals member, his knowledge of his great-grandfather Richard "Dick" Higham brought him into the activity. Dick Higham played and umpired for amateur and professional leagues from 1869 to 1882, and Harry, who is a SABR member, has long been interested in learning more about his famous relative. He finds his association with the Mutuals "a chance to observe what my great-grandfather would have experienced as a player and umpire." He says he "puts on the mindset of the players and 'cranks' (spectators) of the nineteenth century" in order to feel what it was like to be part of that era. Harry recreates himself by putting on the mantle of his great-grandfather Dick Higham. He has, in a sense, become his hero.

First visiting Mutuals games and then joining the group, Harry became their umpire and has traveled with them in presenting demonstration games as far north as New England and as far west as Chicago and Louisville. In 2002 at Hannibal, Missouri, the Mutuals put on a doubleheader against a local Vintage team in celebration of "Mark Twain Days." The vintage teams, like the Civil War reenactors, have thus created for themselves an activity combining baseball with American history.

For fans, vintage ball represents a special way to pursue their interest. By discovering and recreating, both in style and in flavor, the way baseball used to be played by well-known amateurs and early professionals, they have found a way of transmuting their love of the game into a form of historical reenactment. Ed Shuman believes that vintage ball "allows us to play the sport as it was meant to be played, with the same enthusiasm we had when we were kids: for the Glory of the Game of Base Ball!" What could be more revealing of the amateur mindset of these players than a statement like that?

Baseball therefore now comes in various incarnations. Beyond its standard on-the-field major and minor league format, we must include its return-to-youth model, engaged in by pay-for-play enthusiasts and fantasy campers; its statistical model, represented by Sabermetrics, fantasy gamers, and APBA players; and certainly its historical model, represented by vintage baseball. Those who pursue their obsession with baseball beyond such activities as obtaining autographs, building collections, blogging about baseball, and visiting museums can move on to this parabaseball level and become absorbed in these specialized baseball activities, which attract mainly men. For baseball is a manly pursuit.

Success while indulging in spinoffs like fantasy baseball and vintage baseball is predicated on a thorough knowledge of the game: how it's played, who plays it well and how they do it, even the game's history. Fans accumulate this kind of knowledge only over long periods of time and in various ways, showing that the dogged pursuit of baseball in this country cannot be said to take place only on the baseball field; it occurs in homes, offices, baseball camps amateur playing fields, museums, and retail shops all over the country. Baseball's popularity should not be gauged only by the number of people who go to stadiums to attend the professionals' games; countless other baseball activities have to be taken account of.

Is baseball in decline? I think not.

6

Is Baseball the God Game?

Baseball has often been called the American religion. Some fans claim that they experience spiritual feelings while watching it being played. One explained that the game is "full of myth and mystery, an always-fresh and recreating ritual expression of cycles and significations greater than ourselves," thus taking on "the characteristics and value of religion." The "Church of Baseball" referred to by the character named Annie Savoy in the film *Bull Durham* appears to have many active members.

Because of fans' devotion to their favorite players, whom they often call heroes, the Hall of Fame in Cooperstown is regularly referred to as a "shrine" for the "immortals" of the game. Many of us view these expressions borrowed from religious devotion as a bit facetious or at least exaggerated, not to be taken seriously. But according to scholars, baseball does project religious characteristics, with its heroes and anti-heroes, a mythology, a belief structure, and a set of behavior rules for reaching high status, so it could be considered a "folk religion"—a term that seems to rank it lower than "formal religion" but also appears to characterize it appropriately. Baseball's display of religious qualities may explain its power over so many American fans.

Perhaps, too, baseball's religious trappings have inspired players to connect with formal religion. Beginning in 1973, and coinciding with the rise of evangelical Christians in the United States, a Christian organization called Baseball Chapel began sponsoring Sunday service for major league players, one service for the visitors and another for the home team. Attendance varies at these meetings; sometimes more than half the team members show up, along with coaches and sometimes the manager. The varied attendance occurs because some teams include many Christians and others only a few. Baseball Chapel also publishes leaflets to distribute in clubhouses; operates a web site, which includes player testimonies; and sends representatives to teams abroad.

Some religious ballplayers have, under the auspices of a group named Athletes in Action, or with the sponsorship of another group called Fellowship of Christian Athletes, organized their own prayer meetings among team members and pray together on every game day. Clubs have not objected to any of this religious activity. Dan Britton, senior vice president of the Fellowship of Christian Athletes, is quoted as saying that the explosion of club approval for player interest in prayer meetings can be explained by the fact that "coaches look at religion as a rabbit's foot."

These two associations not only sponsor prayer meetings, they organize baseball players into Christian teams, not only at the professional level but at every ability level, from children all the way through amateur and college groups. The FCA, active since 1954, recruits college players and arranges them in leagues whose teams play against other Christian teams all over the States and abroad. During their trips the young people are expected to "witness," or give testimony to their faith. FCA has also set up a baseball training academy for youth teams, where they study "baseball ministry strategies."

Another Christian ministry, the Promise Keepers, directs its message exclusively to men and holds its conferences in stadiums and arenas, perhaps because sports stadiums seem to be "a safe space for men" where they may have what is called "a meaningful religious experience that they could never attain in a church."

Although the stated purpose of these groups is to grow Christians, their actual activities center upon urging players to improve their social conduct, claiming that the use of drugs, random sex, and heavy drinking constitutes anti–Christian behavior. In their assumption that Christianity equates to ethics and morals, the leaders of the prayer groups believe that persuading players to become born-again Christians will cause them to act ethically, especially in their personal lives.

So far, clubs have omitted to say whether that improvement took place. But in some cases, adopting evangelical Christianity has changed players' behavior on the field. Attributing lack of success to "God's will," they became perceptibly less aggressive in their play, so much so that other players and the media criticized their lack of hustle.

Introducing religion into baseball can prove divisive. Problems arose with the new emphasis on team religion: players might decline to participate in club prayer meetings, stating that they prefer to pray at home or in their own churches, or they remark that they are Jewish, or that they "don't do religion." Some observers accused players of misusing religion by asking God for a win in today's game and using Jesus as a good-luck charm. Some club members do pray to God for game success. Before a game, first base coach Don Buford asks, "Lord, help us to win." Of course, ever since the Stone Age, says the editor-in-chief of *Archaeology*, "people have performed elaborate rituals to curry favor with the gods." These rites included summoning the gods, talking directly to them, and asking for help. Today, we call this act praying to God, and it sometimes includes asking God for success in baseball.

Jon Moeller, an FBI agent, served as a volunteer chapel leader for big leaguers until one day he was consulted by player Ryan Church, who asked if Jewish people are doomed because they don't believe in Jesus. Moeller nodded, thus damning Church's Jewish girlfriend. Church described the moment: "I was like, man, if they [Jewish people] only knew. Other religions don't know any better. It's up to us to spread the word." After Jewish community leaders complained, the Washington Nationals suspended Moeller and issued an apology.

Abuse of their position by religious persons who hold advisory or coaching posts is not confined to baseball, of course. In 2008 a Florida high school football coach regularly promoted his faith to his players and encouraged them "to accept Jesus Christ as their savior," admitting that "through football, I can introduce 70 to 100 kids each year to Him." Upon complaint of the Freedom from Religion Foundation's attorney, the coach was "admonished" for proselytizing and for using prayers before and after games; he was also directed to remove religious symbols from the school's football web site and told that he "must not engage in this type of behavior again."

During the period before the Beijing Olympics of 2008, the United States Olympic Committee received complaints that the head coach of the United States Archery Team was pressuring his young trainees to study the Bible and become practicing Christians. Young cadets at American service academies, too, have discovered that to become successful they are expected to pray in public and believe in God. These problems may be signs of the time: when religious people in high positions feel powerful during a time of upsurge in public displays of religion, they may have little compunction about using subtle methods of coercion on their youthful charges.

Baseball has also had to deal with the fact that proselytizing by active evangelical Christian players made others uneasy. When some Colorado Rockies revealed that their club was a strongly Christian organization, the media quoted several players as expressing support for the focus on religion, but some former team members complained that they resented having religion forced upon them. They also asserted that other players had played the role of good Christians (perhaps like the "Rice Christians" of China, supposedly converted by early missionaries) just to stay in the team's good graces. The Rockies, nevertheless, became known as "the God squad."

Another Christian baseball organization, Unlimited Potential Inc., formed in Indiana in 1971 in order to present baseball clinics to youngsters. The stated purpose of the UPI is "to glorify God through the spreading of his good news, the gospel, to youth as well as adults." The founders, Tom and Carin Roy, effect this purpose by establishing evangelistic baseball clinics during which ballplayers and coaches share their testimonies and invite those present "to trust Jesus Christ as their personal Savior."

UPI became active in the 1980s, when in Milwaukee, for example, nearly 1,100 children and adults attended a clinic taught by ten Christian major leaguers, and in Akron when 1,800 gathered for a similar clinic. Local churches in many cities now host these evangelistic baseball events through "clinic ministries," and teams of Christian volunteers travel abroad to thirty countries to conduct them.

Has the movement to bring all players into the evangelistic Christian camp helped baseball improve as a spectacle that fans want to pursue? Sports writer Frank Deford, who has observed and written about the evangelical phenomenon in baseball (he calls it "sportianity"), believes that the sport "does not appear to have been improved by the religious blitzkrieg." Perhaps that's because the Christians base their work on an illogical assumption: that in order to become an ethical and moral person, one must become a witnessing Christian. Historically, of course, Christianity fails to equate to ethics and morality. All of us know Christians who have demonstrated questionable morals and ethics as well as non–Christians whose morals and ethics seem above reproach, so nobody should expect belief in Jesus or God to cause obvious changes in social behavior.

Not that religion has never intruded on baseball before. Organized baseball's legal battles with organized religion for the right to pursue business as usual on Sundays were only gradually. As a player, Branch Rickey found himself in trouble when the Reds purchased his contract early in the last century because he always took Sundays off to attend church with his family, and Cincinnati happened to be one of the few cities that allowed Sunday ball at that time. The Reds always made a lot of money on Sundays, and Rickey was expected to pull his share of the load by playing. When he felt that he could not, he eventually left the team.

Religion could be a worrisome issue to individuals like player Hank Greenberg, whose religious holidays did not always jibe with those of his team: should he take the day off for devotions and please his family, or should he play ball and please his teammates by helping them win the pennant?

Author Susan Dellinger, in researching her book on her grandfather, Edd Roush, learned from him that he was unhappy as a player under manager Jack Hendricks, who took over the Cincinnati Reds in 1924. Roush's discontent stemmed from his impression that Hendricks, formerly athletic director of the Knights of Columbus, favored only his co-religionists among the players and seemed to think little of those who were not Catholics.

But a different and much broader religious development affects baseball outside the locker room. Not only have many baseball players found religion; organized religion has found organized baseball. This development affects fans a lot more directly than does locker-room praying.

Conservative religious groups have successfully infiltrated the national game by holding "Faith Nights." At these games, according to the *New York Times*, Christian ministers speak to urge acceptance of Jesus, Christian hymns are sung, and players who are evangelical Christians "witness" to their faith in God. Most of this activity takes place in the Bible Belt in minor league parks, but big-league clubs have tried it out. Baseball teams, including the Atlanta Braves, the Cleveland Indians, and the Arizona Diamondbacks, have experimented with Faith Nights during which they permitted evangelical Christians to drum up trade for their churches, to persuade fans to accept their religious ideas, and to sell religious souvenirs. When I was in Cleveland in 2006 I happened to click on a channel with a local television show just as a newscaster was announcing that the Indians planned to schedule Faith Nights and asking viewers to call in with their opinions of this plan. With surprise, I found that those whose calls the director aired all professed to be in favor of including religion at games.

Yet national polls reveal that more people than ever claim that they have no religion at all. The change has shown up in every state. Answers to questions on these polls demonstrate that religion plays a smaller part in people's everyday lives than it ever did. Yet baseball fans are accepting religion into their favorite game with seeming equanimity.

Perhaps their passive consent comes because so many fans already pray for their teams. In October of 2008 a TV crew found a group of male Muslim fans of the Chicago Cubs praying for divine intervention so that their team would win its next game. Ricardo Pena, a Muslim, had asked a hundred Muslims to pray at Wrigley Field, but only twenty showed up. "God is the only one who can grant success," said Pena, so "we are going to the boss." A passing fan snapped a photo of a long row of faithful Muslim men praying just outside the baseball park, heads bowed and arms clasped at the front of their bodies. Pena, the group's leader, wore a Muslim-style skull cap and a blue Cubs T-shirt.

This event caused a firestorm of blogs for and against Muslims' right to pray for the Cubs and arguments concerning whether God cared about baseball. When the Cubs lost despite the many prayers for them to win, one fan wrote snidely, "Where was Allah on that one?" Another opined, "Obviously, God is not a Muslim." A Muslim wrote on his own blog, "You know your team really sucks when you haven't won the big one in a hundred years and even Allah can't buy you one lousy postseason win!" Actually, a Greek Ortho-

MECHANICS' INSTITUTE LIBRARY
57 Post Street
San Francisco, CA 94104
(415) 393-0101

dox priest had also blessed the Cubs' dugout; Chicago Sikhs had been praying for the Cubs, too; and the rabbi at Congregation Beth Am in Buffalo Grove admitted, "We've been praying extra hard for the Cubs to win." So perhaps it takes more than supplications to various versions of God in order for a team, particularly the Cubs, to win games.

But the purpose of Faith Nights is not to hold public prayers for baseball success. Their purpose is to persuade fans to become witnessing Christians. At some Faith Nights (occasionally, Faith Days), promoters hold religious presentations just outside the ballpark immediately after the game. On other occasions, Faith Nights occur inside the park, occasionally both before and after, as when the Indians scheduled Faith Night on May 24, 2008, with an Indians pitcher "witnessing" before the game and a Christian concert afterwards.

These occasions go further than mere outings at which church groups get discounts on tickets. According to *USA Today,* "they have become a marketing tool, targeting churches with promotional campaigns."

A company called Third Coast Sports specializes in Faith Nights and Faith Days. Baseball clubs hire Third Coast, a Christian marketing firm from Nashville, to stage these promotions, which often include giveaways of Bibles or bobblehead figures of biblical characters as well as live player testimonials. The Atlanta Braves found that its investment in Third Coast paid off, because on the first two Faith Days held, attendance at Braves Field increased between 10 and 15 percent. Third Coast makes money, too. "Faith Nights," says Brent High, "are the biggest thing we do here. It is big, big business for us." Another Christian marketing firm, Focus on the Family, made a negative impression in Atlanta, however, because of the suggestion during its program that homosexuality is a social problem similar to alcoholism.

Does Jesus belong in the ball park? Does Buddha or Mohammed? The practice of religion in conjunction with a baseball game seems incongruous. Shouldn't organized religion stay out of organized baseball, just as many Americans who uphold the separation of church and state think it should stay out of government?

But organized religion has already penetrated government. Through the pressure of President George W. Bush, the U.S. government gave substantial financial support to faith-based initiatives, and Barack Obama wants an even bigger faith-based program than Bush's. What does that mean? It means that your tax money, and mine, supports certain religious organizations that set up and operate charities to give money, food, and medicine — in the name of their religious group — to people they believe need it and deserve it and to whom they promote their religious doctrines. According to analysts, Bush has poured billions into religiously affiliated social service providers. Your tax money is thus supporting the work of all sorts of religious groups, some of which relegate women to second-class positions (could a woman become head of every religious group?) and some of which discriminate against people who may be a little "different," like gays.

I see religion's penetration of baseball as parallel to the government's "faith-based initiatives." At these religion-flavored baseball occasions, some of the money fans spend to get into the park goes to promote a religious group that they may disapprove of.

Brent High is president of Third Coast Sports, the organization that sponsors Faith Nights. High claimed to a *New York Times* reporter that he went out of his way to avoid "ambush evangelism." But what else would you call this: before a May game in Bridgewater, New Jersey, on Faith Night the baseball club presented a Christian band and a pastor who gave a short speech directly from the baseball field "about the need for connecting with Jesus." Many Americans believe that no such need exists. If I were sitting in the stands that day, I would feel ambushed by evangelical Christians. Spiritual inspiration based on one particular dogma seems out of place at a baseball game.

Blogs like those on *Serious Dismay* point out that others, like me, feel nervous about baseball's adoption of evangelical religion. Because of baseball's historical link with American democracy, the game seems like an inappropriate vehicle for the promotion of a particular version of religion. This is a country where a religion cannot legally be forced upon its citizens, because the founders embedded freedom of religion in law.

Our national game has long been considered a force for democracy, one that promotes tolerance of many religious ideas and people of all varieties. In the early 1900s, when large groups of immigrants to the United States arrived from many countries, their children played baseball together even if their parents were members of entirely different religious groups or no religious group at all. Baseball provided a unifying factor for many children of different backgrounds and thus promoted the growth of democratic ideas. As prize-winning journalist Steve Coll remarks, "Diversity of religious belief is an American strength."

In some places, immigrants taught their children that people who came from a different country or followed a different religious tradition were inferior, or at least enemies. My father, who was never fortunate enough to be exposed to baseball in the immigrant section of downtown Cleveland, where he grew up in the early 1900s, told me that because his parents had come from Germany, he was beaten up regularly by boys whose parents came from Poland. He finally recruited his big brother, an amateur boxer, to show him some boxing moves, and after that he was no longer attacked. But in other places, especially in big cities like New York, children who made contact with those whose families had long been citizens learned to get along by playing baseball together, not only on ethnic and religious teams, which played against other ethnic and religious teams, but also on integrated teams. Although some churches, temples, Sunday schools, and other religious organizations like the YMCA sponsored baseball teams, the sponsors did not expect the children who were team members to proselytize. Team members were not told to "witness" or to scorn others of different faiths or no faith. Public school teams included children from Catholic, Jewish, Protestant, Buddhist, and atheist families.

When as a teenager Harold Seymour started his boys' teams in Brooklyn in the 1920s, he recruited them from every group, considering only their baseball ability. Italian boys played with Irish; Catholic boys played with Jewish. For a while, one black boy showed up to play, but, perhaps feeling out of place, he stopped coming. Seymour's own background (his mother came from Catholic Irish people, his father from Protestant English) reflected indifference to religion; his parents emphasized morals and ethics instead. That heritage probably helped him develop blindness to religious and ethnic differences among the young players on his teams.

Instead of arguing with or fighting against those with different backgrounds or different religious views, children like those on Seymour's teams played baseball together. Newly Americanized children who played together grew up less exclusive in their views of strangers than their immigrant parents were, and they influenced their parents to become more accepting of people from different backgrounds, ethnicity, and religion. Baseball, particularly amateur baseball, thus made a solid contribution to our uniquely democratic style of life.

As children many of us were often warned that it's impolite to try to influence others to believe as we do concerning religion. We were taught that the topics of religion, politics, and money were to be left out of conversations with persons who might hold views of those subjects that differed from our own. But fans at a baseball game represent a captive audience; they become consumers of whatever the club management includes in the entertainment of the evening.

Religious intervention in sport thus represents a divisive force, not an inclusionary one. In a democracy, we do not expect to listen to the expression of some particular religious views when we are paying to attend our favorite entertainment. This never happens when we attend a symphony, a play, an opera, or a Broadway musical. Why should it happen at a baseball park? I think we ought to be free to pursue our national obsession with baseball without being pressured to accept any particular religion.

Those who disagree with this position will point out that I need not attend those Faith Night games, and they will add that many fans who hold evangelical Christian religious views will be glad to attend them. True. But I respond by pointing out that many fans hold religious views different from those of evangelical Christians, or even non-religious views; that makes religious games discriminatory, not democratic. Their planners assume that listeners all hold the same views of religion. In that, they are like the organizers of the ancient Olympic Games, which were held to honor the Greek gods and goddesses. Today's Olympics honor excellence in sporting achievement, not the gods who supposedly dispensed favor or disfavor in the form of winning or losing.

The phenomenon of religion in baseball deserves considerable thought. Why has religion penetrated our national game? As for players' new interest in religion, they explain that they turn to it because of the stress they are under. They feel pressured to succeed each time they take the field, and they may use religion as a crutch, believing that something stronger than they are will help them cope with the demands upon them. Besides, they usually work away from home, with no family or close friends to depend on, so they feel the need for emotional support. The form of religion represented by evangelical Christianity appears to offer a direct and simple solution: depend on God.

As for fans, however, why have so many of them accepted the intrusion of organized religion into their favorite entertainment? For so many years they have pursued baseball in its plain vanilla form; why do they now condone the presentation of baseball flavored with down-home Southern and small-town religion?

I think part of the answer is that some fans view occasions like Faith Night as simply another promotion, like Car Giveaway Night, Fireworks Night, and the day on which dogs get into the park free. They let the event wash over them, taking what they want from it and ignoring the rest. For them, religion has become part of the wallpaper in their mental computers: merely an adornment, not something they need to think about. Others probably feel at home on Faith Night because on this occasion their own personal religious convictions receive recognition in connection with the baseball game they have come to experience.

But if baseball itself represents the American religion, as so many analysts have declared, why does it accept organized religion piggybacked upon it? Perhaps because in recent years the topic of religion has experienced an upsurge in America. Both evangelical activity and the publication of anti-religious books have increased. Religion has moved to the forefront of our consciousness.

That returns us to the question of whether baseball has truly become a religion. Some scholars have no hesitation in ranking baseball as religion. Joseph Price, professor of religious studies at Whittier College, believes that "by all the canons of our modern books on comparative religion, baseball is a religion." Unlike other theologians I will cite, Price obviously subscribes to the belief that if it walks like a duck and quacks like a duck, it is a duck.

But perhaps baseball has merely accumulated the trappings of a religion, with its heroes, shrines, pilgrims, and myths; these trappings may disguise a simple game as a religion. Professor Donna Bowman of the University of Central Arkansas, however, sees more than just resemblance to a religion in baseball; she declares, "Baseball has taught generations of intellectuals and scholars what it means to be connected to something bigger than one's self, something with origins shrouded in legend, a sacred history, saints and villains, and a future bright with hope but constantly threatened by the forces of modernity. In short, baseball has taught us, churched or unchurched, what it means to be religious." That's pretty close to equating baseball with religion; it seems to assert that, at the very least, when watching baseball we engage in religious practices.

Scholars Tara Magdalinski and Timothy Chandler dismiss the notion of baseball as a true religion because "despite even the most ritualistic nature of fandom, sport simply does not address the basic questions that religious communities try to answer." Others agree, at least in part. "Baseball is not a religion," declares Lisle Dalton, professor of religious studies at Hartwick College, about thirty miles from the baseball shrine at Cooperstown. "But if you look at the way people put their emotion and energy, their intellectual ability, into sports, they start to look a lot like what people [in an earlier era] used to put into religion." She then names baseball as "the continuation of religion."

Another who creeps close to proclaiming baseball as religion, Thomas E. Dailey, professor of theology at DeSales University, centers on baseball's "religious power, the force of which can, if we believe it, restore the character of our American culture." Dailey's hedge, "if we can believe it," detracts somewhat from the strength of his assertion. But Professor Dailey also invokes William James to declare that baseball confers one variety of religious experience, and his article on baseball as religion concludes that through our national game we realize "the deepest desires, needs, and potential of human existence and thereby give order and meaning to our lives." That seems like a heavy charge, but it may accurately represent the experience of some fans at a baseball game. A succinct statement of this view is that of scholar Roberta Newman, a professor at New York University, who says that baseball "may be said to serve as the national religion."

A little less wholehearted is Professor Stanley M. Hauerwas of Duke University, a theologian who states rather tentatively that "learning to play or to be a fan of baseball can be one of the means through which we develop some of the skills commensurate with being a Christian." His use of three qualifying terms — "can be," "one of the means," and "some of the skills" — appears to make Hauerwas less convinced than other theologians that baseball has become a religion.

Church historian Christopher Evans of Colgate's divinity school believes in baseball as our "civil religion" (a term some philosophers regard as outdated), although he describes it not in religious words but in nationalistic terms: "At the center of baseball's symbolic power there resides a unique language of civil religion, proclaiming that the game can redeem America and serve as a light to all nations." Seeing baseball as redemptive — presenting a way of saving us from our sins — would make it offer one of the functions of a religion. Hauerwas also sees baseball as instructive in a way similar to what religion is thought to be when he points out ruefully that being a Cubs fan teaches us that "life is not about winning."

As nationalistic as the views of Hauerwas are the remarks of Evans with his co-editor, William R. Herzog of Colgate's divinity school, in their introduction to *The Faith of 50 Million: Baseball, Religion, and American Culture,* where they praise "baseball's enduring stature as a sacred symbol of American identity." They also proclaim "baseball's sacred mythology of individual and group fulfillment" because "baseball has been associated with 'the American dream' and believed to offer an embodiment of it." The link of baseball with "the American dream" is authentic enough, although dreams of success in America, cherished as they might be, can hardly be classified as "sacred." Usually, we think of them in terms of moving up the ladder of status and financial security.

In an article within the book, Evans concludes his examination of baseball as religion not by stating that fans have made baseball a religion but that "American history has framed baseball metaphorically as something transcendent, something permanent, and something sacred." Like other theologians, then, Evans slides in close to equating baseball and religion but ends up attributing to baseball only some of religion's characteristics. And in their conclusion to *The Faith of 50 Million,* Evans and Herzog move even further from the promise of the book's title: "To connect faith and the national pastime [as do the theologians in this book] is not to argue that baseball is something more than a game; it is to affirm that baseball is a game." That, of course, we already knew.

Debates on whether baseball is or is not a religion bore some scholars, like Jacques Berlinerbrau, professor of Jewish civilization at Georgetown University. He poses the trivia question, "How do you know it's Opening Day?" and gives this answer: "When half the (often secular) pundits nationwide are writing columns about baseball being like religion. Like *their* religion."

Well, then, to theologians (who should know), although baseball is not quite a religion in itself, it possesses some of religion's characteristics. One of the basic tenets of some religions is belief in an afterlife. Baseball now furnishes the expectation of that, too — at least, to long-suffering Cubs fans. Those fans who want, even after death, to remain perpetual Cubs fans and be interred among other Cubs fans are in luck. Even if life is not about winning, Cubs fans can make the winning final out by being buried in a Cubs cemetery with other Cubs fans.

If you are a die-hard Cubs fans, you can rest easy by having the urn (emblazoned with the Cubs logo) that holds your ashes buried alongside the urns of many other Cubs fans in a section of a Chicago cemetery reserved for you. "Beyond the Vines," a 24-foot ivy-covered wall designed to look like the one in dead center at Wrigley Field, has been constructed in a section of the cemetery set aside for those who will never, but never, give up on their team. Mounted on the wall next to each urn will be a bronze plaque bearing the deceased fan's photo (wearing a Cubs uniform, if desired) and engraved with the deceased fan's "stats" — dates of birth and death, favorite Cubs game, and favorite Cubs player. The full treatment costs $5,000. But even if you follow a team other than the Cubs, you can buy from the maker, Eternal Image, an urn for your ashes that bears the logo of other sports teams. A Massachusetts funeral home has already sold its first Boston Red Sox casket and expects to inter others with different logos.

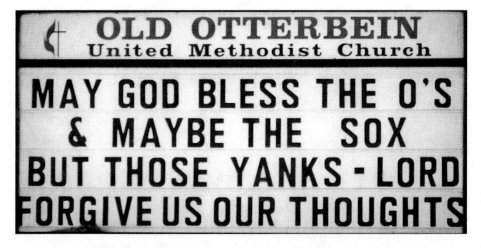

Churches sometimes use baseball messages to attract fans. Here is one message posted in the front of Old Otterbein United Methodist Church, near Camden Yards, Baltimore. A reply of sorts is quoted in the text (courtesy of the photographer, Brad Ciociola).

How do Cubs fans like this idea of passing eternity with other die-hards? One said he would like to get buried there but would not want others to know: "My wife would kill me." Another remarked approvingly, like a fan who has always pursued baseball fervently, "It would symbolize what your passion is, what you enjoyed about your life." For that fan, baseball has surely become his religion.

Perhaps more enlightened is one church's playful use of baseball to attract attention via a clever rhyming prayer. Old Otterbein United Methodist, a church across the street from Camden Yards, home of the Baltimore Orioles, sometimes posts rhymes like the following on the sign in front of the church:

MAY GOD BLESS THE O'S
AND MAYBE THE YANKS
BUT AS FOR THE SOX
IT'S HARD TO GIVE THANKS.

Not all congregations view baseball this liberally. When the Reverend Mr. Jon Adams, the minister at Parkview Church in Lilburn, Georgia, presented a sermon with baseball as his theme and used the phrase "Step Up to the Plate" to urge members to use their spiritual gifts, a group of members complained to the head office. Upon being queried, Adams expressed regret and promised to "take great care in the future."

Attempts to link baseball with religion may never succeed, but they help reveal the depth and breadth of the American obsession with the national game.

7

Baseball and Our Other
National Sport: Business

Every year eager fans buy hundreds of thousands of baseball caps, jerseys, and T-shirts. Baseball is good for the casual clothing business, because one way fans pursue their passion for baseball is to demonstrate their devotion to their favorite teams and players through their choices of clothing.

Some wear simple T-shirts with slogans supporting their teams; these shirts enable fans to become walking billboards for their clubs. Others invest in baseball caps and jerseys like ones worn by the professionals so that they will look, and perhaps feel, like members of their favorite teams.

For if baseball remains our national game, business endures as our other vital national activity. Baseball itself became big business in the nineteenth century, but even in its amateur days it sought advertising. Owners of companies who contributed money so that the town team could obtain equipment and uniforms expected to see the company name, "Martin Music Store" or "George's Garage," emblazoned on the players' shirts. Now a company's name, instead of appearing on the back of a player's shirt, can be displayed on a baseball park because an insurance group or a beer producer has purchased the right (with a limited shelf life) to see its name there.

Fans in large numbers began to wear baseball clothing in the 1960s and early 1970s, when the T-shirt fad exploded into a permanent item of sales. The Shirt Shed, a company that includes many Major League Baseball products in its inventory, now projects annual sales of a hundred million dollars.

To many baseball devotees, however, buying a cheap T-shirt with the words "New York Yankees" printed on it seems no longer sufficient. They want to display their pursuit of their favorite game by wearing something closer to what their heroes wear. Consequently, the baseball clothing market has broadened to include historically authentic uniform pieces, especially jerseys and caps. Fans have learned to select specific styles — a team's road cap or home cap, or a jersey worn only in a particular year. The fans wear these pieces of clothing at ball games, or as leisure wear on weekends, or even on casual Fridays at work.

Some sophisticated fans prefer to wear a baseball cap that no team has ever worn. Spike Lee, the film director, ordered a New York Yankees cap in red, a color the team has never used, and when others saw him wearing the cap at sports events, they began ordering the same item.

Children, too, wear baseball clothing. A New Yorker related what happened to her after the 2008 season when waiting in line at a Dunkin' Donuts shop while wearing her Yankees cap: behind her stood a "very young boy" in Yankee gear, whom she engaged in conversation. "Ah," she said, "a fellow Yankee fan. Gee, our guys didn't do so well this year, did they?" Smiling shyly and fingering his uniform shirt, he replied, "Their clothes are still in fashion, though."

Now "throwback" clothing has also come into prominence, for real fans want to show their knowledge of baseball history by wearing replicas of the jerseys or caps or jackets worn by the 1935 Detroit Tigers or the 1910 New York Highlanders. Authenticity has become the haute couture among uniform-wearing fans. Some even search out copies of caps worn by Dutch teams or those of the Czech Republic. They share their lists of styles, names of companies, and eBay finds on sites like *Yahoo! Answers* and *Baseball Fever,* where they also chat about when and where they display their clothing ("I wear my Blue Jays cap every time I take my dog out for a walk") and talk about their problems ("I wear my throwback every Saturday. My girlfriend hates it, but I don't care. Soon she will be gone, but my love for the Tigers will last forever!").

Another gimmick has proved highly successful among baseball fans, although it has little to do with baseball: teddy bears. A company called Build-a-Bear has opened stores in several Major League Baseball stadiums to give fans a chance to create "their own little team mascot." Maxine Clark, the company's chief executive officer, says the store in Philadelphia's ball park was "driven by the owner" and "incredibly successful from the get-go."

Teddy bears, says Clark, have long been "a universal sign of comfort and love and trust," and now they have become a sign of "passion for the sport." Ballpark Build-a-Bear stores appeal to families, who wander in during games to discover that they can buy a teddy bear and dress it as a mascot for their favorite ball club. Only 20 percent of buyers, however, are above the chronological age of twelve.

Many other businesses provide ways for baseball fans to feed their passion. Inside the park, especially during a long game, fans get hungry and clamor for their traditional baseball food: hot dogs and beer, supplemented by snacks of peanuts and Cracker Jack. After too many years of using beer bottles and glasses as missiles against hapless umpires, however, fans were punished by being forced to walk to booths under the stands to buy their beer in paper cups, which lack the inherent danger of glass. Nor will the clubs allow them to bring their own beer — but some fans find ways around that prohibition. Once a fan waiting outside Shea Stadium saw a group of college-age men drag a big box of beer and ice over to where a rope with a loop was being mysteriously lowered from inside the stands; the young men fastened the loop around the box, and their pals inside hoisted it slowly and carefully up and over the side. Only one bottle was lost in the process, and "the box's successful transfer generated a round of applause and cheers" from watching fans, for Americans love seeing rules circumvented.

Hot dogs, the traditional high-protein munch, have undergone some updating. No longer do they emerge from hot, greasy water to be smeared with a little mustard and placed in drying white buns; fans' taste buds have matured. So many devotees have traveled to several ball parks and tasted the local clubs' offerings that they can now engage in ranking a ball park's dogs according to flavor; the famous Nathan's Hot Dog served at Yankee Stadium usually receives a high rating and is being served at the new structure, along with French, Japanese, Hispanic, and other ethnic and regional offerings. Clubs seem to be competing for honors in creating the most elaborate hot dog: one minor league team, the Gateway Grizzlies of St. Louis, decorates its Black Angus frankfurter with two strips of bacon, sautéed onion, sautéed sauerkraut, cheddar cheese, and a choice of six relishes. The variety of food offerings available now means moving well beyond hot dogs with items like grilled salmon in Seattle's Safeco Field and Gilroy garlic fries at AT&T Park in San Francisco; these specialties now rival traditional ballpark food for fans' attention. Parks today offer a broad range of restaurant fare including current fad food like baked stuffed potatoes, ethnic foods like tacos and sushi, and local favorites like brats and barbecue. The new Citi Field includes shrimp rolls, pulled pork, and corn on the cob in its cuisine.

With vegetarian specialties claiming a niche in the food market, some fans look for, and find, meat-free hot dogs and other veggie fare. At least a dozen ballparks now offer soy dogs for vegetarians and others whose stomachs reject the questionable content of today's meat frankfurters. An on-line e-letter, *Cool Cleveland*, reported in 2004 that a vegetarian organization, PETA — People for the Ethical Treatment of Animals — had selected Cleveland's Progressive Field (it was Jacobs Field at that time) as the Number One vegetarian ballpark in America, offering crowd-pleasing veggie pierogies, burritos, knishes, and burgers. Now that Major League Baseball includes some vegetarian players and at least one who sticks to vegan food, more fans may investigate how one can become a successful athlete while avoiding meat and consuming plant protein instead.

Fans who prefer to bring their own food to a game can still display their team devotion by packing it in a New York Yankees MLB lunch box bearing the team logo (the intertwined N and Y), a product with a ten-dollar purchase price; or they can tote a cooler with the Yankee logo purchased for thirty-five dollars, or an insulated hot drink mug bearing most any team logo, but the mug will set them back forty-five dollars.

Part of the price of these items decorated with team logos goes to Major League Baseball, which grants contracts to companies for the use of club logos. A company that uses the name or logo of a major league team in its advertising without permission finds itself at the wrong end of a legal action, since team names have become valuable properties. Major League Baseball also pressures small local leagues with ties to the big leagues to stop using trademark team names like "Cardinals" and also to use only those suppliers licensed to produce uniforms and equipment to organized baseball — or risk losing their connection for trademark violation. Names can be valuable, so even those pursuing baseball through volunteer-run organizations like the Cape Cod League must watch their step.

In Cooperstown itself, before or after watching a game at Doubleday Field, fans flock to the Doubleday Café or the Short Stop Restaurant. Evidently, the majors lack legal control over those names. I prefer to order my baseball nourishment online from the Cooperstown Cookie Company, which bakes deliciously rich cookies in the shape of baseballs and sends them to clients in attractive tins. These tasty treats have become popular additions to baseball-themed parties as one more way fans can demonstrate their connection with the game.

Fans can select baseball-related souvenirs in shops, like the one in Cleveland's Tower City, where I bought a fat, Bic-like pen bearing the threatening visage of the Indians' mascot, Chief Wahoo; all merchandise in the shop has some relationship to the local team. Or they can go online to web sites like the one called *FansEdge,* where they find more than a hundred thousand "items for the fan." To decorate their homes with gadgets that relate to baseball, they can purchase for under fifty dollars a beautiful Waterford crystal pen tray decorated with four copies of old baseballs, including the 1870 "lemon peel ball." For decorating their cars, they can buy bumper stickers like the one featuring the word "Braves" with a picture of a tomahawk, probably symbolizing the famous Baltimore chop. Fans who want to show off their devotion to the White Sox can purchase, for their mobile phones, a ringtone that chimes a few notes of the team's fight song, "Let's Go Go White Sox." Through Turner Licensing, MLB itself sells team-logo items like calendars, notepads, Christmas cards, and puzzles.

Although I think of myself as a non-fan, I, too have succumbed to the desire for baseball gimmicks. For an office decoration, I found a catalog offering an oversized and overstuffed pillow bearing my name and decorated with big black painted "stitches," so that it looks (something) like a baseball; people entering the room notice it instantly and realize that I identify myself with the game. For distributing to clients, fans who own businesses can buy baseball-themed promotional items to give away, like the usual key chains. If they want something special for a giveaway, business people might select the inflatable beach balls decorated to look like baseballs, which can be picked up for a little over a dollar each; but of course promos are priced to sell in large batches, so to obtain the beach balls at this price they must buy four thousand of them.

Some fans, like Steve Yerid of Westport, Massachusetts, have installed in their homes a "sports den" displaying their collections of baseball cards, baseball clothing, and other valued traded and purchased sports items. Building on the "sports den" fad, MLB's new *Insiders Club Magazine* advertises a roomful of baseball-related furniture for "the perfect sports den," including leather recliner chairs ($999 each) and baseball-themed wallpaper ($388).

Probably no aspect of our business life has benefited from fans' pursuit of baseball more than the media. Although not designed to be worn or displayed, books about baseball have become favorite objects of fans' desire. Through books they can devour stories about their favorite heroes and teams, relive exciting games, pick up information about infamous scandals, read about thrilling pennant races, find out about long-ago leagues, learn why players use the tactics they do, get coaching tips, and discover the history of baseball. They buy baseball encyclopedias and guidebooks, statistical records, collections of interviews with baseball people, histories of baseball in a particular city or state, records of baseball as played in certain industries, and even books about umpires. When you become a member of the MLB Insiders Club, you discover that you have joined a book club, with new MLB-produced books delivered to you periodically (you'll be billed).

The Baseball Almanac, which keeps all kinds of records, estimates that more than 70,000 books have been published about baseball, but at this writing, when I ask Amazon.com for books on baseball, I receive the names of nearly 175,000. Every effort to list them all has quickly been hopelessly outdated. Ron Kaplan, a sports writer and feature writer who specializes in baseball reviews, declares that "more words have been written about the national pastime than all other sports combined." The publisher of the book you are reading right now has published more than 400 books on baseball history and, in order to describe them all, finds it necessary to use a catalog separate from the one listing its other books.

Although the number of Americans who read books declined considerably in the 1990s, analysts find no indication of a drop-off in the reading of baseball books. Librarians cannot keep up with the number of baseball books being published; they soon begin to run out of shelf space and discover that they have to become very selective about what they furnish their clients. "Libraries and the individuals we reach seem never to tire of reading about the sport," says Gary Mitchem, acquisitions editor at McFarland, who has noticed no decline in the number of baseball books published. Mitchem continues, "If anything, the number has grown over the last decade, at least in the scholarly market." In sum, "for McFarland, baseball is one of the steadier-performing lines." Ron Kaplan, who watches the market for baseball books, feels confident in the future: "I believe that people who love to read about a given subject will always do so."

Debates about "the best" baseball book are futile; what is best depends on what a reader enjoys. Some prefer personal interview books, such as Donald Honig's *Baseball When the Grass Was Real*. Others enjoy hilarious revelations, like Jim Bouton's *Ball Four* (and Bouton's oral presentations are just as funny as that book). Others like descriptive writing that the fans who love to attend games can identify with, like Roger Angell's *The Summer Game*. Still others prefer a good biography, like Bob Creamer's *Babe*. In fiction, Bernard Malamud's *The Natural* stands out and still sells well, according to Amazon.com, although its popularity may come in part from its big-screen treatment with Robert Redford in 1984. That leaves biographies and autobiographies, statistical studies, histories, humor, poetry, encyclopedias, and dictionaries, all of which have their devotees among baseball readers.

For humor and charm, despite H. Allen Smith's cleverness, I still lean toward Ring Lardner. His *A Busher's Letters* and *You Know Me Al* uncannily echo the style and substance of letters that young, unsophisticated men actually wrote to Harold Seymour in the 1930s from the minor league towns where they were sent after Seymour had successfully recommended them to the teams' parent clubs. Life follows art.

Baseball biography, however, sometimes makes for iffy reading. Not all biographies stick as close to the facts and a careful interpretation of them as does Judith Testa's *Sal Maglie, Baseball's Demon Barber*. I felt it necessary to point out, in my review in 2002 of a *New York Times* bestseller, *Joe DiMaggio: The Hero's Life*, by Richard Ben Cramer, for the *International Journal of the History of Sport*, that although the DiMaggio book makes for revealing and absorbing reading, it must stand outside the genre of biography, since at times it drops back to an era when writers, less rigorous in their work, included words that the characters were supposedly thinking. Cramer, an experienced writer, obviously used this technique deliberately. He often put words into a person's mouth, not using quotation marks but writing as if he were that person. He slipped into the person's mind and revealed what (he believed) the person was thinking. This technique makes for good writing — on the part of a novelist, but not of a biographer, who is supposed to confine himself to what happened. He could not possibly know what DiMaggio or his friends were thinking at any particular time. Fuzzing up the line between fiction and biography does readers a disservice.

Autobiography, too, must be judged carefully. In writing about themselves, some writers have begun to blur the traditional boundaries between fact and fiction, reverting to the puffery of the early nineteenth-century biographies. After Doris Kearns Goodwin, a formerly respected historian who has written touchingly about her childhood baseball experiences, was discovered to have used the passages of other published books in several of her own, she tried to explain away the plagiarism, claiming it was unintentional and due to negligence. Now we wonder if she really experienced the baseball events she told us about.

These kinds of lapses — pretending to know something that cannot be known, or depending solely upon memory to tell about one's life, or using another writer's work without attribution — have become all too common in the rush to publish, including the rush to publish baseball books. The authors' carelessness or intentional plagiarism makes the rest of the genre suspect. I have begun to worry whether readers believe what I wrote in my own baseball autobiography, *A Woman's Work*, although to write it I avoided depending completely on my memory of the last fifty years; instead, in order to be sure I reported accurately on what I was doing at any particular time, I traveled to Cornell University in the middle of winter (slipping and sliding on snowy hills), asked to see the Seymour Collection in Cornell's archives, and pulled out my notes on the work I performed with Harold Seymour. As a result, I not only checked on my memory, I discovered notes I had made about many forgotten adventures that I was therefore able to include in the book.

To some scholarly fans, the most interesting publications are the early baseball guides, especially those published annually before and just after 1900. Not only fans but research libraries and historical societies have become collectors of these guides, because besides presenting seasonal statistics about the major league clubs, the books include all sorts of colorful historical commentary about leagues, teams, and players, amateurs as well as professionals, so these publications are especially valuable for baseball historians. Those who collect these guides know that a publication like *Beadle's Base Ball Guide for 1860,* known also as *Beadle's Dime Baseball Guide,* actually did cost ten cents that year but is rare enough now to sell for at least forty dollars.

Baseball fiction seems to be gradually gaining in popularity on nonfiction, especially when the stories reach Hollywood and fans can see them interpreted on the big screen. Baseball commentator Peter Bjarkman ventures the opinion that those stories including magical elements — he may be referring to works like *The Natural* by Bernard Malamud, in which an aging player wins with a magical bat, and *Shoeless Joe* by W.P. Kinsella, a book that became the fantasy film *Field of Dreams*—"seem somehow better at capturing those metaphysical complexities of baseball which have elevated this beloved American game to the status of unrivalled national institution." *Field of Dreams* also perpetuates our fixation upon and our nostalgia for our pastoral origin.

For a long time *Bull Durham* has held its place as the number one baseball film, not only on Amazon.com but in the hearts of many fans. *Sports Illustrated* ranked it as the greatest sports movie (not just baseball movie) of all time. Why has it struck such a chord with knowledgeable fans? The first reason, I think, must be verisimilitude. The actors knew how to play the game; the director himself played minor league ball for five years. The setting, a rundown minor league ball park, seemed real because it was. And the inclusion of a "baseball annie" (Annie Savoy) as a character, as well as an over-the-hill player who must teach his tricks to a neophyte — these situations offer the very smell of reality. Somehow, the dialogue rings true, as well; it depicts realistic tensions among realistic characters. Yet the story enters the realm of fantasy, too, because, according to one fan, "the plot revolves around what every baseball player dreams of: Sex with an incredible and mysterious woman and making it to the highest echelon of players." So the movie is about making it and making out. That must be the pinnacle of success desired by American men who pursue the manly sport of baseball.

In today's adult baseball fiction, the protagonist represents a fan as often as it does a player. *The Celebrant,* by Eric Rolfe Greenberg, with a narrator-fan who wishes he were Christy Mathewson, rates tops in baseball fiction by many who pursue this kind of baseball experience — including the talented author of *Shoeless Joe,* W.P. Kinsella. Like Darryl Brock's *Havana Heat,* Greenberg's *The Celebrant* evokes a particular period in baseball and accurately uses baseball events to tell his story. *The Celebrant* (and did you notice the religious flavor of the title?), instead of concentrating on the ballplayer Christy Mathewson, reveals the feelings of a fan whose devotion to Matty dominates his life and brings him to the highs and lows of emotion. Greenberg uses religious words and phrases like "worship," abbey," monk," "high priest," and "confess my faith" to describe fans' attachment to their heroes as well as emo-

tional terms like "rapture" and "ecstasy" to describe fans as they celebrate
their team's "glorious victory." Use of such words reveals the intensity of emotion that fans can experience as they pursue their favorite sport/entertainment.

Children's and adults' novels alike often resort to magical thinking. Scientists have found that the habit of turning to unreality arises from feeling
insecure and out of control. Perhaps fans, distressed over their inability to
become baseball stars, feel comforted when they experience baseball stardom
vicariously through books, or read about fans who do.

Nowadays, fans can read and comment on baseball "blogs" instead of or
in addition to purchasing books. Blogs (web logs) make it possible for fans
to express their opinions to a large public about anything happening in baseball. Blogs may consist of discussions of individual teams, players, or events,
or they may concern topics like technology or baseball shirts; their great
advantage is that fans' opinions count in conversation on a topic, which is
known as a "thread." Searching the internet for a blog with an attractive
approach to the subject or an interesting thread is part of the fun. A web site
called *sportsfanlive.com* adds an innovative mapping device as an attempt to
help its contributors find each other geographically so that they may congre-
gate or at least meet at the same sports bar. Quotes selected from multiple
blogs appear at *baseballblogs.org,* where fans can decide which baseball blogs
to read or join. Being interactive makes blogs quite different from books,
which are static; books may offer a lot more solid information than blogs,
but they accept no backtalk. Readers find it useless to say to a book, "You
guys are completely and utterly clueless," as they can (and do) say on a
blogspot.

Some fans may not realize it (and others may not want to admit that
they do it), but some of them read baseball poetry, from the whimsical ("Shall
I Compare Thee to a Triple Play?" by Keith Eisner) to the piece with a sharp
point ("Oscar Charleston's Lament" by Daniel Bronson). The latter grace-
fully introduces the idea that Charleston, often referred to as "the Black Cobb,"
resented that appellation, pointing out gently that observers might more accurately have called Cobb "the White Charleston." In four short, well-written
stanzas this poem presents an important idea: our prejudice (or, in sociolog-
ical terms, our cognitive bias) skews our view of reality. Baseball poetry has
moved far beyond the simple recitation of the events of a game, as in the
beloved "Casey at the Bat." Many poems written in recent years describe the
way we connect the formative events of our youth with our baseball experiences; they therefore help explain baseball's power over Americans.

Other fans include music in their pursuit of baseball. To satisfy their
interest, composers have since the 1860s been writing, and groups have been
performing, songs like "Base Ball Fever" and "The Base Ball Polka," early hits

among the "fanatics" or "kranks" of the time (today they're sometimes known as "seamheads"). In the current baseball music scene, nothing seems to have caught the admiration of fans more than "Van Lingle Mungo," a ballad by singer-songwriter Dave Frishberg that celebrates ballplayers' names, many of them as mellifluous as the one in the title. Among baseball recordings, my first favorite became "The Brooklyn Baseball Cantata," with the lead sung by operatic baritone Robert Merrill; I bought the recording in the 1940s, when I began learning about baseball's colorful history and thought the "cantata," with a story based upon the events of a real game, to be charmingly presented.

Fans who want to pursue their love/hate relationship with the New York Yankees in their greatest years could for a long time enjoy the wonderful Broadway show of the 1950s, *Damn Yankees*. The show is based on the Douglass Wallop novel *The Year the Yankees Lost the Pennant*, in which the hero, instead of praying to God for his team to win, sells his soul to the Devil, thus (almost) following the classic Faustian theme. Baseball fans long admired, then envied, and many finally hated the pin-striped New Yorkers of the era of DiMaggio and Mantle. *Damn Yankees* gave them the opportunity of expressing as many of these emotions as they wished while they were enjoying the tuneful songs and sexy dances in a show explaining what can happen to a middle-aged fan who wants both to be a star ballplayer and to seduce a beautiful woman. According to Mark Lubbock, a specialist in light opera, *Damn Yankees* became "the only successful musical comedy built around the American national pastime of baseball." The show won many awards. Smaller theatre groups all over the country have produced it, and promoters have twice revived it on Broadway. The song originally sung by the seductive Gwen Verdon, "Whatever Lola Wants, Lola Gets," became familiar on the airwaves because many well-known vocalists recorded it.

Because I was living in New York when *Damn Yankees* opened, I had the luck to experience the original production on Broadway, but at that time I failed to realize that this show reprised the dream of the typical American male fan, only in this version (unlike the similar *Bull Durham* plot thirty years later) the hero realizes that desiring to live a fantasy like that ultimately corrupts the soul. By the time the 1950s turned into the 1980s, living one's fantasy appeared perfectly acceptable; traditional morality never entered into the consideration of the main characters in *Bull Durham*. Perhaps Peter Bjarkman has the correct interpretation of baseball literature in his remark about fantasy being the better genre for presenting baseball plots.

Even current efforts at presenting baseball stories often include fantasy, as does *Mornings After*, a drama by Gene "Two Finger" Carney, a writer and SABR member from Utica, New York, which features musical touches by the musician Lowell Kammer of Niagara Falls. The show concerns the old-time pitcher Addie Joss of the Cleveland Indians, who died early in his promising career, and a character patterned after another real player, Paddy Livingston, who lived to age 97. In the play Paddy seems haunted, perhaps possessed, by the tragic figure of Joss. So this play, too, is flavored with fantasy.

Children, however, may have been the first consumers of baseball stories; in the early twentieth century hack writers churned out dozens of cheap novels about bold young fellows (meant as role models for youngsters) who won baseball games, exposed cheaters, and became the town heroes. Some of these books, like the later adult books, depended partly on fantasy to solve problems, as in the ancient Greek dramas when the god in a machine (*deus ex machina*) was lowered to the stage to rescue the hero in the nick of time. In *Billy Mayes's Great Discovery*, Ralph Henry Barbour presaged the storyline of Bernard Malamud's *The Natural* by giving his hero, Billy Mayes, a magical bat.

The boys of the early 1900s also devoured supposedly factual stories about the real players of the day, including autobiographies, many of them ghostwritten. Boys collected periodicals like *Tip Top Weekly*, a magazine that published exciting stories about fictional characters like Frank Merriwell, an impossibly virtuous young fellow who always won his games against great odds.

The number of baseball periodicals seems to have declined, and some that used to publish only baseball articles have broadened to include other sports. *Baseball Digest*, the oldest baseball magazine, now often appears in both paper and online versions to satisfy a shifting audience. *Baseball America*, a biweekly, may be the biggest paper-based periodical now devoted entirely to baseball, although it, too, publishes an online version. The swimsuit edition of *Sports Illustrated*— photos from which are now offered as a series of near-pornographic picture books — remains its best seller. *The Sporting News,* an old standby newspaper that used to be called "the Bible of Baseball," long ago began including other sports.

Magazine articles on baseball can rise to literary heights. Roger Angell, himself an excellent reporter of baseball events, calls a piece by John Updike (his fellow *New Yorker* contributor) "the most celebrated [sports] piece ever." Angell is here referring to a splendid little memoir Updike wrote about Ted Williams's final appearance in a ball game, an article Updike tagged with a headline rather than a title: "Hub Fans Bid Kid Adieu." In it Updike praised Williams for his celebrated quietness by saying that "of all team sports, baseball, with its graceful intermittences of action, its immense and tranquil field sparsely settled with poised men in white, its dispassionate mathematics, seems to me best suited to accommodate, and be ornamented by, a loner." Is there a better description of the national game?

The periodical market seems to be skewed toward the celebration of heroes and the game itself. Even the Hall of Fame at Cooperstown now publishes a fan magazine, *Memories and Dreams*, billed as "the inside story of the heroes, the fans, the innovators and the great moments of our National Pastime." Similar is a new periodical launched by Major League Baseball itself. As part of a fan's membership in the new MLB Insiders Club, he or she receives a club magazine claimed to offer "behind-the-scenes access" to Major League Baseball, along with a separate directory of big league ballparks, travel tips, and other fan resources, as well as features for fantasy league players, plus discounts on MLB-licensed merchandise. MLB's new effort should benefit itself more than the fans: it can enable the established clubs and leagues to come into direct and personal contact with each serious fan.

Other creative people who make their living by feeding on the desires and yearnings of baseball fans include artists and photographers — and sometimes the two terms identify the same person. Some serious artists specialize in baseball scenes and people, but none has yet gained the everyday popularity of Norman Rockwell with his famous baseball paintings, especially the one that appeared on the cover of the *Saturday Evening Post* April 23, 1949, showing three umpires checking the sky for rain. Other well-known artists like Claes Oldenburg, Elaine de Kooning, and Robert Rauschenberg have all paid attention to baseball. In fact, *FulcrumGallery.com* lists 3,188 items of baseball art for sale; some, of course, are photos (you can perpetuate the lost Ebbets Field by hanging its picture on your office wall), some of which are obviously commercial while others have real artistic qualities. My physician, a Yankees fan, displays on his office walls pictures of baseball action in oversize photographs of the type *Sports Illustrated* and other sport magazines publish.

To see a large collection of fine art, folk art, sculpture, and memorabilia all relating to baseball, fans can visit the Lehigh University Art Galleries in Bethlehem, Pennsylvania. In 2003 the American Folk Art Museum in New York City presented a fine exhibition called "The Perfect Game: America Looks at Baseball." After Jim Bouton, the ballplayer and author, saw the New York exhibition, he wrote, "For a few hours I was a kid again." Museums would not go to the trouble of preparing such exhibitions if they weren't sure of their drawing power.

Most fans appreciate baseball cartoons, too, especially those of Willard Mullin in the 1950s in which he tried to objectify the Brooklyn Dodgers, portraying the team as a disreputable-looking bum that to him represented their secondary nickname. Millions read the daily "Peanuts" cartoon strips, which feature baseball often.

But what they hear seems even more effective than what they see in enabling fans to enjoy the national pastime. For many years radio broadcasts of baseball games constituted the sound track of our culture. In nearly every neighborhood during the summer, the voice of the announcer for the games of the nearest big-league club could be heard emanating from every home's open living room window. In the summer of 1948, when the Indians contended for the American League pennant, "one could take a walk around the block and never miss a batter." It seemed that just about everybody in Cleveland, including my family, felt it necessary to listen to radio announcer Jack Graney's play-by-play. On the day of the playoff game with Boston at Fenway Park, Monday, October 4, 1948, teachers permitted students listen to the game at school; office employees likewise neglected their work to listen.

Older fans remember the days of radio with nostalgia because radio accounts of a game, by leaving much to the imagination, allowed us to "be our own cameras." In our minds arose pictures emanating from small hints of the way everything looked and thus increasing our awe of what must be happening. Some announcers presented "re-creations," or descriptions of games they had never seen, complete with sound effects, and the excitement in their voices convinced us that what they were describing was really occurring.

That changed when we could both hear and see the game, especially when so many watched Bobby Thomson hit a home run on live television in 1951 to unexpectedly bring a pennant to the New York Giants, much to the delight of many fans. "We saw history happening," said Sal Marchiano, who has been reporting sports on a New York television station for forty years, and "that's when baseball and television came together." The Thomson home run became "baseball's first TV event." The "shot heard round the world" became a legend partly because fans, perhaps as many as seventy million of them, saw it happen before their eyes. The exciting moment drove home the idea that fans could enjoy their game on an entirely new level inside their own homes, and sales of television sets boomed. That same year CBS Television broadcast the first baseball game in color, the Brooklyn Dodgers playing the Boston Braves in Boston, and four years later the World Series appeared in color on television. Now almost every American household boasts at least one television set. By creating a graphic way for fans to pursue their obsession, televised baseball helped sell those instruments, all the while expanding the professionals' fan base.

Now television sends out much more than the games; it devotes entire channels to sports news, including baseball news. In addition, it presents ambitious baseball documentaries, like those of the historian Ken Burns, and other films dramatizing baseball. Even "Mr. Monk," the neurotic detective played by Tony Shalhoub in a humorous television series, went to a ball game during an episode aired in 2003.

Films, many of which are now featured on television, have been using baseball in their plots since at least 1899. Fans could enjoy the sight of Babe Ruth and John McGraw lending their (limited) acting talents to some of these early silent films, like *Headin' Home* (1920), *One Touch of Nature* (1917), and *The Ball Player and the Bandit* (1912), all of which fans can view today on a DVD called *Reel Baseball*, produced by Kino International Corporation. Ty Cobb acted in *Somewhere in Georgia* (1916). When about mid-century studios began to film baseball biographies with real actors instead of real ballplayers, poor baseball scenes resulted, since the actors portraying the baseball heroes, like Jimmy Stewart (as Monty Stratton), William Bendix (as Babe Ruth), and Ronald Reagan (as Grover Cleveland Alexander), could not even move like ballplayers. Gary Cooper (as Lou Gehrig) proved the exception.

On a certain level, if not an artistic one, fans can still appreciate these commercial attempts to recreate baseball people and events. Because of the increased sophistication of today's fans, today's more ambitious filmmakers strive to portray baseball's history accurately and historically. Producers Don Casper and Jim Hughes of Crystal Pix, themselves knowledgeable about baseball history, utilized several recognized baseball historians as well as well-known players and authentic backgrounds in order to produce *Signs of the Time: The Myth, the Mystery, the Legend of Baseball's Greatest Innovation*, which explores the origin and development of umpires' hand signals. Pat and Bill Kittel of BaKit Productions have been working on a documentary about SABR and its members. Even Major League Baseball produces documentaries, notably *Baseball Discovered*, which discusses the earliest instances of baseball play in England and was produced in 2008 by filmmaker Sam Marchiano.

But fans devoted to their game need not wait for documentaries to appear; they can get current baseball news on the premier television channel devoted to sports, ESPN, or check NBC Sports, Fox Sports, and CBS Sports. Those fans who want to follow their own particular teams even when away from home can, for a fee, also subscribe to the channel that carries the teams' games.

Now Major League Baseball has created its own channel, the M.L.B. Network, devoted completely to baseball, especially MLB-sanctioned material. "We want to be the authentic home of baseball," says Tony Petitti, president and CEO of the new network. "We're another tool [with which] to enjoy the game." Is this perhaps overkill? Will fans actually watch all this baseball content? Jason Kanetsky, a media agent for the network, contends that there are so many avid fans around the country that "you can't have too much baseball." I think he's right.

Fans can even pursue baseball knowledge at the college level, since institutions of higher education from Maine to California now offer courses in baseball as it relates to history, law, literature, fiction, and math. At the University of San Francisco, among other places, one can pursue a sports management course at the graduate level. Professors prepare textbooks for these courses. There's even an American Sport University, located in San Bernardino, California, where students can earn graduate degrees and prepare for work in sports organizations. And the Society for American Baseball Research offers some baseball course syllabi through its web site.

In the 1940s Harold Seymour presented to the faculty of Fenn College (now Cleveland State University) a course syllabus on "Baseball and America" that he wanted to teach, but the faculty turned him down: baseball was not yet a respectable subject for study. When he taught at Finch College in New York City in the early sixties, Seymour simply inserted a lecture on baseball history into his current events course, supplementing it with an adventure in which he escorted his students to Yankee Stadium to see a game, on which he commented extensively. To borrow a metaphor from football, one could say he made an end run around whoever would have blocked him from teaching about the significance of baseball history.

Not only does most every business you can think of, including the education business, try to use baseball either in its advertising or as an actual sales item, so too does the United States government use baseball in its productions. In 2001 the Post Office produced a 20-stamp pane featuring "Baseball's Legendary Playing Fields," even though some of the pictured parks no longer exist. In 2008 it came out with an aid that Americans probably don't need: to accompany a 42-cent stamp portraying a player in nineteenth-century costume and commemorating the hundredth anniversary of the song "Take Me Out to the Ball Game," the Post Office sells a book presenting the lyrics of the song you hear every time you go to a ball park, along with a CD to play so that you can sing as you read — just in case you forgot the words etched into every fan's memory.

8

Brakes on Our Pursuit

Although fans still believe baseball to be quintessentially American and consider the successful practitioners of the game to be heroes whose exploits are worth praise and imitation, analysts who do the math have discovered that nowadays, more fans prefer to watch other sports. Several studies of attendance at big-league parks show that baseball interest has dropped significantly since the mid–1990s. Polls and surveys reveal that fewer fans reply "baseball" when asked, "What is your favorite sport to watch?"

To sports writer Harvey Araton, the most important signal of baseball's decline is the lowered interest in watching the World Series. He points out, "Professional sports tend to be judged by their big-event performance, and the World Series as a premier event continues a downward trend in the ratings and, worse, in the position it holds in the national dialogue."

By "national dialogue" Araton may refer to interest, as judged by the talk around water coolers, in coffee shops, and at bars — places where professional football and basketball talk appears to dominate. The news media reflects that difference in the amount of relative coverage given the sports.

How can that be? With all the baseball books being read, baseball museums being patronized, baseball souvenirs being purchased, and fans finding places to play the game themselves, how can baseball possibly be in decline? The complicated statistical games lasting an entire season that fans play; the obvious emotional involvement fans display in the fortunes of their teams; the religious fervor with which they treat the game and its stars — surely these activities reveal deep interest that should translate into game attendance. Why do fewer fans attend professional games and fewer of them watch the biggest attraction in their sport, the World Series? Have the actions of players, clubs, and owners done something to put the brakes on fans' pursuit of the national game?

Maybe not. Some analysts attribute the change to alterations in the character of our society. Newly available entertainment attracts young people in particular, who have "many more distractions than we had as kids," as Ron Kaplan remarked. They have, for example, discovered the variety of interesting activities offered by the internet: blogging, leaving messages at interest groups, playing games, researching with search engines, texting, emailing, and building personal web sites. Baseball-themed internet resources make up only a small fraction of what this new medium has to offer. In addition, television exposes them to the thrills available from watching other professional sports like exciting football and faster-moving basketball.

The interests of older fans differ from those of younger. Editor Gary Mitchem singles out an aging fan base as a change that affects baseball attendance negatively. Older fans, he points out, enjoy print-based newspapers, magazines, and books about baseball more than the young do. Mature fans appreciate nostalgia, and they delight in reading about player records and in savoring baseball history. Their interest, he says, is what makes baseball "king in the world of books" rather than king at game attendance.

Changes in fans cannot be the whole reason for the drop in baseball's attendance. Differences in the presentation of the sport must bear some blame. Players should shoulder some of the burden for the way baseball is perceived. Their unethical tactics during games, their bad behavior in and out of the park, the strikes that cause game cancellations, the huge salaries that players demand, and the scandals in which they have boldly engaged, all inspire anger, contempt, and deep disillusionment among devoted fans.

Cheating on the field is nothing new. In fact, the professional era in baseball was born from a wave of cheating by amateurs: using ringers, putting players on the city payroll as a way of paying them under the table, and offering "gifts" to talented amateurs for playing against other amateurs. This activity caused such an increase in paid players during the nineteenth century that soon team backers, acting defensively, decided to hire entire teams to play for salaries. With the striking success of Harry Wright's Cincinnati Red Stockings of 1869 as outright professionals (they beat all comers), what used to be cheating became acceptable and even admirable.

Other kinds of dishonesty soon followed. The degree of cheating deemed acceptable in playing the national game would hardly be tolerated in some others. "All sorts of subtle illegalities," says Professor James Keating, are "embedded" in the game. In fact, the leagues' many changes in the rules of play often came about because players had found ways to get around earlier rules. Beginning at least in the 1880s players not only threw directly at batters, they tripped and blocked runners, and they purposely knocked down infielders. A catcher might toss his mask into the base path right in front of a runner trying to score. The revered Connie Mack admitted after his career that while catching for his team he often "tipped" the hitter's bat. Doctoring the ball, stealing signs, and changing the topography of the field to favor the home team — these forms of cheating became common among the professionals. Umpires found detecting and controlling them to be difficult. Fans and writers call this kind of play either "smart," "clever," "wily," "tricky," or "dirty," depending on which team the fan or writer favors.

Cheating can be a cause of fans' negative perceptions — or the subject of their approval. Groundskeepers still slight the rules, as they have for many years, by changing the features of the infield and outfield to give the home team the advantage. According to researcher Peter Morris, nineteenth-century groundskeepers manipulated the grounds in Baltimore so that the home team's bunts, made on heavily watered dirt around home, became singles; grounders took "wicked bounces" on a parched infield; and runners advanced while their singles stopped rolling in wet grass. "Pitchers," said Morris, "became either better or worse, depending on the lay of the mound."

Manipulating the field to benefit the home team is not unusual. When I was growing up in Cleveland in the 1920s and 1930s, I gradually realized, from stories in the local papers, that for years the Cleveland Indians' groundskeepers had been preparing the field in favor of the home team's players; they boasted openly to local reporters about their achievement. Many fans consider the tricks of groundskeepers perfectly acceptable. I recall hearing Cleveland fans marveling about the clever tactics of the local groundskeepers and approving their initiative in making the field serve the strengths of the home team.

This kind of cheating continues today. Not long ago my local newspaper featured an article about George Toma, groundskeeper for the Minnesota Twins, explaining, "If the visiting team steals too many bases, Toma will soften it up to slow them down. He'll even add sharp granulated sand to grind a slide into second base to a halt. He tips the baseline edges to encourage bunts to roll fair or foul, customizes toe holes for specific hitters in the batter's box, and — depending on which team has a pitcher who throws sinkers — tweaks the hardness of the dirt in front of home plate to control the ball's bounce into the infield." Toma's work seemed so important to the team's success that the reporter, Tristan Spinski, called the groundskeeper the home team's tenth member. Spinski's admiring tone provoked no objections from readers; not one letter to the editor objected to that sharp, granulated sand sprinkled around second base — after all, it's going to hurt the other guy. Owners can hardly pretend to be unaware of these efforts, but I've never heard any protest against them. And helping the home team win by changing the shape of the diamond probably turns away few fans.

Other forms of cheating like stealing signs and doctoring the ball seem less acceptable to fans. Using a hollow bat or pickling it in resin are both illegal in baseball. Using the hidden ball trick or the potato play is generally thought of as "underhanded" but more irritating than wrong. Delaying the game to keep one's team in the lead engenders boos from the audience but is difficult for umpires to rule upon accurately.

In 1920 the rule-makers finally outlawed throwing the spitball, believed to be a danger to batters, although they permitted a few pitchers to continue using it. Others reportedly refused to stop throwing spitters. Edwin "Preacher" Roe, a spitball pitcher, made no apologies for using the pitch. A year after he retired, he wrote an article explaining his position: "It never bothered me none throwing a spitter.... If no one is going to help the pitcher in this game, he's got to help himself." Pitcher Bob Gibson underlined this sentiment: "Rules or no rules, pitchers are going to throw spitters. It's a matter of survival." This way of thinking seems prevalent among players today. It's the same attitude that led to the use of steroids: *I'm going to do what I think I need to do in order to get the advantage, since all other players are doing the same thing.* This attitude is expressed clearly in a 2008 Broadway play, *Back Back Back*, when a character named Raul, playing a baseball star who takes what in the play are called "vitamins," asserts that "baseball is no longer a team sport but a showcase for individual accomplishment, and anything that levels the playing field is fair game."

Devoted fans have become used to the many instances of cheating in baseball and the need for rules to prevent their occurrence. Any observer unfamiliar with baseball who reads the game's elaborate rule system could be surprised by it. "After all," outsiders might comment, "everybody knows the difference between right and wrong. Do you really have to legislate baseball ethics? Must you pass a rule to guard against every unethical thing a player might possibly do?" The answer is "yes." The infield fly rule, for example, evolved to prevent a fielder from intentionally misplaying a fly ball and then effecting a double play by throwing out runners who were anticipating a caught ball. Analysis of the rule by an attorney, William S. Stevens, points out that the rule gave baseball a technical remedy for sneaky behavior that would not have occurred in amateur days.

After the Giants won the National League pennant in 1951, perhaps in part because of the elaborate mechanical sign-stealing system they installed secretly, baseball outlawed sign-stealing by mechanical means. Said Sal Yvars, the catcher who helped pull it off, "I didn't feel guilty about anything. I was just doing my job."

The endless declarations by newspapermen in the nineteenth and earlier twentieth century that "baseball builds character" have little to do with reality. The notion that sports built character arose long after sports had already developed in this country; scholars point out that we play sports not to develop our character but as an escape from life's responsibilities.

Cheating in baseball sometimes inspires critical columns by sports writers and occasionally bothers fans enough to write letters to the editor; after all, cheating represents an attempt to gain an unfair advantage over one's opponent. But cheating generally bothers fans less than other occurrences. Peter Beinart of the Council on Foreign Relations claims fans care about cheating "only in the abstract.... We cheer when our teams cheat. That's because all we care about is winning.... Fans aren't moral universalists; they don't care about being fair to the other guys."

Fan annoyance with cheating, if any, remains fleeting. What really puts a brake on fans' pursuit of baseball is anything that keeps their favorite game from being played. That means player strikes and owner lockouts. Over the era 1972–1994, seven long stoppages in season play frustrated, even infuriated, many devoted fans, especially when one occurred in 1981 and resulted in the cancellation of 712 games. During those periods of no baseball, newspapers kept reporting declarations of angry fans that they would never watch professional baseball again but would transfer their loyalty to football or other sports. Many did return later, however, as is obvious from the way attendance figures rebounded somewhat, although not to pre-strike levels.

Anger at striking players often intensified with the media's frequent revelations of the huge salaries players can demand, especially since 1975, when the lifting of the reserve clause made free agency possible, for when a player is free to move to another club, he can negotiate a higher salary. Everyone seems aware that ballplayers now make a great deal more money than the average worker. While the average American salary more than doubled between 1978 and 1987, the average baseball salary more than quintupled. Then, between 1987 and 2002, the average American salary doubled again — and the average baseball salary quintupled again. By 2002 the average pro baseball player's salary had become a whopping two million four hundred thousand dollars, while the average Joe or Jane brought home forty thousand.

How could the average middle-class fan avoid feeling jealous and angry? Many of us have wondered whether something is wrong with a society that permits such a preposterous difference between the earning power of a teacher, nurse, or soldier — all of whom contribute much to our country — and the salary of a professional baseball player. To many fans, paying a fellow millions of dollars for playing baseball seems unconscionable, obscene, crazy — especially compared with what they themselves can make through working at their trades or professions. They feel cheated.

How can owners possibly pay such huge salaries? They can do it because they make a lot of money. Low-priced tickets cost sixty dollars instead of sixty cents and seem more in line with the cost of seats at the opera. "In baseball," says analyst William C. Rhoden, "salaries tend to reflect the income of the previous year, and baseball has enjoyed several good years." Moreover, baseball makes money even during a recession. "Historically," states Don Fehr, executive director of the Major League Baseball Players Association, "baseball has been recession-resistant.... If you look at baseball's income numbers beginning with the late 1970s, even though we went through bad recessions in the early '80s, in the late '80s, and in the early '90s," baseball's income remained almost the same. The president of the Boston Red Sox, Larry Lucchino, declared during the world economic crisis in the fall of 2008 that clubs' spending to hire expensive free agents would be "largely unaffected." At the same time, the president of the New York Yankees, Randy Levine, defended his club's huge salary expenditures by saying that because the owners believe that "the Yankees are a sacred trust to their fans," they must reinvest in it at a rate calculated to be far more than have the other 29 major league teams *combined.*

But huge baseball salaries have hardly put a brake on fans' pursuit of baseball. As author Stefan Fatsis points out, "The shock over how much money elite players make has gradually dissipated." Economist Andrew Zimbalist believes "big-city teams signing big-name players to lucrative contracts won't prompt angry comparisons to the plight of the working class." Fans may complain, but they remain fans. Historically, what has cut devoted baseball fans to the quick is not overblown salaries but the exposure of the ultimate in cheating: players who conspire to let a rival team win.

The most striking example of cheating remains the Black Sox scandal of 1919, after which several players of the Chicago White Sox were expelled from baseball. "Say it ain't so!" was supposedly the cry, echoed in the hearts of many, of a boy who wanted to disbelieve the news that his heroes were cheaters.

But long before 1919 baseball experienced several similar cases of crooked players who succumbed to the temptations of gambling and gamblers. Betting was rampant at the beginning of the century in pool rooms, saloons, and other gambling centers, including baseball parks, and not only on the part of fans. Players, and sometimes owners, bet on their own teams and on games of other teams. Major League Baseball's investigation of some cases of player crookedness came up with too little proof; charges were dismissed. MLB hushed up other charges. Probably the worst offender of the era was player Hal Chase; despite many complaints against him, MLB put up with him for years because of his playing skill — which he did not always use.

Another disappointment for fans was the Cobb-Speaker case, in which Major League Baseball permitted the two star players Ty Cobb and Tris

Speaker, idolized by many, to resign in the face of accusations of crookedness. Smoky Joe Wood, also involved in the Cobb-Speaker case, had already left MLB. Ty's distant cousin, Ron Cobb, believes today's press gives Cobb a bad rap; he told me, "Of course we all know he was no angel. But he was far from the ogre that the modern press portrays." That could be. Nobody admired his mean personality, of course, but his admission to having tried to bet on his club after being told it was "a sure thing" is a lot more serious than accusations of being an "ogre." Yet sportswriters elected both Cobb and Speaker to the Hall of Fame in Cooperstown. Do the writers represent fan opinion? Probably.

Fans seldom think deeply enough about these cases to realize that owners bear some blame in them, too, for their efforts to keep the news of cheating under wraps. These and other early cases established precedents for baseball's attempt to cover up the biggest scandal of them all, the "fixed" World Series of 1919. Writers have produced so many articles, documentaries, movies, and books on the subject that even if we wanted to forget it we could not. As one publisher has declared, for more than eighty years the 1919 scandal has "lingered in the collective consciousness." In fact, the way it's remembered in various circumstances is the subject of one of the best books on the scandal, *Saying It's So*, by Daniel A. Nathan, a book I reviewed favorably for the British journal called *Sport in History*. Yes, British sport historians, too, find the topic fascinating; in 2003 I received a query from a student at the University of Aberdeen in Scotland asking for information to help him research the scandal.

Whenever the subject of player misdeeds arises, the Black Sox scandal becomes the event cited as the worst of them all. But like those who tried to conceal earlier scandals, the central characters who tried to cover up the "fix" — Charles Comiskey, the White Sox president, and the other Major League Baseball officials — seldom stand out as the persons remembered in the scandal; instead, we recall Shoeless Joe Jackson, who has become either the crooked liar or the goat, depending on the way his experience is read. Those who study and evaluate his story believe that after accepting (or rejecting) a bribe, he actually played to win. In any case, Jackson has become the principal figure in a real-life drama, a fallen hero banned from the game he loved and in which he starred, living out the rest of his life in resentment and obscurity.

In the sixties, while Harold Seymour and I were preparing our analysis of the Black Sox scandal as a chapter in *Baseball: The Golden Age*, Eliot Asinof was writing his seminal treatment of the event, *Eight Men Out*. Seymour got himself invited to Asinof's home to discuss the topic, reporting afterwards, with surprise, "Asinof knows more than I do about the scandal." Asinof gathered a great deal of information about the events of the Black Sox and wrote about them dramatically in his book.

Since then Gene Carney emerged as the resident expert on the Black Sox, uncovering all sorts of unexpected details. Carney said, "The more I learn about it, the more there seems to be learned. Certainty about things related to the fix and the cover-up is elusive." Another revelatory book about the scandal, Susan Dellinger's *Red Legs and Black Sox*, tells the experiences of Dellinger's grandfather, the player Edd Roush of the Cincinnati team, rival of the White Sox in the World Series, a book in which Dellinger reveals that Roush knew very early that the fix was on and even knew of attempts by gamblers to corrupt Cincinnati players as well.

Jackson is still the center of interest about the scandal, and his life has inspired many writers. W.P. Kinsella's *Shoeless Joe*, a novel, became famous as the basis for the fantasy film *Field of Dreams*. Researcher David L. Fleitz and writer Howard Burman are among those who have written Jackson biographies, Burman's in the form of historical fiction. Jay Bennett, a scientist who specializes in baseball statistics, showed in an article that Sabermetrics supports Jackson in his constantly repeated claim that he played up to his full potential in every game of the 1919 Series, and the producers of the television program *Numb3rs* were alert enough to cite Bennett's article in one of the program's episodes. The Baseball Reliquary has inducted Joe Jackson into its Shrine of the Eternals; the Hall of Fame at Cooperstown has not, although his admirable playing records should have qualified him.

In any case, it's clear from the evidence that a group of conspirators made a determined effort to control the outcome of the 1919 World Series and that some players agreed, at least at first, to conspire with them, while the owners, who knew about the attempt, kept quiet about it until they could cover it up no longer. Baseball will never live this event down, and whenever a history of questionable player behavior occurs, sports writers dredge it up again. It is a permanent, if subliminal, brake on fans' love for the game.

The Pete Rose case caused some fans to feel disgust for the player, but Cincinnati fans stuck by him. Rose, after first denying vehemently that he had bet on baseball, admitted it fifteen years later. The commissioner banned him from baseball, angering local fans, who defended him because he was a home-town boy. A helicopter pulling a "We Support Pete" banner circled the city while thousands of Cincinnatians waited hours in line to buy the book in which he admitted his guilt. "If he played for any other team," said fan Jeanne Loreaux, "I wouldn't have liked him, or what he did to baseball. But he's from Cincinnati. He's our Pete." The city of Cincinnati helped sponsor a Red Sox exhibit in which Pete's record hits, represented by a three-storey-high wall in which baseballs were embedded, formed the centerpiece. Moreover, before Game Four of the World Series in 2002, when Pete Rose was introduced, fans gave him a "loud, long ovation" and chanted "Hall of Fame! Hall of Fame!"

The support of Cincinnati fans for Pete Rose seems similar to the support for Joe Jackson by the city of Greenville, South Carolina, Jackson's home, except that Jackson never admitted any guilt and may not be guilty. Rose's case has inspired less literary effort. ESPN produced a film about Rose called *Hustle*, which reviewer Virginia Heffernan found a "potent drama," "true to the dismal facts" and without any "elevating moments," a presentation in which Rose comes off as "an amoral sociopath." Cincinnati fans seem unmoved by criticisms of Rose, and from everything I've read, he is still beloved in his home town.

Rose obviously needs to be his own person even if doing so hurts both baseball and himself. But keeping him out of the Hall of Fame — his playing skills surely qualified him — may not be the right punishment. Was Babe Ruth a virtuous person? Was Ty Cobb? The Cooperstown establishment may be punishing itself by neglecting Rose and his drawing power among fans who appreciate the Charlie Hustle style of successful baseball playing.

The kind of cheating that probably discouraged most devoted fans from pursuing their favorite game in recent years is the use of drugs. Reflecting trends in the general society, players used "greenies" (pep pills) and other drugs as early as the 1960s, according to Jim Bouton, the ex-player who in the 1970s first revealed player peccadilloes, and the number of drug users may have gone as high as 80 percent. Yet as late as 1995, commissioner Bud Selig claimed that if baseball had a drug problem, he was "unaware of it."

MLB delayed banning performance-enhancing drugs until 2002 and failed to begin drug testing until 2003. Four years later, finding it could no longer manage the cheating and the lying about it, MLB asked a congressional leader, George Mitchell, to conduct an investigation. Mitchell, unfortunately, also maintained close ties to baseball through the Red Sox and through ESPN, so his judgment could hardly be considered disinterested. His twenty-month investigation did reveal, however, that eighty-nine players, including prominent ones like Roger Clemens, had strong links to illegal drug use, and that illegal drug use had been widespread for more than a decade. Yet Mitchell recommended better testing and more aggressive investigation, but urged commissioner Bud Selig to forego disciplining any but the most "serious" cases.

By that time two independent, prize-winning San Francisco journalists had produced a book, *Game of Shadows*, exposing the rampant use of steroids in baseball. The two writers, Lance Williams and Mark Fainaru-Wada, came out with a searing indictment not only of BALCO, the drug house that produced and gave steroids to many players, but also of MLB and the players' union for avoiding their responsibility to stop the illegal and harmful use of such substances as human growth hormones. Nobody wanted to officially recognize what was happening. Baseball had entered what newsmen had begun calling "the Steroid Era."

Fans reacted negatively, especially at first. Revelations of drug use shrank fans' enjoyment of their favorite game in several ways. First, players were obviously breaking hallowed records by unnatural means, using supplements unavailable to stars like Babe Ruth. Was Bonds's success in breaking the Ruth and Aaron home run records supposed to be as respected as Ruth's? After all, in baseball, statistics are vitally important. Second, the revelations of doping shocked those fans who had used ballplayers as role models for youth. With an echo of "Say it ain't so!" dismayed parents protested as they discovered that their heroes had let them down. "The owners, the managers, the trainers, and the players — nobody is immune from blame," declared one blogger. "And that includes the fans. We let ourselves be hoodwinked." She might have mentioned specifically the clean players who knew about the drug use but said nothing.

In a monthly baseball newsletter I was writing and publishing at the time of the Mitchell hearings, I pointed out to my subscribers that fans and commentators were concluding that the drug problem had grown too big and had been going on too long for anything to be done about it. I predicted that past offenders would not be punished. Unfortunately, I was right. Mitchell recommended "letting go of the past." Commissioner Bud Selig imposed no suspensions or fines; guilty players were asked to perform community service, such as speaking to high school students on the dangers of drugs. Shouldn't they have been doing that anyway? They ought to be emulating cartoonist Robb Armstrong, who produces the comic strip *Jump Start* and spends a lot of time visiting schools, advising students to pay attention in class and avoid experimenting with drugs.

As the baseball drug scandal unfolded, fans began to express more sadness than anger. A newspaper headline summed up their feelings: "Parents Feel Betrayed by Millionaire Role Models." When Alex Rodriguez admitted that he had used drugs when he was "young and stupid," fans proved ambivalent. Phone lines to talk radio shows were jammed with fans waiting to state their opinions, which ranged from calling the player's apology "hollow" to declaring that fans may forgive but not forget. The following month, a national poll showed that 60 percent of fans questioned remained resentful of Rodriguez, but when he showed up for spring training in Florida only a couple of fans shouted critical remarks. As sports writer Terry McDonell points out, fans eventually forgive cheating players who subsequently perform well on the field.

Many fans react to the news of player culpability with simple whining. As baseball researcher John Thorn commented, a revelation of drug use "makes them feel bad about themselves for being credulous. It's like someone has dumped on the family scrapbook." Sports writer Chuck Klosterman put it this way: "We were all fools and now we have to pretend we weren't." A fan wrote a letter to the editor complaining, "When I was growing up in the 1970s, parents encouraged their kids to participate in sports to help keep them away from drugs. Now the most prominent drug abusers are professional athletes." One of the best examples of whining is the resentfulness shown by James Traub in the *New York Times Magazine*: "We want the sport, like other endeavors we care deeply about, to be worthy of our love. Is that too much to ask?" Obviously, it is. Resignation became the reaction of some, as with a reporter named Wallace Matthews, who declared that sports fans need no longer wonder about the ethics of any pro players: "It's official," he declared. "Nobody plays clean any more."

Much of the controversy boiled around Barry Bonds, who lied about the drug use that became obvious with the noticeable changes that drugs induced in his body. Moreover, sports writers were depicting Bonds as meaner even than Ty Cobb, with an "in-your-face" style that repelled interviewers. "I cheat because I'm my daddy's son," he is quoted as saying, thus blaming his famous father, Bobby Bonds, for his own transgressions. To sportswriter George Vecsey, Bonds became "an odious human being "...a cheat, a bully, and a whiner." Chuck Klosterman called Bonds "a self-absorbed, unlikable person who has an adversarial relationship with the world at large." Writers subjected him to "crude news treatment," and some fans acted "nasty." His negative personality may have aided the indictment for perjury that removed him from MLB by giving him free agency. For whatever happens, MLB and its supporters want above all to save baseball, and Bonds represented a threat to the status quo.

Yet we must remember that the controversy arose less because of objections to drug use and cheating than because of concerns about fairness; some players used drugs to enhance their playing skill and others did not, so those who relied solely on their natural talent to produce many hits, react quickly, run very fast, and make great catches were penalized. Professionals in many sports, says Michael Shermer, who studies and writes about drugs in sports, "have come to believe that they cannot remain competitive if they do not participate" in the use of drugs. This belief, he states, is supported by MLB's failure to establish clear rules and enforce them as well as by its "historical tendency to look the other way." Moreover, prosecutors proved willing to accept light pleas from defendants who admit they were guilty of deliberately breaking the rule. ("We knew we weren't taking Tic Tacs," said Alex Rodriguez in 2009.) Journalist Clyde Haberman believes that the drug scandal, combined with dissatisfaction over clubs' excessive spending of taxpayers' money on salaries and unnecessary parks, has shaken fans' faith in the game and that their "discontent runs deep." Evidence of their feelings surfaces when cheers turn to jeers.

Those of us who know baseball history are reminded of what Harold Seymour and I dubbed "the Twilight Era," when in the 1850s some amateur clubs began to break the rules and give some players a salary; those clubs that continued to follow the rules and relied on amateur talent paid the penalty by losing games to professionals. So other amateur clubs broke the rules and made themselves into professionals in order to level the playing field and compete on the same basis as those who had already turned pro. The comparable step for the owners to take today is to forget the rules against drug use and permit all players to alter their natural abilities with drugs (or even surgery, if they like), so that everyone gets the same chance. In fact, healthcare consultant Ted Park believes that "it is impossible to determine what is and is not an unacceptable artificial enhancement. With advances in medicine, biology and even prosthetics, the broad gray line will only get wider and murkier." The next step may be genetic enhancement, already nicknamed "gene doping." It can be done *in utero* to create a super-baby, and Don Fehr, director of the players' union, said it "will make what we do now look quaint."

MLB has already taken the first step toward establishing a new equality by "forgiving" those who broke the rules in the early part of the Steroid Era. Perhaps eventually MLB will find it impossible to control all attempts at physical enhancement and legalize everything players do in order to "get that edge on the other guy."

Would fans sit still for that? Would they pay to see games in which players had greatly enhanced their physical abilities with drugs and other methods? Perhaps we can make that judgment by checking on the way they react when watching "juiced" players perform. An editorial in the *Naples Daily News* asserted that fans had proved "remarkably indulgent of steroid allegations about their own teams." Despite their initial angry reaction, those who watched Barry Bonds while he was hitting his 73 home runs in 2001 seemed to writer John Heilemann "remarkably blasé"; to Heilemann, the heavy use of drugs in the general society (for anxiety, depression, aging, excess weight, hair loss, difficulty with erections) contributes to fans' eventual acceptance of drug use by players, once they get past the initial shock of the players' boldness in breaking the rules and their disappointment in players for failing to be perfect. Some writers have pointed out that for an even longer time we have been using exercise machines, herbal supplements, protein shakes, and vitamin cocktails to improve our physical performance. What are they if not external and artificial aids to fitness?

After their first dismay upon knowing for sure that their heroes have fallen, Americans have generally reacted to the steroid problem in baseball the way they typically react to problems: with rather snarky humor. They seem to agree with writer George Vecsey that "flinching in negative body English is a waste of time," so instead they have responded with jokes based upon irony or sarcasm. Late-night showmen David Letterman and Jay Leno used the situation for their one-liners. A comic strip called "Hi and Lois" showed a child sorting his baseball cards into three piles: "drug-free," "suspected steroid users," and "confirmed cheaters." Clever comments on the gross expansion of players' muscles with unapproved supplements abounded. Illustrator Steve Brodner prepared for his blog a caricature of a bat-toting ballplayer wearing humongous shoes, over the caption, "New revelations [show] that slugger Barry Bonds'[s] feet mysteriously grew 2½ sizes." Steve Kelley drew for the *New Orleans Times-Picayune* a huge man in baseball uniform being interviewed by a reporter about steroid use in baseball; the large fellow replies, "Don't ask me ... I'm just the bat boy." Artist Barry Blitt produced a *New Yorker* cover that showed Alex Rodriguez signing his autograph for children — a standard-looking piece of art until the viewer realizes that all the children have grown the same huge forearms that Rodriguez displays. Jim Bouton, wryly assuming that lying and cheating players would receive prison sentences, predicted in 2006 that prison ball would show sudden growth: "Prisons will become the new sandlots" and bumper stickers will be revised to claim, "My kid plays third base for Sing Sing!"

Irritated acceptance seems to be the attitude behind these reactions. Fans eventually accept all kinds of changes in baseball, good ones as well as bad ones. They finally accepted the advent of black players and those of Asian origin. White parents seem more accepting now of black youth in the Little League, although in the past black children had some harrowing experiences. They could hardly have had a worse discrimination experience than the one that a group of twelve-year-olds had to go through in 1955 when the Cannon Street All-stars of Charleston, South Carolina, were prevented from playing because of their color. The controversy began when the state Little League director Danny Jones, who was white, was "stunned" when he learned that manager Ben Singleton of the Cannon Street All-Stars, who was black, planned to send an all-star team of black boys to the city tournament. To prevent black children from participating, Jones called off the tournament. Singleton then prepared his team for the state tournament in Greenville. All 61 of the white Little League teams then withdrew from the South Carolina tournament to protest the black team's entry.

Are we actually expected to believe that it was the white boys who refused to play against blacks? I don't think so. Obviously, the white parents made their children into little racists. And the result was that those parents prevented their white children from having the experience of engaging in a tournament with the blacks, who were awarded the state championship by default.

The All-Stars then got ready to enter the Little League's regional tournament in Georgia, one that included eight state champions, the winner of which would travel to Williamsport to take part in the Little League World Series. But the Rome organizers declared that the Cannon Street team could not play in the regionals because the rules required that a team could not continue if it had "advanced by forfeit."

Meanwhile, Jones circumvented them by resigning as state Little League director and forming a new organization, Little Boys Baseball, Inc. (later renamed Dixie League Baseball), setting up a tournament for the boys on the dates formerly chosen by the Little League, and publishing a rule requiring that the program be carried out "on a racially segregated basis." Jones signed up 537 teams in 122 leagues for the 1956 season to assure that Southern white boys would not have to play Southern black boys.

Little League officials in Williamsport proved sympathetic to the plight of Ben Singleton and his players. They decided to invite the Cannon Street team to the national tournament — not to play, but to watch! The black team was game enough to come, its backers thinking that they might be able to persuade tournament directors to let the team play. When the black kids visited the playing field in street clothes during the white players' batting practice, they were standing in left field when a baseball came the way of the Cannon Street boys. The team's best player picked it up and fired it to the white catcher. Play stopped entirely. Fans "wouldn't stop staring" at the skill of that boy.

When the team members were seated in the stands, the announcer introduced them, and as they stood up to acknowledge the cheers, they heard the chant begin: "Let them play! Let them play!" But the league directors were not persuaded, and after the tournament the Cannon Street boys phoned home crying. To this day the players, grown up and having become contributing members of their community, resentfully point out that they could have become the first African American team to win a Little League title. But Creighton Hale, founder of the Little League, stands by his decision preventing them from participating: "I thought we did them a favor" was his illogical comment.

I can't imagine how black parents feel when they see their children hurt by having their dreams destroyed in this way. If I were a black parent, my gratitude for the favors granted by Little League would be zero, and the memory of the Cannon Street boys would put a brake on my enthusiasm for baseball.

Today, some white fans can accept a black player on an otherwise white team and see their children play on Little League teams with and against black children. But how will they feel when gay members of MLB come out and reveal their true selves?

Baseball, you'll recall, is "a manly sport." In fact, the word "macho" may apply better; Robert Lipsyte aptly calls pro sports "hyper-masculinized." That means players must act ultra-masculine even if they aren't. And doubtless, some aren't: writers who cover the baseball clubs assure readers that baseball already has some homosexual players who are afraid to make themselves known for fear of harassment. When stories intimating that a pro player is gay appear in the papers, the player hastens to deny it, whether he is or not. If a player is gay, he realizes that admitting it means he might be "driven from the team" by tormenting, persecuting team members.

William D. "Billy" Bean, the ballplayer who after his career became a gay activist (not the statistics-using manager Billy Beane), has explained how difficult it was for him to bear the anti-gay remarks of teammates and coaches while pretending constantly to be someone he was not. Finally, convinced that baseball was not ready for a gay player, he quit at age 31. He felt that "the game wasn't mature enough to deal with a gay ballplayer." A football player in the same position said he "tried to be tougher than any player" in order to fend off any suspicion. Living a lie took a toll on his health. As tennis player Martina Navratilova explained, "When you're in the closet, the soul suffers."

The only baseball player who admitted his homosexuality during his career was Glenn Burke, and that admission went down badly, especially with the owners. Burke's friendship with manager Tommy Lasorda's gay son made the Dodger administrators suspect he was gay, and the club offered to pay for his honeymoon if he would marry! The Dodgers traded him to Oakland, but a year later manager Billy Martin announced to the world that he didn't want any "fags" on his team. After suffering an injury Burke was demoted to the minors, and soon afterward he left baseball. Burke remained angry: "I got cheated out of a career," he said, and Martin's remark "broke my heart."

In 1988 Dave Pallone, who for ten years had umpired in the National League, was released, purportedly for poor performance. Pallone, a gay man, believed his firing was actually related to his sexual orientation. Today Pallone speaks before groups like corporations and students about respecting everyone and treating them equally.

The Burke, Bean, and Pallone cases happened back in the seventies and eighties; players should have gained a bit of sophistication and toleration since then. In fact, two players have been quoted as declaring that in their opinion MLB clubs are ready to accept gay players. What about the MLB power structure? Although it has made no remarks welcoming gays to the ranks of players, MLB responded appropriately to recent openly anti-gay remarks made by a couple of players. The Atlanta Braves even helped support the city's bid to sponsor the Gay Games by holding a pregame event, and other clubs have held "Out at the Ballgame" nights in which gays who buy blocks of tickets get to offer their own pregame entertainment like a presentation of the National Anthem by the Gay Men's Chorus. Dug Funnell, a gay sports fan in Cleveland who teaches hearing-impaired and handicapped children, has sent out thousands of letters to people connected to baseball trying to "raise their consciousness" about the pain of gay players and the homophobia of the sports community. He points out that baseball has retained players charged with assault, felonies, solicitation, statutory rape, and illegal financial actions, not to speak of those who admitted selling, buying, and using illegal drugs; he asks, with perfect logic, should those players be more acceptable to baseball than gay players? Funnell has received letters of support from some players and believes the atmosphere on teams has "warmed somewhat." Burke claimed that when he played back in the mid-seventies, at least ten other gay players were playing, so logically, at least that many men who are secretly gay are playing now. How must they feel in the virulently anti-gay atmosphere of a men's baseball team? Funnell, although he sees increased tolerance in baseball, does not urge any gay big leaguer to come out of the closet because "there's still too much homophobia in the sport, especially in the locker room." Evidently, the outlook isn't brilliant for the "different" guys today.

But are the fans ready to root for gay players? When the *Oakland Tribune* polled fans on the question of whether they would accept an openly gay player in MLB, 51 percent claimed they would while 49 percent said they would not. No doubt these numbers will continue to change. If players and fans can learn that black men have rights, maybe they can learn that gay men have them, too. Writers point out that the social climate is shifting, that television has been emboldened to embrace gay characters, and that in some states gay marriage has been legalized. Most straight people are now acquainted with at least a few openly gay people and realize that they are not monsters. But even those who believe acceptance will eventually happen point out that gay players would still be subject to hecklers' catcalls and boos. "Society has grown increasingly tolerant of homosexuality," said Jim Buzinski of *Outsports.com*, "but this does not translate into being totally comfortable with it." Society has proved able to accept Hollywood's gay cowboy, but accepting a real gay ballplayer in the Manly Pursuit will doubtless take a lot longer.

Jim Bouton believes that many players are ready to accept gay colleagues and that "if he's good enough" the others will eventually have to; besides, as with the introduction of Jackie Robinson, "you can't wait for every single player to accept a gay player." A poll of ballplayers taken in 2008 by the *Tribune* newspapers and reported on a gay sports site claims that 74 percent of current ballplayers would accept a gay teammate. If the players manage to overcome their homophobia, can fans be far behind?

Homosexual players have not yet become an issue of contention with fans, but tactics of the clubowners have. Especially does the owners' establishment of high ticket prices, which generally increase each year, engender a lot of water-cooler objection. Fans complain of having to spend as much as three hundred dollars to take their families to a game and paying five dollars for a bottle of water. Moreover, owners have created another way to extract money from fans: selling them "personal seat licenses," which cost as much as twenty thousand dollars, simply for the right to buy season tickets. Other clubs draw the ire of fans by demolishing hallowed and still-serviceable ball parks like Yankee Stadium and Shea Stadium, using public financing to construct new ones next door, and selling luxury suites at these stadiums for as much as $600,000 a year when most fans find a seat at the park too expensive.

Many old-time supporters saw the now-extinct "House that Ruth Built" as a living museum; Ralph Nader called it "a national treasure," pointing out that George Steinbrenner of the Yankees, instead of making improvements on his park, decided on destroying it for private gain. New York taxpayers, according to several estimates, gave each team, the Yankees and the Mets, a "nine-figure donation" to construct the new parks. Fans soon began protesting that they are, through the taxes they pay, helping to build stadiums they do not want. According to *New York Times* writer Harvey Araton, "nobody has been swindled like the Yankee Stadium community." Criticism of the idea of building new stadiums appeared to dissipate when the two new pleasure palaces opened in 2009 and fans, along with reporters, swarmed inside to check out the amenities, take photos with their cellphones, and admire the attempts to retain some of the historical details and flavor of the former buildings. As usual, fans' annoyance began to fritter away when new events distracted them.

Franchise-transferring angers fans, too, at least for a while. Devoted followers of the Brooklyn Dodgers still wince at the thought of having lost their beloved Bums to the West Coast fifty years ago when owner Walter O'Malley moved them to Los Angeles. Outraged fans see changes like these as cynical moves on the part of greedy owners who put the prospect of higher earnings ahead of fans' enjoyment. Using the common response of Americans to disappointing events, an embittered Brooklyn fan channeled his anger into a joke: "If you had Hitler, Stalin, and O'Malley in a room and you only had two bullets, what would you do?" The answer is "Shoot O'Malley twice."

Baseball parks have become even more commercial and less related to the neighborhood as a result of owners' sale of "naming rights." Club owners now sell to huge commercial entities the right to have ball parks named after them for a set number of years. As a result, your neighborhood ball park, instead of being called by the name of the team that occupies it or the name of the city in which it stands, now advertises a power company or an insurance firm. This artificial and commercial decision imposed on fans alienates them instead of helping them identify with a club that the owners want them to consider "their team." Citigroup, the shaky financial institution that requested billions in government aid, will still pay four hundred million dollars over twenty years to have the Mets' new ballpark named Citi Field, although Massachusetts Representative Barney Frank accurately calls the naming rights ploy not "marketing" but "ego boosts" for businessmen.

Fed by the fury of taxpaying fans over this situation, New York politicians for a while demanded a different name for the park. Sports writer George Vecsey would have preferred that it be called Jackie Robinson Stadium, after "a legitimate New York sports hero." Some disgruntled fans referred to it as "Bailout Park." A wry poem in a baseball journal ends with the poet wondering if the new Yankee Stadium would be named for Viagra "in a climax of poetic justice."

Tom Goldstein, editor and publisher of the *Elysian Fields Quarterly*, asserts that he has become too disillusioned to go to the ballpark now because of the "humorless, sterile atmosphere that corporate baseball exudes," with every marketing decision designed to appeal not to Everyfan but to the rich. Because owners are "monetizing every aspect of the game" instead of treating it as something that belongs to all of us, some analysts believe attendance will continue to drop and baseball will soon stop being the national pastime.

Players, too, irritate many fans. To some, the players, like the owners, seem self-absorbed, forgetting that they are public personalities — skilled performers hired to entertain us. They break laws as well as drug rules, getting themselves in jail for lying, fighting, and even stealing. Frank Josza summarizes their conduct as a display of "disgusting behavior and bad manners." Offended fans eventually begin to react to these events in the usual way: with humor shading into irony. For example, when reporters discovered the married player Alex Rodriguez dating a "busty blonde stripper" in New York, Boston fans taunted him by showing up at Fenway Park wearing yellow-haired masks. Tim Marchman of the *New York Sun* said he responded to the A-Rod story by doing what anyone else would do: "I laughed and laughed."

Yet fans themselves often fail to act in civilized fashion, many of their tricks "committed in the name of home-team loyalty and fueled by beer." George Vecsey asserts that this behavior is not confined to mere towel-waving or using bad language; fans throw packs of mustard at those who root for visiting teams or even rough them up; one rooter was actually mugged during the 1986 World Series for wearing a Red Sox jacket at Shea Stadium. Perhaps the most spectacular example of bad behavior on the part of fans is the mean way they treated a Giants rookie, nineteen-year-old Fred Merkle, a century ago at the Polo Grounds for committing a technical violation of the rules, the same violation that other players had been permitted to get away with "for as long as anyone could remember." When the umpire called him on it at a crucial point in a game that might decide the pennant, the game had to be replayed, and his team lost. As a result, according to player Mordecai Brown, "from the stands there was a steady roar of abuse." Brown said he "never heard anybody or any set of men called as many foul names as the Giant fans called us that day." Moreover, Merkle became known as Bonehead Merkle, "the man who lost the pennant" with "a mistake that was not a mistake." Constant fan heckling caused him to lose weight and become depressed.

Is baseball in decline? Perhaps it is, if you limit your estimate to actual game attendance. As I've shown, fans never limit their pursuit of baseball to just showing up at the baseball park. Dismay over "bad actors" and other flaws in their favorite game put only temporary brakes on their pursuit of baseball. Thousands of them continue to collect souvenirs, play baseball board games, take part in intricate season-long statistical fantasy leagues, travel to baseball destinations in the States and abroad, admire exhibits at museums, attend baseball camps, join teams that take part in historical baseball play, shop for baseball-themed household items, buy and wear specialized "throwback" baseball clothing, watch baseball films, and read all kinds of baseball-related publications as well as checking and contributing to baseball internet sites. They even embrace "heroes" who cheat. In such ways is baseball made part of the general culture.

The baseball card business shows graphically what is happening to baseball. For several years, sales of cards plunged 15 percent annually, and Topps, the big name in the field, saw its sales dip disastrously. Card companies realized that their sales problem lay not with baseball itself but with the aging of baseball fans. Card sales dropped because children who grew up collecting baseball cards are old now. Today's boys differ from those of the past, who had fewer choices among enjoyable free-time activities. In the current culture, children like interactive gadgets like Game Boys and MP3s as well as complicated cellphones. Besides, they can find players' records easily on the internet. So the card companies are introducing fans, especially adults, to new gimmicks in the traditional collecting and trading of cards.

Both the Topps and the Upper Deck card companies have begun including in some packs of cards an actual hair from an historical figure, like Marilyn Monroe. These rather morbid items become saleable on eBay. Fans buy boxes of cards for thousands of dollars in the hope of finding one card of value in the whole box. The newest device is the three-dimensional card: hold it in front of your web cam and you will see a three-dimensional avatar of the player. All it takes to revive sales, the manufacturers realize, is newer and better gimmicks. Michael Eisner of Topps presents a lofty view of the trading card business as "a cultural, iconic institution ... [that] conjures up an emotional response that has a feel-good, Proustian kind of uplift." And he may be right, although "Proustian" seems like a stretch.

Fans still show up at stadiums, too. Even when money is tight, professional baseball, to a greater degree than other pro sports, continues to draw fans; some attendance analysts take an upbeat view, claiming that baseball has proven to be "relatively immune" to recession. Family spending on baseball often becomes the alternate choice in a slow economy when compared with an expensive trip the family might take instead. Besides, as Richard Lapchick of the National Consortium for Academics and Sports explained, "the public in general does not care that much about the athlete's salary. They want that escape. When people are depressed about life or the economy or whatever it happens to be, they gain solace from being able to escape at a sports event."

Baseball has integrated itself so thoroughly into American life that its disappearance is impossible. Boys are still brought up understanding that familiarity with baseball is part of being an American. The "Manly Pursuit" has become part of us all. Now it needs only to embrace the half of the population left behind by the professional era and become a bona fide womanly pursuit as well.

PART TWO.
A WOMANLY PURSUIT

9

Can Women Be Baseball Stars?

One warm afternoon in the late 1980s, when I lived in Keene, New Hampshire, I was walking in the park when I came upon a baseball game in progress on the public diamond. I stopped for a moment to watch. Two uniformed teams were locked in an intense competition in front of excited fans seated on wooden bleachers. As I stood there, I slowly realized that as familiar as the tableau seemed, something was very different about it: all the players were women.

Transfixed, I hung around longer than I had intended. What I saw surprised me. This was no pickup game among a group of pals trying their hand at something for fun. It was serious. I saw no joking around, just complete focus and determination. I soon realized that what they were playing wasn't softball; it was baseball.

The women on the diamond before me displayed good hitting and excellent pitching, hard throwing and strategic running. I viewed some exciting plays and saw definite signs of teamwork. Mutual support was reflected in infield chatter and calls of encouragement and praise. In the background welled the rooting and cheering of fans.

Then the thought struck me: this is real baseball. Women can play real baseball. Some women want to pursue their interest in baseball by actually playing the game. Not just watching; playing.

It was then that I realized the significance of this thought: more of us women might be fans if we got to see real baseball played by excellent women players. They could be our role models. In fact, if I had seen women play baseball skillfully when I was a girl, I might have been inspired to try playing myself.

I was reminded of this thought more than ten years later while reading Susan Johnson's book, *When Women Played Hardball*, and learning that she

I learned only late in life that playing baseball might have been fun. Here I am experimenting with the bat and ball awarded me by Justine Siegal of the Women's Baseball League for my work in women's baseball history (courtesy of the photographer, Brian Myers).

had become a fan largely because as a girl she lived in a city where she could watch the teams of the first women's professional league, the All-American Girls Professional Baseball League of the 1940s and early 1950s. As a girl who loved to play the game, Johnson found herself admiring these skillful women players, who took part joyfully in what was supposedly a men's game. "The women were the scene," she asserted, remembering the thrill of seeing women "do something I, as a tomboy, could identify with and respect." Realizing that the community valued something that people of her gender could do, she recalled "how good it felt to join with other fans in cheering for our team." Those fans saw women using "physical courage, intelligence, and a fighting spirit," all the while working as a team to achieve "a game well played."

When I thought about Johnson's reaction, I realized that the women of the league had become her idols. What would happen, I wondered, if American women could always look up to female professionals who played the American national game with skill and pride? After all it's American women's national game, too.

What would happen might be the same thing that happened when the All-American Girls Professional Baseball League began playing in small Midwestern cities during World War Two and after: thousands of women ballplayers came to try out for a spot in a league that could handle only five or six hundred players; thousands of fans, about half female, came to watch the games and cheer the players on; and thousands of other women and girls in many cities and towns became inspired to play ball on their own teams.

Fans who originally came to watch out of curiosity ("Can women really play this game?") stayed to applaud the play and admire the players. Many became regular fans, and some followed the teams on road trips to other cities. The women's teams had become local heroes.

At these women's professional games, those who thought only men could play well could hardly credit what they were looking at. "You had to see it to believe it, and [even] then you didn't," commented Chet Grant, one of the teams' managers. Two big-league scouts, invited to a game that Leo Schrall coached, professed amazement at what they saw. One said, "My God, Leo. I'd never have believed that if someone were to tell me on a Bible. I never saw girls play baseball like that. That's not softball, that's baseball!" Wally Pipp, a great-fielding first baseman for the Yankees in the twenties, called Dottie Kamenshek of the Peaches "the fanciest fielding first baseman I've ever seen" and claimed that she represented "a piece of baseball property that might bring some dough, if the majors were game enough to trying using girl performers." Charlie Grimm, too, saw dollar signs when he saw one of the players, Dottie Schroeder, in action. Grimm, then managing the Chicago Cubs, declared, "If that girl were a man, she'd be worth $50,000 to me." Max Carey, who played major league ball for the Pirates and became a Hall of Famer, evaluated the final game of the 1945 championship series between the Peaches and the Belles by saying, "Barring none, even in the majors, it's the best game I've ever seen."

Sports writers soon began writing straight news stories about the women's games, minus the usual side remarks about the women's appearance. Instead, as one writer put it, they revealed that the "strong, accurate arms" and "healthy cuts" that the women took at pitched balls "were revelations to most of the onlookers — including this one." He added, "They play for keeps, too, as evidenced by the manner in which they slide, crash into each other, and generally carry on as though they were out for blood."

The major theme of these admiring remarks is one of astonishment, with undertones of envy. Charlie Grimm's wistful "If that girl were a man..." reflects the same dismay as *Sporting Life* in its remark fifty years earlier about the black player Bud Fowler with his "splendid abilities," a remark that began: "If he had a white face...."

Now that skin color no longer prevents excellent players from qualifying for OB, should gender continue to do so? Jackie Robinson entered organized baseball in 1946, after the professional Negro Leagues had been in operation for a quarter of a century. The women's professional league, on the other hand, closed a half-century ago. Perhaps it's taking longer for women to break into organized baseball because certain barriers to their inclusion seem higher than those black men had to overcome. Are women ever going to make it to the Show?

To answer that question, we need to step back and see how far women have come in their goal of complete inclusion in the American national game. Doing that will tell us how high the obstacles to women still remain.

Most fans remain unaware of the long history American women have enjoyed in baseball. Bat-and-ball games have littered history and prehistory, but one of the main predecessors of the British game of baseball is stool-ball, a baseball-related game played by Britons of both genders in the seventeenth and eighteenth centuries as part of the continuation of ancient spring fertility celebrations. (Who used a stool every day? English milkmaids.)

Not until the 1740s did the game become associated with children through English publications designed to illustrate their games. David Block, the intrepid researcher, makes the educated guess that boys and girls "observing the frolicking pleasures of the multiple-base version of stool-ball" probably adapted it to their own abilities.

At some point English base-ball (the hyphen was used for a while) was exported to the colonies, where "more rigid standards for ladylike behavior" apparently denied girls the opportunity of playing. Boys were burdened with no such restrictions, and their ball games, including base-ball, were described in early books produced for them. From American boys' play, the game returned to adults, as young men began to take it up in cities, on college campuses, and in military camps.

So although girls and women played base-ball in England, at least from the 1820s onward, the game in the American colonies became off-limits to them — as far as we know, since nobody has yet found evidence that American females played baseball during the colonial era. Burdened as they were by the Puritan ethic, the colonists had trouble shrugging off the idea that "weak feminine bodies" housed souls susceptible to "Satanic possession," and that any activity by women that Puritan men deemed questionable became evidence of possession by the Devil.

But before the Civil War, even the restrictive ideas inherited from John Calvin, especially his objection to the use of the body for exercise, had eroded, and sports, including ball playing, had insinuated themselves into some schools, where girls could see baseball being played. Already in 1823 a newspaper called baseball a "manly and athletic game ... innocent amusement [with] no demoralizing tendency." When girls saw boys playing ball games, how could they resist trying to play it themselves? Some women's journals published before the war began loosening up earlier rigid opinions, urging that girls and women be allowed to enjoy exercise.

After the Civil War, baseball spread widely among boys and young men. Continued warnings that women were too weak and delicate to play games led to a challenge by feminists: if women are too weak, let us strengthen them by providing calisthenics and gymnastics — which they did, by means of the elite colleges being opened for well-off women in the Northeast. Women's college sports often grew directly out of their gymnastic programs.

Fans today generally don't realize that women formed baseball clubs back in the 1860s and 1870s, many of them completely on their own. Researchers have documented the existence of such early Civil War–era clubs in Michigan, Illinois, Massachusetts, Connecticut, and New York State. Nobody told women that baseball was a womanly pursuit, one that would develop their physical and mental powers; instead, they were lucky if they found opportunities to play. Men's baseball of course progressed and improved faster than women's. The men, free of any cultural restraints, started forming into clubs at least twenty years earlier than did the women; no objections on the part of the opposite gender hindered the development of their clubs and leagues, as it did for women, for men dominated the culture and expected women not only to know their place but also to stay in it.

What lay at the foundation of men's view was their view of women. Playing baseball failed to fit the image of women that men preferred: small, weak, soft, dainty, dependent, and unable to think or move fast — more like children than adults. This false assumption made white men treat women's play as farcical, just as they did black men's play; white men ridiculed both as parodies of their own activity. Only bold women could "shake off the social restrictions of traditional femininity" and compete in physical activities where they could "play hard and be aggressive," as Professor Carly Adams puts it.

The story of women's entrance into baseball therefore had to be one about exceptional women. Scholar Stephen Lehman calls them "persistent, skilled individuals — pioneers — who were set apart not because they were the only ones who could play or umpire or manage, but because they were the few who couldn't be stopped by all the social, cultural, and political barriers placed between them and the realization of their baseball talents." Lehman's assertion infers the existence of many women unrecorded in history, women who would like to have played baseball but didn't quite have the nerve to face down the opposition.

Those who did have that much nerve played in long skirts or, around the turn of the century, in the new bloomers named after Amelia Bloomer, which gave them more freedom from the yards and pounds of cloth dictated by the styles of the day; moreover, bloomers resembled the knee pants used in men's baseball uniforms. Bloomer Girl teams became well-known, especially in New York, New England, and the Midwest, touring the country and flourishing until the end of the 1920s. Some skilled men players joined their teams, at first dressing as women and later not bothering to do so.

Most Americans have never heard of the individual women who became star players because those who ran the men's leagues, although they occasionally became aware of the skill of these women, avoided recognizing them until much later.

As a result, those Americans who know all about old-time major league pitchers have no knowledge of early women baseballers who proved successful not only against other female players but also against male semipros, town teams, touring teams, and minor leaguers. They are unaware, for example, of the success of a team called the Philadelphia Bobbies against men's teams in the twenties and thirties and the team's tour of Japan in 1925. They haven't heard that Ed Barrow signed Lizzie Arlington to pitch in the Atlantic League in 1908. They don't know that the Cleveland sports reporters thought pitcher Alta Weiss had everything that the Indians needed early in the twentieth century and that the *Cleveland Press* reporter wondered, in print, why the Indians didn't consider hiring her. Even most New England fans haven't heard about Rhode Island first baseman Lizzie Murphy, who played competently with and against many excellent men's teams from 1918 to 1935. Fans are unaware of the skill of umpire Amanda Clement, who earned the respect of male players out West in the early 1900s. They never heard of pitcher Maud Nelson, whose strikeouts of male players received major attention in the Boston papers and who formed and managed several highly successful women's teams. Fans who know every detail of Babe Ruth's exploits are probably unaware that in 1931 he was struck out by a woman baseball player named Jackie Mitchell. Yet even if fans come up blank on hearing names like those, they might have heard of Mildred "Babe" Didrikson Zaharias, whose sports superiority during the thirties in many fields made it clear even to MLB that, although she spent most of her energy winning top honors in other sports, she might easily have turned into a fine big-league baseball player.

How did these women develop enough skill to compete against experienced male players? First of all, they watched. Newspapers from the 1840s on reported groups of women viewing with great interest the progress of men's baseball games. When the newly professional Cincinnati Red stockings were attracting women fans in 1869, some of them showed their devotion by flashing red stockings when they raised their skirts to step from a carriage to the curb. In the stands, some women of this era didn't merely watch, they kept score and made bets. By the time professional baseball had reached its glory years of the 1920s, many women could keep up with Grace Coolidge, wife of the U.S. president, who listened to radio broadcasts of games, knew baseball trivia, kept score at the many games she attended, and even went over to the presidential telegraph room of the White House to check on who won a particular game. At least one woman, Mrs. Elisha Green Williams, not only kept score, she actually served as official scorer for the Chicago White Stockings from 1882 to 1891, but nobody knew about it; she and the club owner kept it secret, for who would believe a female official scorer? No other women were known to hold such a position until the thirties, when Mrs. Helen Snow served as statistician for the Western Association, Mrs. Ora Bohart acted as statistician for the Arkansas-Missouri League, and Emma Dreskell became official scorer for a minor league club.

Men did approve of women as fans; they thought women's presence at games improved the behavior of players and fans alike, and the players never objected to being cheered on by enthusiastic rooters, especially if the rooters were pretty. But cheering men's exploits failed to satisfy some women; they wanted to play the game themselves. A few even cherished the idea of playing in the big leagues.

In this desire they ran into the tradition preventing women from participating in anything that took courage, strength, determination, and perseverance. Never mind if women were strong enough to scrub floors, clean toilets, cook meals for large groups, care for the sick, run the household, work in the fields or factories, and birth as many as ten children; men thought they were too weak to play sports. Baseball was therefore inappropriate for them.

From the beginning of their interest in pursuing the national game by playing it, women and girls ran into dismay, objection, ridicule, and outright prohibition. The privileged young women who ventured to play while attending the exclusive women's colleges in the late nineteenth century did so semi-secretly; they tried to keep their adventure to themselves, lest their parents should hear of it. The teams of young women who toured around the country to play exhibition games in the 1870s and 1880s were variously skilled or unskilled, and were generally laughed at for their boldness more than they were encouraged or applauded for trying to play. Not until the 1890s and afterwards did truly talented women's teams, especially the professional Bloomer Girl clubs, elicit grudging praise. By then a good number of women had grown up playing baseball on playgrounds, in college, or among family members — or even at "training schools" for delinquent girls, places where the sport was not banned and where girls were actually encouraged to "let their hair down," both literally and figuratively.

About the time the twentieth century opened, girls began to receive the opportunity to play baseball in public and private schools, although they were usually confined to a modified form of the game. In school, girls' games were kept separate from the boys.' But on neighborhood playgrounds, many girls were persuading boys to let them play on the boys' teams and perfected their playing that way. About this time newspapers began to print sporadic stories about individual girls who excelled at pitching or other baseball skills; these girls made news because men considered them highly unusual.

Then businesses and industries began to sponsor recreation for women as well as for men, and their games often included baseball. In the 1920s in particular, industrial ball for women became popular in the Northeast, Midwest, and Upper South, where the textile mills sponsored teams and leagues. For industries to give women workers a chance to play had nothing to do with benevolence; the policy was based solidly on self-interest. At William Wrigley's gum company in Chicago, the physician in charge of the Medical and Welfare Departments lauded company-sponsored women's baseball as a good investment, explaining that it reduced absenteeism and kept labor turnover down. Industrialists let women pursue baseball because doing so helped them pursue profits.

Meanwhile, along came softball, originally invented by men as a way that they could play baseball indoors. Softball would eventually prove to be both a hindrance and an aid in women's pursuit of baseball fun.

The indoor version of baseball was played differently in different parts of the country, but in the twenties and thirties organizations got together to standardize the rules. As the rules solidified, so did the determination of those who assigned themselves the job of regulating sports for girls and women that they should be relegated to this game, soon called softball, and that they should never play baseball again.

Their ruling arose largely from the baseball opinions of Professor Gladys Palmer, the self-appointed spokesman for a self-appointed group named the Sub-Committee on Baseball of the National Committee on Women's Athletics of the American Physical Education Association. Palmer and her Sub-Committee declared that the "intricate technic [technique] of the game is too difficult for the average girl to master," that "the throwing distances are too great," that using a standard hardball makes "the danger of injuries ... unnecessarily great," and that the same advantage of playing "the men's game" can be enjoyed in a "more simple" and "less strenuous" game, the one that by the mid-twenties was becoming softball. Palmer saw to it that girls and women were directed into this simplified form of the national pastime, which "eliminat[ed] much of the highly technical detail."

Not realizing that she was insulting herself as well as others, Palmer asserted that girls and women could not master the intricacies of baseball. She also believed that playing softball instead would increase women's enjoyment in watching "the men's game." So Palmer's goal was twofold: to move girls and women into a different, easier game and to make women into better spectators when they watched men playing the national game. In this way she consigned half the population to a pool of national spectators.

Yet Palmer's view of women and baseball showed that she recognized the events of history. She admitted that "girls have been playing baseball for some time" and added that she understood the game's advantages to girls: "It teaches them what the boys have learned from time immemorial in their sand-lot games: the ability to think quickly, to coordinate thought and action, to exercise good judgment and a certain faculty in divining in advance the thoughts and actions of others." She also admitted that baseball developed loyalty, self-confidence, and a sense of responsibility and good sportsmanship in girls and women. Nevertheless, she and her sub-committee colleagues ruled that baseball was too difficult for them and that from now on schools and colleges, along with community recreation sponsors of sports for girls and women, should offer them only softball.

Palmer's sub-committee also ruled against interscholastic competition; only intramural games were allowed, so schools were not to permit challenges to other school teams or competition for a championship. Moreover, her organization disapproved of the development of individual "prowess," thus discouraging the development of highly skilled athletes. Women and girls were not allowed to become stars; presumably, they were to look to the men for their models. In the late thirties Palmer began to soften her views, advising college directors and teachers to pay some attention to the development of those with expert skills and to give some consideration to the development of intercollegiate sport, but the national group that controlled amateur and college athletics, by then entrenched in its position, rejected her suggestions.

For women, softball became queen, sponsored by recreation associations, businesses, and educational institutions. Women's teams, leagues, and championships were everywhere. Intercity, regional, and national tournaments produced stars of the game, completely negating Palmer's wishes. Only in colleges were most young college women soon prevented from playing softball — or anything else — against other college teams.

The use of a smaller diamond and a softer, larger ball as well as an underhand pitching delivery helped make this simpler game popular, and the Depression of the thirties, during which everyone looked for cheap recreation, heightened its appeal for men, too. Women who loved to play baseball turned to softball as their second choice because of the many opportunities to play.

By the early thirties, baseball had become reserved for men only, and softball had strengthened its position as the only appropriate ball game for women. From then on, girls and women who loved to play baseball were on their own, isolated and without support. Women had been taught that they could not compete in the national game, and many of them believed it. But not all. Perhaps some of them hadn't heard that baseball was too difficult for them. Or maybe they possessed so much desire to play that they didn't care what others claimed.

Who were those brave souls that defied convention to pursue baseball as players? They were akin to the early female pilots, female medical doctors, female lawyers, and female soldiers. When the gifted flier Harriet Quimby became the first American woman to receive her pilot's license, the year was 1911. In those days women aspiring to fly were subject to the same type of abuse as women who tried to engage in sports: men sabotaged their planes and lied about their accomplishments; pilot Glenn Curtiss told everyone openly that "woman's place was on the ground." (In those days men knew instinctively where "women's place" was — anywhere they did not want to see women participating on an equal level with men.) Myra Bradwell easily passed the Illinois bar exam in 1869, but the state's Supreme Court denied her access to her profession because of her gender, declaring that the mission of a woman was confined to being a wife and mother. Female medical doctors encountered similar barriers: Elizabeth Blackwell took her degree after studies made unpleasant by objecting students, and during her residence at a Philadelphia hospital the male residents refused to have anything to do with her; in her practice she faced what she called "a blank wall of social and professional antagonism," and to give other women the chance to study medicine she finally had to open her own women's medical college. Female soldiers served semi-secretly in both the Revolutionary and Civil wars — at least 400 of them in the Civil War — and some even earned military pensions, but when their gender was discovered on the battlefield they earned scorn as prostitutes, although many were wives of other soldiers.

Early women ballplayers had to be as tough as the early female golfers, tennis players, mountaineers, runners, jockeys, high jumpers, and long-distance swimmers, who plunged into competition at a time when sports were considered questionable careers for women. When Gertrude Ederle announced her plan to become the first woman to swim the English Channel, the *London Daily News* sneered that in contests of physical skill, speed, and endurance, women would forever remain "the weaker sex," but Ederle performed the swim faster than any man had done before her. When Julia Holmes decided to climb Pike's Peak with her husband and other men in 1858, "nearly everyone tried to discourage" her from trying it, but she was confident: "I believed that I should succeed." And she became the first woman to do it. Alice Marble loved to play baseball and became angry when her brother suggested she "stop being a tomboy" and turn to tennis, which she considered a "sissy sport," but she changed her mind after adopting an aggressive style that made her into one of the best tennis players in the world. Like others, Marble channeled her sports skills into a different sport when her favorite game, baseball, proved to be a dead end for her gender.

For a long time men kept women out of the modern Olympic Games; not until 1900 could they participate. Helen Stephens, after winning gold medals in Germany during the 1936 Olympics, received an invitation to a personal audience with Adolf Hitler, but his attentions were not merely congratulatory. She related the encounter this way: "Hitler comes in and gives me the Nazi salute. I gave him a good old Missouri handshake. He shook my hand, put his arm around me, pinched me, and invited me to spend the weekend with him." Men do things like that to women, including sportswomen, when they think they can get away with them.

Like women who tried to enter other fields, early women baseballers who grew up playing with the boys and later joined women's teams defied the conventions of their times. Susan E. Johnson, who has interviewed many such players, describes and explains their determination this way: "What is extraordinary about these girl ballplayers is not that they acquired their love of baseball so young, but that they remained true to it; they kept playing ball when they grew old enough to know better." The explanation for their success lies, she believes, in their luck in having supportive families as well as working-class origins, which made fewer demands for "ladylike" behavior. Sometimes it was a girl's mother rather than her father and brothers who helped her along.

And how did the neighborhood boys view these girls? With varying degrees of acceptance. At first skeptical, the boys might eventually let them join their baseball games and, when the girls showed skill, often permitted them to continue. Or, if not enough boys showed up for play, a girl might grudgingly be allowed to take part. One day when Alice Pollitt was in elementary school she saw the boys playing together and "just naturally went out there, everybody making fun of me, you know. I had a skirt on, but no glove. I caught a fly ball, went up to bat, and hit the ball. Those boys were amazed."

When girls of this era tried to play baseball supervised by grade-school and high-school teachers or coaches, they were usually blocked, since few institutions offered or permitted girls' baseball or let girls play on boys' teams. The most the girls received was practice in "leadup skills"— throwing a baseball, running bases, and catching a ball. One girl, Alice Beeckman, actually won a place on her all-boy high school team in 1928 and played excellent ball in the team opener, although her presence on a boys' team was criticized.

In the Depression years of the thirties, some town and city recreation programs offered girls' and women's baseball, but most girls and young women who loved the game had to scale back their goals and turn to softball, sponsored heavily in the twenties and thirties by local and national groups. And in some ways softball helped the cause, since when the professional women's baseball league started in the forties, it could recruit softball stars and gradually retrain them into baseball players, as the professional league itself gradually became a baseball league rather than a softball league.

Some girls and young women never gave up playing ball in the thirties. Susan Johnson tells about the experience of Dorothy "Snookie" Doyle, who played softball in school and various baseball games with the boys in the street. Sometimes they refused to let her play, and then she would feel sad. Her aunt soothed her by saying, "Some day, Snookie, they're gonna have a league, a girls' league, and then you're gonna be able to play." Doyle's aunt was engaging in the usual feminine reaction to discrimination against a girl: instead of teaching her niece that she could fight for her rights and helping her do it, Snookie's aunt counseled her to wait and hope. This is the way girls are brought up to become women who are timid and fearful instead of confident and aggressive. They are taught to accept the status quo, in the belief that they can do nothing about it.

Over the centuries, women have internalized the notion that they must demur to men's desires about their behavior. They know, as a British professor announced in 1889, that "the woman must not develop her faculties in any way unpleasant to the man.... Strength, courage, independence [are] not attractive in women.... [Women's] rivalry [with men] in men's pursuits [is] positively unpleasant." Unpleasant to men, that is.

In 1925 the American Legion opened a comprehensive junior baseball program for local, state, regional, and national championships. By "junior" the Legion meant not "children" but "boys." It seemed that nobody in the Legion thought girls might want to play baseball. The Legion's move was self-serving: because the program opened in an era in which fear of Communism became rampant, the Legion believed its effort would promote "Americanism" and admitted forthrightly that it used baseball as "bait" to train boys to accept the status quo unquestioningly as well as to prepare them as future soldiers. By 1935, about 500,000 boys were taking part in the Legion's baseball program, which received financial support not only from private donors but also from Major League Baseball; after all, MLB benefited by scouting for good players among Legion graduates.

When the Little League opened in 1939, its organizers professed a focus different from the Legion's: they believed the opportunity for boys to play baseball in a rigidly organized way would combat juvenile delinquency, which appeared to be the problem of the times. With a view to strengthening the family unit, they recruited the boys' fathers to coach; assuming that the mothers knew nothing about baseball, they relegated women volunteers to tasks like holding bake sales and serving as cooks and waitresses at picnics.

Unlike girls, boys found wide opportunities to play baseball. Besides playing Legion ball or Little League ball, they could join church teams or those set up by Boystown Clubs, and if their fathers worked at large companies like Goodyear Tire & Rubber they could get into programs set up by employers. Service clubs like Kiwanis followed suit in setting up clubs and leagues for boys. Camps and city playground leagues provided more opportunities, but generally for boys alone. Knowledgeable coaches opened commercial baseball schools, but only boys whose parents could pay were welcomed. Poor boys, if they happened to be delinquents or paupers or orphans, could play at reform schools. (Delinquent girls could play at the training schools set up for them.)

But some girls found ways to use and even develop their baseball skills, making a place for themselves on America's baseball scene. Thus do women discover that if they want to do something badly enough, they must fight for it. Sometimes this determination gains them the support they need to succeed.

10

Girls and Women Who Excelled

With some girls and women, the prevailing culture of prohibition against playing baseball never really affected them, for their desire to pursue their dream was too important to them. Those were the girls and women who helped change the culture of sports, chipping away at the foundation of the concrete wall separating them from their goal.

In 1928 the American Legion, that bastion of Americanism, suddenly encountered the problem of Margaret Gisolo, a fourteen-year-old girl who loved to play baseball. What could be more American than the desire to play the national game? And because the Legion hadn't considered the fact that girls might want to play, it had passed no rule against their participation. Gisolo, an excellent player who had managed to get into a Legion team because of her skill, called attention to her gender by starring in the county championship game for her team. So in 1929 the Legion remedied its oversight and specifically banned girls from participating in its baseball leagues.

Gisolo eventually hooked on with independent professional women's teams, including one operated by Maud Nelson, and ended with a varied sports career that included teaching college physical education. Since Legion ball was, and still is, known as an important stepping-stone for entrance into organized baseball, its decision to prevent girls from playing effectively cut off half of American children from access to organized baseball's minors and majors.

As for the Little League, from the beginning it clearly stated its program as an opportunity for boys, but some girls resented the slight to their gender and tried to participate. Nine-year-old Donna de Varona could hit the ball farther than some of her brother's twelve-year-old friends, but the Little League rejected her 1956 application to play. That same year Donna Lopiano, an eleven-year-old who had dedicated herself to pitching and starred for her team, suddenly discovered she would not be able to play in Little League; she cried for months. Two years later another girl, pitcher Donna Terry, disguised herself as a boy and traveled to Puerto Rico with her team of Little League All-Stars. Terry won her game, but when she revealed her gender she found herself out of Little League. When Dot Richardson was recruited for her local Little League team, the coach, admiring her throwing arm, told her he would have her hair cut and rename her "Bob," but Dot refused to pretend to be a boy. For girls like de Varona, Terry, Richardson, and Lopiano, changing sports was their only option, so from then on it was softball for Terry, Richardson, and Lopiano, while de Varona went on to become what *Sports Illustrated* called "without question, the best all-around woman swimmer in the world."

For Mamie "Peanut" Johnson, moving from the South to New Jersey gave her a chance to join the Police Athletic League, where she was the only girl on the local team. When she was seventeen, Johnson, a black woman, attended the tryouts for a place in the AAGPBL but wasn't permitted to show what she could do. She ended up pitching successfully in the Negro Leagues. Toni Stone, another talented black female player, wrote to the AAGPBL for a try-out but received no reply. She spent much of her career in semipro and touring teams like the House of David before being invited to join the Negro National League.

Black girls and women suffered extra discrimination because of their color, but historically, exclusion of white girls and young women from a sport they love and in which some of them can excel has been based on alleged health concerns. Physicians and physical education instructors have dreamed up all sorts of medical and physiological reasons to keep girls from playing baseball. Their objections have long since proved to be without foundation. In fact, a review of the "experts' advice to women" over the last 150 years reveals these so-called experts to have been dismally and perpetually inaccurate in their counsel.

The real reason for girls' exclusion, as modern analysts now realize, is the assumption that because in America baseball became a men's game first and was heavily promoted for boys and men, it belonged to men exclusively. Permitting girls and women to play undermined men's ownership of the sport and thus brought their "manliness" into question. After men had appropriated the national game, commentators began characterizing it as "a manly sport" that developed "manly virtues" like courage, confidence, and endurance. They assumed that these virtues could not possibly be womanly as well; invoking the failed premise of Freud, they asserted that women who displayed them were trying to act like men. Discoveries in both psychology and physiology have helped destroy Freud's male-centered notion of "penis envy." In fact, women who play baseball want only their freedom to be women. Anyone who watches them play soon realizes that.

Girls and women who loved to play baseball continued to try to participate in the thirties. People truly devoted to what they believe to be right cannot easily be diverted from their goals. Galileo, for example, although he accepted the Roman Catholic Church's decision that he was guilty of heresy for asserting that the earth and other planets revolve around the sun, never gave up his reliance on the evidence demonstrating that they do. Girls and women appeared to accept the decision of the sporting goods magnate Albert Spalding and other cultural icons forbidding females from playing baseball, but not all of them gave up their attempts to take part. As Marilyn French points out, "Women can behave within the boundaries allotted them and yet not be defeated." Some girls who found themselves sidelined simmered with discontent and kept in their minds the idea of a girls' league; others never stopped dreaming of their early goal of playing in the minor and major leagues. And a few of them came pretty close to reaching their hearts' desire.

By the turn of the century, some women had developed their skill in playing baseball to at least the semipro level, and others had joined professional traveling teams. Unable to penetrate organized baseball, they played with and against the many pro touring teams that crisscrossed the continent before and after 1900. These teams, although not part of organized baseball, were certainly professional: they enabled their players to make a living at baseball.

Those who have studied Maud Nelson report her to be among the most talented of these women, for she not only played from 1897 through 1935, she started, trained, managed, and booked many successful teams, like the American Athletic Girls, the Western Bloomer Girls, and the All Star Ranger Girls.

Many female players who became known for their baseball skill trained with Maud Nelson. One of them was Lizzie Arlington, born Elizabeth Stride or Stroud, who pitched so well in 1898 against a men's team, the Philadelphia Reserves, that she became the first of four women known to have signed minor league contracts. Ed Barrow, then president of the Atlantic League and later with the Yankees, signed Arlington to play for Reading, Pennsylvania, and on July 5 she pitched in a regular minor league game against Allentown. She saved the game in the ninth inning, giving up no runs, but Barrow thought that too few customers paid to see her, so he let her go. Arlington continued playing by hooking on with Bloomer Girl teams.

Amanda Clement used her baseball skills mostly in umpiring. Drafted to umpire a game in which her brother was playing, Clement proved so successful that she made umpiring her career. Those who watched her work saw a tall, stately woman who walked athletically and officiated confidently, an umpire who commanded the players' respect and never hesitated to eject those who acted up. For six years she worked semipro games in five western states, earning from fifteen to twenty-five dollars a game. As a player she also excelled in basketball, tennis, the shot put, running sprints, and jumping hurdles; in 1912 she threw a baseball farther than anyone in the world had done up to then. About 1906 the *Cincinnati Enquirer* quoted her as asserting that "all the official baseball umpires of the country should be women" because players generally "avoided speaking rudely to a woman" and because fans would tone down the insults they shouted to umpires. That would eventually prove to be an idealistic assumption.

Although college women started baseball teams on campus in the early part of the twentieth century and by then were receiving some support from college physical education staffs, they were kept from thinking of baseball as part of their futures by staff members who taught them repeatedly that they were in college for one purpose only: to prepare for marriage and motherhood. Some failed to forget baseball, however: daughters of wealthy parents in Philadelphia organized their own baseball clubs in the early 1900s and played on private estates and at a local country club.

But those privileged women usually played just for fun. The only highly skilled girl ballplayer of this era known to come from a privileged upper-middle class background is Alta Weiss, daughter of a small-town medical doctor who noticed her pitching skill and bought a semipro team for her to star with. Dr. Weiss also built a private gym so she could work out and play during her high school years. His daughter developed an effective fastball, curve, knuckleball, sinker, and spitball. Pitching at seventeen in the resort town of Vermilion, Ohio, she soundly beat the area's sandlot clubs. When a local semipro manager booked her to play in Cleveland's major league park against a fast semipro Cleveland team, she won her game and garnered rave reviews from the Cleveland papers, whose sports editors then opened a half-serious campaign to get the Cleveland American League club to sign her.

Alta Weiss's continued pitching successes enabled her to pay her way through medical college, after which she yielded to her father's demand that she practice medicine with him. This decision sounds to me like one made as part of a quid pro quo: *I financed a short baseball career for you; now it's time for you to do the right thing and submit to my desire that you join me in practicing medicine.* Although her main talent probably lay in baseball, Alta Weiss apparently reverted to the expected role of middle-class obedient daughter.

It was primarily children of blue-collar workers who pursued their baseball skills during much of their working lives. While Alta Weiss was piling up wins in the Midwest, Lizzie Murphy, daughter of a mill worker, was doing the same in New England. A professional first baseman for men's teams in the Boston area, Murphy, while playing in a 1922 Boston charity game, became the first woman known to play with and against major leaguers. Murphy developed her skill playing industrial ball in Rhode Island, where rivalry among textile mill teams remained intense for years. Residents of Warren, Rhode Island, loved seeing her take part in games when her teams played at the home ball park.

Recently, I met a woman who grew up in Warren and remembers how Murphy drew the local fans to the baseball park. Like Alta Weiss, Murphy was not an oversized woman. Just five feet six and 122 pounds, she was nonetheless strong enough to hold her own on men's teams, particularly a professional touring team that played all over New England and into Canada. The club owner told the press, "She's worth every cent I pay her. She's a real player." Murphy wore the regulation uniform and looked for no favors because of her gender. She seemed to be trying to avoid standing out from the others so that her gender would appear to be an unimportant aspect of her playing. Murphy commented that once the other players saw she could play baseball, they accepted her. "Playing ball is the same as everything else in life. Mind your own business and concentrate on what you are doing and you will be all right." Murphy always concentrated on what she was doing and lasted for seventeen years with her pro men's team before retiring at forty-three and marrying a mill worker.

Some fans know the Jackie Mitchell story because it involves big names, like Babe Ruth, Lou Gehrig, and Tony Lazzeri, who couldn't, or at least didn't, hit her pitches in a 1931 game she worked for the Chattanooga Lookouts, a Double-A league team. Newspaper reporters ridiculed her, calling her accomplishment a fluke and her appearance a circus event. When Judge Landis, then commissioner of Baseball, canceled her contract because he believed baseball was "too strenuous for a woman," scout Joe Engel, who had signed her, declined to fight for her, so she was out of organized baseball. It was Engel, really, who permitted her candidacy to die; evidently, Mitchell just wasn't important to him. She went on to play professional ball for seven years with the House of David, a well-known touring team.

Minor league owners didn't give up on top-notch female players. They kept pecking away at the wall separating women from success in organized baseball. Soon after Mitchell's game for Chattanooga, another young woman, Vada Corbus — sister of Luke Corbus, who played for the Joplin Club of the Western Association — was signed to catch for the team, but it's not clear if she ever did. Then in 1936 Frances "Sonny" Dunlop signed to play for the Fayetteville Bears of the Class D Arkansas-Missouri League, appearing in a game against the Cassville Blues. Because she took part without advance publicity, her participation couldn't be prevented. Whether Dunlop continued playing afterward, however, is doubtful. In 1952, when Eleanor Engel was signed to a minor league contract, George Trautman, head of the minors, not only voided her contract ("such travesties will not be tolerated") but also, with the support of Commissioner Ford Frick, banned women from playing professional baseball. Engel was shocked and hurt both by Trautman's insulting rejection and by the hostility of male players. But shock and hurt meant nothing to those who wanted to keep baseball masculine.

What this sequence of signings shows is that despite blocks to their progress, in the twenties and thirties some women became so highly skilled in playing baseball that an individual club owner might find himself tempted to take a chance on a woman even though her gender could quickly be discovered and the player rejected by the league president or by the commissioner. This same sort of thing happened to males just before and after 1900, when major league owners became aware of the skill of Cuban players and couldn't resist hiring them. If their skin was a little darker than that of the rest of the team, owners got around that by describing them for American racists as American Indians.

Meanwhile, as Harold Seymour and I showed in *Baseball: The People's Game,* up to World War Two organized baseball ignored women. Despite the early growth and development of women's ball, women remained outside the pale, or rather, boxed in, inhabiting a sort of annex to baseball's main living quarters.

So for women baseballers, the twenties and thirties were the years for joining their own touring clubs and for developing individual stars, a few of whom almost crashed the barriers erected by organized baseball to keep out everyone that the most reactionary among them thought to be unacceptable.

Why don't we know a lot more about these females in baseball history? Two reasons: First, men are in charge of baseball news. Although some women have attained reporters' positions, men are still the directors of the media. Why would they seek to celebrate women's success in something they have always viewed as an expression of manliness? If they did, more women might decide to try taking part and thus (as the men see it) undermine the male prerogative. Second, it's notoriously harder for women to tell about their attainments than it is for men. Betty Spence, president of the National Association of Female Executives, claims that "from boyhood on, males are encouraged to talk about their accomplishments while girls are typically discouraged from that behavior." It used to be called bragging; girls were supposed to avoid "putting themselves forward." Not until historians, and particularly women historians, began digging into women's past has women's performance in the field of baseball started to be revealed and even proclaimed.

While a few women pursued baseball doggedly as best they could during the thirties, many others were taking the easier road and participating in the softball leagues that were proliferating all over the country and that continued in popularity after the beginning of the war.

Softball became a bridge to the formation of the first successful women's professional league. In Chicago, Philip Wrigley, who had inherited his father's gum company, noticed that within a hundred-mile radius of Wrigley Field a thousand women's softball teams were playing. He offered his field for their championship game and saw attendance rise greatly. Wrigley also noticed the drawing power of a league in his own city called the Chicago Metropolitan Girls Major Softball League. The gum entrepreneur began to think of cashing in on the popularity of women's softball, especially since he and the other owners had begun to worry that MLB might be cancelled or greatly curtailed because of the war. Moreover, Wrigley was prescient enough to realize that "in two or three years' time it's possible that girls' softball may be recognized by the press and radio as of Major League possibilities and be treated as such." If softball rose to major league quality, as he predicted it might, Wrigley wanted to be in on the ground floor, so he decided to organize his own women's professional softball league.

To construct his professional league, Wrigley built a tight ship: the league's contracts, instead of including a reserve clause as in MLB, resembled those of the movie industry because they merely included an option clause, and players would belong not to their clubs but to the league, which could shift them around at the end of the season for the purpose of equalizing competition. Instead of placing clubs in big cities, where they might compete against MLB teams, Wrigley chose smaller Midwestern cities like Gary, Indiana, where citizens were heavily involved in war work and might look for the kind of entertainment that the league could provide.

As a member of his board Wrigley chose the man who was the only other forward-looking owner in MLB: Branch Rickey, who had already instituted the modern farm system, which put player recruitment and development on an entirely new basis. On the satellite clubs Rickey owned, young players "ripened into money." Nobody has found evidence that Rickey worked to bring women into baseball, but by 1943 he was already secretly working on plans to open organized baseball to black players, and in a few short years he would boldly bring us Jackie Robinson.

Wrigley's scouts combed the softball ranks for recruits. Can anyone imagine how the young women felt about offers to join his organization? They were absolutely thrilled. Although many were still in their teens, and for a lot of the girls it would be their first time away from home, they were eager to use their skills in playing ball, and their anticipation and joy usually overcame their homesickness. They had all played either baseball or softball, and many had played both, so as the league gradually changed its rules to become closer to baseball, most of them were able to adjust to the different pitching style and the longer base paths. The girls took part in the league's progress with delight, and they enjoyed themselves so much that a great many recalled the experience later in words similar to these: "I didn't want it to ever end. I enjoyed every minute of it."

In explaining why young women joined the league, a player named Lois Youngen remembered their reasons this way: "They came because they simply loved to play baseball, they loved to win, they loved to make a great catch, they loved to feel the crack of the wooden bat on the ball and to know it would be a base hit. Not the rules and regulations, the uniform, nor charm school could keep them from playing baseball ... [which] was more important than the money (as long as you had enough to survive), more important than having to take directions from a man, and more important than letting a 'strawberry' keep you out of the lineup." In other words, these players felt exactly like male players about baseball.

The league gave several hundred young white women who were ardent about playing baseball a chance to pursue the game. It could have recruited black women, too, for they had long established their own separate teams in softball and baseball, but the few who applied failed to be accepted. The league's directors, who did discuss the matter of hiring blacks, may have thought that supporting and promoting a girls' league was enough of a departure from tradition for the public to handle, for they decided that any black players hired would have to show "exceptional ability." Probably as a result of this extra restriction, nobody known to be black was hired for the league.

Along with gradually changing from softball to standard baseball (by 1948 overhand pitching was required), the league changed its name to reflect that switch, eventually becoming the All-American Girls Professional Baseball League. In keeping with the culture of the time, the league's name continued to use the word "girls" instead of "women." And in fact many of the youngsters who joined were so young that they would even by today's standards be considered "girls."

Wrigley's shrewdest decision was his insistence on femininity: the players had to use make-up, adopt a feminine hairdo, conduct themselves in a manner consistent with 1940s mainstream feminine behavior, and wear a pastel uniform with a short skirt instead of trousers or knickers. Instructors from a "charm school" assisted them with their appearance. Chaperones assigned to each team acted as confidantes as well as guides, rules enforcers, house mothers, and sometimes coaches. The girls' feminine appearance fit in with the then-popular image of attractive young women. It reassured men that these ballplayers were not competing with them, and families who attended games out of curiosity drew the conclusion that the league was probably not made up of homosexuals; seeing masculine-looking girls on the field might have cut family attendance.

But weren't there some homosexuals on the teams? Players revealed later that the league did include a few lesbians but that they were persuaded to avoid approaching the youngsters (Dolly Brumfield White was only fourteen), who were mostly unsophisticated about sex as well as centered completely on pursuing baseball. Any players who refused to give up wearing "mannish" haircuts were let go; everyone on the teams had to at least appear to be "straight."

Besides offering a fast brand of ball which eventually turned into standard baseball, the players also earned the public's respect by seeming to conform to current standards of behavior both on and off the field; any rule-breaking was discreet. Fans came out to games in big numbers. In their team towns, the players became celebrities, receiving gifts and attentions from local fans and certainly from male admirers, including servicemen. Pepper Paire of the Fort Wayne Daisies claimed she had a boyfriend in every town; one romance, with a pitcher, broke down when Paire's team beat his and she got three hits off him, the last one right through the box ("I parted his hair!").

The league's clubs played few games against men's teams, basing their decision to concentrate mainly on women's play in the belief that competing with men smacked of gimmickry and carnival events. The directors wanted to establish the idea that the women players were not trying to act like male players. And the women appeared to agree with this decision. The prevailing feeling in the league was camaraderie, and not only among their own team members. (What other professional league has a league song?) Players often broke the rule against fraternizing with members of other teams. After all, women tend to be highly sociable. That's why their networking is so successful.

It's a question whether these women's teams would have competed well in regular play against strong men's teams. The consensus appears to be that they would have held their own with some minor league clubs. A Peoria resident, Dick Bogard, managed to see all the teams of the league play and asserts today that they could have competed successfully against at least against those in the lower minors. In addition, some of them, like Dottie Schroeder, would doubtless have done well if the league's players had been hired as individuals to play with men on a men's minor league team. Pepper Paire of the Fort Wayne Daisies claimed that although "we didn't have the power men had, we played just as skillfully. We could beat an average men's team any day of the week, and we often did."

But the women themselves seemed uninterested in moving to a men's team in organized baseball, and the league's administration appears never to have considered transferring one of its teams to an OB league or selling individual women's contracts to OB. In fact, when the Fort Lauderdale team of the Florida International League tried to buy Dottie Kamenshek's contract from the AAGBPL, Kamenshek, one of its best players, refused to consider the move. She believed that women would be at too much of a disadvantage in organized baseball because they would have to compete with men more than six feet tall and outweighing them by 60 or 70 pounds. As pitcher Jean Cione explained, the women of the AAGPBL "couldn't run as fast, hit as far, throw as hard" as the men's teams they occasionally faced. She points out, however, that today a lot of women players are bigger and stronger than those of fifty years ago; women playing men today would not find themselves so outweighed. Besides, as observers have noted, strength that comes from weight and size is only one of the factors that make a good baseball player; some small men have been successful at the game.

Like Philip Wrigley, the women of the AAGPBL appeared to adjudge their organization as a separate unit impermeable to men's baseball. They loved the idea of playing with and against other women because they knew they had the skills to do it. To them, playing regularly with or against men was a doubtful proposition. With women, they were comfortable. Only unusual women like Alta Weiss, Lizzie Murphy, and Jackie Mitchell had developed the complete confidence in themselves that enabled them to face the challenge of men who might be much stronger. During the time these unusual women played, no professional girls' league was available, so playing baseball against men was their only option if they wanted to be part of a pro league.

For girls and young women without much experience in life, those who joined the AAGBPL met other women who were confident in themselves and who became the role models for the neophytes. A young player named Carol Owens marveled, "I saw strong, risk-taking women ... and that helped me to know it was okay to be a strong, competitive, and risk-taking person myself."

Besides establishing the player standards he wanted, Wrigley and his representatives promoted the league heavily, and the players generally cooperated with the league by adhering to the rules, traveling long distances for spring training, making free individual appearances at events, playing for free at military camps and veterans' hospitals, endorsing local products and businesses without charge, and joining in charity games and exhibition tours. In all, the league proved successful, establishing an enthusiastic fan base mostly in the Midwest. Merrie Fidler, the league's historian, has discovered that its success inspired a startup copycat, the National Girls Baseball League, Inc., in the New York area, to organize a four-team league; its creator was the disaffected, retired major-leaguer Lou Haneles, along with another former player, Eddie Ainsmith, who had managed in the AAGPBL. Evidently, the NGBL never got off the ground.

So if audiences loved the AAGPBL and its success inspired competition, why did it decline and finally fold? Social changes like the inroads of television detracted from the league's drawing power. The biggest negative influence on the league may have been the United States government, which after the war started a relentless campaign to persuade women to return to their former positions as homemakers so that returning veterans could get jobs. But many internal problems, like changes in organization, team mismanagement, and the directors' inability to agree on policies, affected the league's stability. Especially did withdrawal of promotion cut attendance. By 1950, according to historian Merrie Fidler, the league was already doomed.

With the end of the All-American Girls Professional Baseball League, its players withdrew to their private lives. The baseball women seem to have been suddenly swept into prominence as heroes only to be swept back into obscurity again. Significantly, they stopped talking about their baseball experience, realizing that it was an aberration, a blip on the screen of normality; people to whom they mentioned their participation in a professional baseball league appeared hardly to believe them, anyway. Soon the whole thing receded into history, nearly forgotten. The sad and wistful remark of Sue Macy, who wrote an excellent young adult book about the league, serves as its epitaph: "The story of the AAGPBL shows that baseball once belonged to women, too."

But it should continue to belong to women; after all, it's their heritage, too. And in some ways, even after the demise of the AAGPBL, baseball remained their purview, with the efforts of a few girls and women who in recent years have managed with great difficulty to play school, Little League, and college ball, and with the temporary success of the one professional team, the Colorado Silver Bullets, that survived for any length of time. The Silver Bullets came into being because a staff member of the Atlanta Braves named Bob Hope (not the actor) had seen women playing softball in Florida and thought, "These women could play [softball] as well as Class A minor league teams [could play baseball]. I saw no reason why the best women couldn't play [baseball] at that level, and surely some women could play better than some men. In baseball, finesse, quickness, and mobility are the issue, and women are more flexible and in better shape than male players." Earlier, in 1984, Hope had tried to get a women's team called the Sun Sox into the Florida State League, but his effort proved unsuccessful, even though sixty women showed up to try out. Scouts ranked six of them as ready to play immediately. But the league, unwilling to take a chance, awarded the Florida franchise to a team from Tennessee. Hope was stunned, calling the decision "a human rights issue."

In 1993, with backing from Coors Brewing Company, Hope formed the Colorado Silver Bullets, a touring team that played men's minor league, amateur, semipro, and college teams in the 1990s. An astounding 1,800 women showed up to try out for twenty available spots on the team. Some were top softball players, and many had played some baseball when they were younger. When Phil Niekro, a former major league player, accepted the job as manager of the club, he commented, "Women should have every opportunity to play competitive professional ball. I think we are going to surprise quite a few people with the ability of these athletes and the caliber of ball they can play." Publicity and media interest followed, but the team never developed the following that it might have had. Just as the Silver Bullets began to be a winning team, Coors withdrew its sponsorship. Some rumors hinted that Coors did not want its product thought of as a "woman's beer." Probably, with two touring teams — or, even better, with a league of such teams, as with the AAGPBL — interest might have been sustained. As it was, the team proved to be an anomaly, with competition that varied too much for fans to build up an interest in it.

If the AAGPBL could attract sponsorship, re-establishing a fully professional women's league might be easy. Many women play baseball today in amateur leagues. The women who played in the AAGPBL fifty years ago, buoyed by their sudden rediscovery in the 1980s through Penny Marshall's Hollywood film *A League of Their Own*, were inspired to institute reunions and a tighter organization as well as support for emerging women's baseball programs. They would applaud and, to the extent possible, support any new move toward a professional league.

So why should baseball not be open to both types of participation by women: on mixed teams in mixed leagues as well as on women's teams in women's leagues? Keeping an unbreachable wall around organized baseball is as outdated as it is as unfair. Those women who possess the skill and confidence to play in leagues adjudged to be representative of the best brand of baseball should be able to take part at that level if they so desire. It's certainly time that reactionary males bury their ancient prejudices. Women, like black men, are tired of the discovering that in order to compete in any field they must actually be better than their white male counterparts. Why isn't "just as good" good enough?

What it finally took for girls and women to begin making inroads into organized baseball was for the law to become involved. And for that to happen, the women's movement of the 1960s and 1970s had to help. Social changes began to occur with legal protests by little girls (with their families), high

MECHANICS' INSTITUTE LIBRARY
57 Post Street
San Francisco, CA 94104
(415) 393-0101

schoolers, and college students who were tired of senseless rejection and just wanted to get the same help in playing baseball that the boys received. What the girls and women learned in the courts was that males, including judges, still believe that "baseball is a manly game" and that, as sportswriter Frank Deford put it, in trying to play baseball, girls were not only "monkeying with men's baseball but with men's childhood." Women's childhood seemed to warrant no consideration. This situation is beginning to change.

11

Girls Are Children, Too

You'd be surprised to find out how many girls enjoy playing ball. I was. Girls are much like boys in that they don't all want to be Alta Weiss or Mickey Mantle or Lizzie Murphy, but if they try baseball and like playing it, they want to pursue it for fun. But pursuing it on an organized basis proved difficult for girls. Not until the 1970s did many of them and their supporters begin to realize that the passing of Title Nine of the Education Amendment of 1972, along with the Equal Protection Clause of the Constitution's Fourteenth Amendment, might assist them in receiving the same opportunities to play baseball that boys and young men did, not only in educational institutions (most of which get federal money) but in every other organization set up to promote children's baseball. Some of those sports organizations, like the Little League, received only federal recognition, not federal money. So because Title Nine addresses educational institutions receiving federal funds, non-scholastic organizations like the Little League were affected only by extension.

Although not federally funded, the Little League occupies an important position among youth leagues, which often pattern themselves after it. In 1964 Congress actually declared the Little League to be tax-exempt, even though it was set up to serve only half the children of the United States and excluded the rest with a rule that read, "No Girls Allowed."

Children's and young women's attempts in the 1970s to pursue opportunities to play baseball in school, college, and other organizations resulted in an unexpected and appalling backlash among men. In New Jersey, two thousand teams voted to suspend play rather than let girls join. The New Jersey Assembly was presented with a petition signed by fifty thousand people asking to keep girls off baseball diamonds. A Babe Ruth League in North Carolina ejected a thirteen-year-old girl because its national organization threatened to revoke its charter if the girl wasn't ousted.

The issue of girls in amateur baseball spawned what Professor Sarah Fields called an "astonishing" number of lawsuits about whether girls should play baseball, accompanied by expressions of male dismay and anger. Over the three-year period 1972–1974, supporters of the girls filed fifty-seven actions against Little League baseball alone and still others against various youth and high school baseball leagues. The National Organization for Women (NOW) took an active part in these lawsuits.

Lawsuits to allow children to play? Such intensity seems absurd, but there was a serious reason for the legal action. As Professor Fields puts it, "The lawsuits arose because America's identity was linked to baseball, and to allow females access to America's game was to foreshadow female access to all aspects of American culture, and not all of America was ready to change without a fight."

Surprised and displeased statements from the judges who were asked to adjudicate these cases enlighten us about their reasons for wanting to continue the ban on girls. In the case of Pamela Magill, age ten, for example, the judge, instead of addressing the law, stated that he believed girls should not play baseball because they might get hurt; he also seemed to go along with Magill's local league in its contention that if girls played, boys would quit. What he believed, of course, was not at issue in the case; nor was any credible evidence for his belief presented in his courtroom. In the case of Allison Fortin, also aged ten, another judge decided, without evidence, that girls would get hurt playing with boys. No proof of girls' physiological differences that would prevent their participation ever came to light in these cases. Obviously, what lay behind these judges' decisions was not facts but assumptions about girls' "proper" behavior in society.

The Little League and similar local leagues pressed their case against girls by insisting that baseball is a "contact sport," that girls are too frail physically to play baseball, that playing ball would threaten girls' bodily privacy because coaches could no longer give players an encouraging pat on the rear and that they would embarrass players whose clothes needed to be loosened after injuries; besides, they would lose too many objecting boys from their teams if the boys had to play with girls. (Who trained boys to object to girls? Often, it was those same coaches.) Moreover, as one coach put it, coaching girls was a waste of time because they would never play professionally. (If they did play professionally, of course, they might compete successfully with men.) Not until cases reached the higher courts was it made clear that the objections of the youth leagues and coaches were baseless and frivolous.

Masculine prerogative lay at the bottom of the leagues' views. Men, in their opinion, owned the game. If females gained access to something men saw as belonging to them alone, as Professor Fields put it, they threatened men's "power, prestige, and identity in American culture." And not until 1974 did the Little League give up and change its rules to allow girls. Not all Little League teams complied with the change, and the courts had to threaten at least six organizations before they opened their leagues to girls.

Yet the 1974 ruling appears to have done little for girls who want to play baseball. By 1998 the number of girls in organized youth baseball was estimated at about one girl per league! This situation indicates that coaches expect girls to be much better than the average player in order to make the team. Professor Jennifer Ring has detailed for us the way her own talented daughter was repeatedly "marginalized" by coaches who gave precedence to their own sons and the sons of other men they wanted to please, boys whose skills were often inferior to those of Ring's daughter.

High schools usually provide softball for girls in the belief that females should be relegated to this game. Some proponents of this view even argue that softball is equivalent to baseball and that girls should stick to that game. Not until 1989 did a court agree with most players and rule that the two games are not substantially equivalent, so girls should have the right to try out for high school baseball teams if they want to. Now more than a thousand girls play high school ball nationally, but most of them find great difficulty in getting a chance to show what they can do and in becoming accepted by the coach and the other players.

Title Nine opened the way for educational institutions to solve the problem of girls' desire to play baseball and other sports by offering separate teams for girls and boys. This sounded like a logical solution, but segregation by sex resulted in unequal opportunities and certainly unequal facilities for the two sexes, just as segregation by race did.

A case that illustrated these issues is that of Linda Williams, a high school senior in Texas, barred from playing on the boys' baseball team even though there was no girls' team to play on. The organization governing her school had separated all girls' and boys' sports, and no girls' baseball team existed, so Williams signed up to play on the boys' team. She was told her team would forfeit any games in which she played, so she quit. But the judge for the federal district court ruled that Williams had been denied her rights under the Equal Protection Clause of the Fourteenth Amendment. Her team members were overjoyed at her return. Williams responded sensibly by saying that she wasn't sure whether all girls and boys should be on the same team, but "at least girls ought to have the opportunity."

And that's exactly the point. The two sexes should have an equal chance to play. The former system gave boys every advantage while girls were neglected because administrators incorrectly assumed lack of interest and ability on the part of girls. The result was that boys' teams built traditions over a period of many years while girls sat admiringly on the sidelines or were invited to don sexy satin shorts to lead cheers for them. Many girls, who were products of the same culture, assumed that the administrators acted correctly in failing to offer team sports for girls. Any girls who did express a desire to play those sports popular with boys received only perfunctory assistance, if any. Some were told to raise their own funds by holding bake sales.

Now the courts have made it clear that girls who can qualify to play sports can take part either on all-female teams or on male teams. Girls, ruled the courts, may voluntarily segregate themselves, but they may not be coerced into segregation.

Because bringing the fairness principles of Title Nine to scholastic sports is idealistic, applying it to the reality of high school and college sports has proved a nightmare of inconvenience, disruption, and expense. That's because men's high school and especially college sports have been allowed — no, encouraged — to grow into huge semiprofessional empires garnering regional and even nationwide interest while women's sports were neglected. And one result of the disruption is deep resentment on the part of males, especially in the athletic departments that used to be primarily male preserves. The director of the National Collegiate Athletic Association warned, "Impending doom is around the corner if these [Title Nine] regulations are implemented." He meant that the business empire built for and around college men, especially football and baseball players, was in danger of collapse financially because sports funds might have to be shared with women, who had in the past received only a fraction of the support men did.

But the impact of Title Nine on women's scholastic athletics in general has been positive, leading to a 400 percent increase in the rate of women's participation in college sports and an increase of more than 800 percent in high school participation. As sporting opportunities open up for females, more women become aware of them and decide to take part. For the women, surely that will mean better health, more pleasure in play, more experience with teamwork, and more confidence in their abilities. Too bad those improvements must come at the cost of angering young male athletes and their coaches.

School and college administrations have nobody to blame for this negative result except themselves; they have permitted the sports empires to inflate inappropriately because those bloated structures have helped publicize their institutions and earn money for them. As a result, some institutions have become sports teams with schools or colleges attached. At the University of Southern California, for example, the highest paid staff member is not the president but the head football coach, who makes nearly four and a half million dollars, which is about four times what the university president makes. To reorder their priorities, these institutions must tone down the promotion of sports and put strict academic requirements on every student, seeing to it that athletes do not play unless they adhere to the same standards as all other students.

Schools and colleges must also reconsider the questionable educational value of regional and national tournaments, which have little or nothing to do with becoming an educated person. Students who cannot live with these appropriate requirements and restrictions should leave and turn professional. Loyalty to one's alma mater ought not to require becoming, or cheering on, athletes who spend most of their time on sports rather than on their studies. I am hardly the first to point out that college sports for males are grotesquely magnified; the problem has inspired criticism since the 1920s, so it's long past time to see that all educational institutions emphasize education over everything else. I favor government oversight to check on colleges' success with placing intellectual development ahead of sports, since they obviously cannot or will not manage this problem themselves.

Sports originally entered the curriculum in order to improve students' health. It remained in order to improve the educational institutions' financial health. I see the idealistic goal of reordering college sports to bring them into line with educational goals as similar to the idealistic desire to furnish health care for all. For fifty years, various groups have made unsuccessful attempts to insure and protect the health of all Americans. We have let Europeans and Canadians move far ahead of us in this respect because of the objections of entrenched organizations. We could and should also see to it that school and college sport contributes to the health of all even if it means removing entrenched sporting structures. Giving women equal access to sports teams is a start toward equalizing opportunities for all students to develop their physical potential.

Some will complain that this goal is mere idealism. What is an idealist? Definitions emphasize the desire to have things as they should be regardless of practical considerations or the disapproval of others. I am proud to be both an idealist and a pragmatist because I think the two positions can be balanced, that change in the desired "ideal" direction can be managed in practice if enough citizens become convinced of its importance.

Many female baseballists have been idealists, believing that if they worked at it hard enough, they would be able to reach their goal, whether it was playing on a boys' team, gaining acceptance to Little League, or playing baseball in high school. They have had to also become pragmatists in order to pursue their goals. Even joining a men's baseball team in college has become possible for a few who want it badly enough. Some have reached their goal, at least for a while, until the abuse they took became too much to bear. What others want is a chance to play professionally in organized baseball.

After Julie Croteau fought to play high school and college baseball, she commented, "Discrimination is really hard to prove," but "you have to stand up for things you believe in." Croteau left a good job as assistant baseball coach at Western New England College in order to try out for the Colorado Silver Bullets; she made the team and played for them their first year. The day the Bullets beat the male Watertown, New York, All-Stars 3–2, filmmaker Lois Siegel asked Croteau for her advice to girls; it was "Fight! Fight like hell." But Croteau's experience with the professional Bullets failed to lead to an offer from organized baseball. It was pitcher Ila Borders who managed to play three seasons of men's professional ball, not in OB but in independent leagues.

Borders had starred in kids' baseball from her earliest years. Her teammates in Little League, once she showed her pitching ability, accepted her, but the parents, especially the mothers, hated seeing their sons lose to her as pitcher or hitter. Borders was such a good player that in junior high her teammates accepted her easily. In high school, because the school fielded a girls' softball team, the local high school prevented her from playing baseball, so her parents moved her to a private school, where Borders not only made the baseball team, she became its star. But when she entered a private college, opposing players abused her with profanities, and her own teammates hurt her deliberately during practice. Threats and an evening physical attack followed.

Determined to continue with her career, Borders changed colleges, and after graduation she was signed for men's professional baseball, playing mostly in the independent Northern League, outside organized baseball, for three years. The fans appreciated her, cheering her from the stands, but the opposing players didn't enjoy trying to get a hit off her, and they hated it when she struck them out. Feeling isolated, Borders became reclusive and began to question her goal of playing in the majors, finally leaving independent ball to reconsider her options. Her last manager called her "one of the most courageous people I've ever met or seen play the game."

Would you or I have the courage Borders displayed to face the resentment, jealousy, and anger of established male players? What young women who want to play professional ball must expect is what Ila Borders put herself through in order to play baseball on a professional level.

Some high schools and colleges still block women from playing baseball. Only about a thousand high school girls a year find acceptance on a varsity or junior varsity team, and only a very few college women do. These institutions set up varsity baseball teams, but they are meant for males, and the idea of organizing varsity women's baseball teams or welcoming women into men's varsity teams has evidently not occurred to coaches. So girls who have been playing since grade school find their baseball pleasure cut off when they enter their teens.

Women's lack of acceptance as ballplayers goes back to male belief in male entitlement — their assumption that they, and they alone, should take part in certain sports, the national game in particular. Until men and women stop teaching their children this humbug, girls will never get a fair chance to prove what they can do.

Meanwhile, success in "separate but unequal" leagues appears to be the only way to demonstrate to the public that many girls and women can play the game well, on a level that approaches the professional. In those leagues women are not held back because of their gender and can feel comfortable facing the opposition, knowing that they will not be criticized or attacked for the wrong reasons. Women who want this experience are not waiting for chewing gum magnates or beer manufacturers to form leagues for them; they are creating their own leagues, some of them with the help of men who believe in them, and they are showing everyone that the All-American Girls Professional Baseball League was not really an anomaly. Women still play the national game at a high level of skill.

The Women's Sports Foundation means well, but it is inaccurate in its stated assumption that "women have simply not had the opportunities to play baseball." Actually, they've been playing it since the 1860s and are still playing it; they make their own opportunities. The foundation errs, moreover, in assuming that women stick to softball and that, for success as pro baseball players, they must make the "transition to baseball." As a matter of fact, many women ballplayers have never engaged in softball and state that they would not want to play that game as long as they have the chance to play baseball.

Where are all these women baseball players today? Playing on girls' and women's teams operated by Justine Siegal for the Women's Baseball League and by Jim Glennie for the Women's Baseball Federation, as well as on other assorted leagues throughout North America. As an example: for ten years beginning in 1996, the Great Lakes Women's Baseball League, founded by John Kovach and Jim Glennie, operated with at least four clubs, including one from Manitoba, Canada. Now the WBL, the WBF, and the Pawtucket Slaterettes have risen to the top of the heap as places where women can pursue the national game.

Leagues available to women include the Eastern Women's Baseball Conference, known as the longest-running adult women's baseball league. Now in its eighteenth year of playing hardball, the EWBC fields six teams each year — about ninety players — from the metropolitan areas of Baltimore and Washington. JoAnn Milliken of the EWBC wishes more people would "pay attention" to women's baseball. This is a non-profit league, and games are free. In the EWBC fans will see something never viewed in MLB: tampons shoved up the nose to staunch the blood after a wild throw. Catcher Jo Ann Kruger of the Baltimore Blues says this trick "works great."

Justine Siegal of the WBL has become a great force for women's baseball today. Starting at an early age in Ohio with tee ball, she quickly moved up to baseball and played every chance she got. Those chances declined as she got older, but she refused to take the advice of others and switch to softball. Siegel states, "I was 13 when my baseball coach looked at me and said, 'I don't want you here. Girls shouldn't play baseball.' I didn't listen." Now in her thirties, Siegal has been playing baseball for most of her life.

Justine Siegal was the first woman to play for the Cleveland Adult Baseball League. In 1997 she formed her Women's Baseball League, which started playing in 1999. In 2003 her work went international. Now she not only plays, she coaches, manages, and runs her own league as part of an organization she calls "Baseball for All." Moreover, she earned a master's degree in sports studies and has began work in a Ph.D., helped coach a women's college baseball team (Springfield, Massachusetts) and a men's pro team (the Brockton, Massachusetts, Rox), serves in the National Guard, and raises a small daughter with baseball goals of her own. Justine Siegal has pitched and coached on five continents and in three international championships. Plenty of competition for her teams is available because thirty countries around the world offer some level of baseball for women.

Those of us who know Justine Siegal are used to hearing startling news of her latest doings — that she has taken a team to Japan or Australia, or she has just started a girls' baseball camp, or she has opened a league for youngsters aged ten to thirteen, or she has arranged a "Friendship Game" that two dozen college women from ten New England colleges played at Springfield College. Siegal set up this college baseball experience with the assistance of Robin Wallace, head of the North American Women's Baseball League, in order to try to jump-start intercollegiate women's baseball so that a college league can begin playing within months of this event. Siegal is the archetypical Type-A person, the busiest and most proactive woman in her field.

Another focus of women's baseball interest centers in Rhode Island, where Lizzie Murphy once pleased New Englanders with her skill in playing on men's pro teams. Now in the same state we have the Pawtucket Slaterettes, a league of girls and women who have been playing for thirty-five years. Your history books mention Samuel Slater, who established a textile mill in Pawtucket and helped create America's industrial revolution. The Slaterettes follow in his footsteps with a league founded to help create a women's baseball revolution.

The Slaterettes operate all over southern New England and have begun

Justine Siegal, with the cooperation of Robin Wallace, arranged a "Friendship Game" at Springfield College on May 3, 2009, so that two dozen women from ten New England colleges who love to play baseball could take part in a college women's contest. In this group photo, Siegal appears standing at the far right, in braids, with a cap bearing the letter S for Springfield, and Wallace stands second from left, in black jacket and white pants (courtesy of the photographer, Richard Reddy).

competing in national tournaments. Establishing four divisions gives children as young as eight a chance to play and to eventually advance to the upper divisions. Women in the top age bracket play with MLB rules. The Slaterettes present baseball playing opportunities to about two hundred girls and women each year. Deb Bettencourt characterizes her organization as a "recreational league" because it includes women new to the game who are just looking for some exercise. Since the league has been operating for so many years, a lot of the current players are daughters of former players, so Deb likes to claim that "we breed ballplayers here."

Jim Glennie's determined work with ballplayers in the American Women's Baseball Federation, which began when his daughter wanted to play baseball, has resulted in participation of women in many baseball competitions. Since 1992 Glennie's organization has sponsored seventeen regional and national tournaments, including the first four Women's World Series, which included the national teams of countries like Canada, Australia, and Japan. He keeps a database of players interested in trying out for the USA Baseball women's national team and directs potential candidates to tryout sites.

Roy Hobbs Baseball, an organization operated by Tom Giffen in Florida, includes sponsorship of some women's tournaments. If you know the Bernard Malamud novel *The Natural* and the subsequent film version starring Robert Redford as the character called Roy Hobbs, you realize that the league is named for a fictional player who makes a magical comeback after an accident. Giffen says that for most players, the league represents not a magical comeback but "the idea that they can still play, still compete, still contribute, still enjoy the dugout and what it means to be teammates, and escape from the real world to the athletic world of their childhood.... They are just happy to play and, even in their sixties, exercise their competitive juices." Giffen obviously knows the real value of his league for women as well as for men.

In 2002 Giffen asked Dolly Brumfield White, a former AAGPBL player, to hand out gold medals to the winners of the final game in a Fort Myers, Florida, women's tournament playing standard American League rules under the auspices of the Amateur Athletic Union, and he asked me to hand out medals to the team that came in second. I discovered that the game I viewed between the Ocala Lightning and the Chicago Storm was the culmination of a series in which an astounding 162 teams had taken part, playing in venues all around Fort Myers. That's a total of around twenty-five hundred women, aged sixteen into their forties, all gathered into one area to play ball. I had never dreamed so many women even played baseball; nor did I realize that they played as well as they did in the game I watched. It's events like these that can open the minds of people who question women's baseball ability and devotion to the game.

Giffen still sponsors tourneys for women's groups that find themselves able to schedule competitions at a time when his organization can accommodate them, but he says the number of participants has begun to drop. In 2007, a hundred and sixty women (ten women's teams with an average of sixteen women each) participated in a tournament he set up for them, but in 2008 conflicts with other tournaments and limits on the discretionary time and funds of many would-be participants cut down on their number. A tournament that Giffen sponsored in Tucson attracted fewer than a hundred women compared with more than a hundred and fifty in the previous year. Perhaps a tournament fails to inspire women players as much as a formal league would, but today there is no professional league.

Giffen believes that both the declining economy and the aging of some women, who he fears are beginning to give up baseball, may be the causes of the decline in numbers, along with USA Baseball's lack of promotion of women's baseball. USAB's participation, asserts Giffen, now seems confined to recruiting a women's national team and sending it to another country. And its increase in fees charged to participating teams hardly helps.

What, I wondered, is USA Baseball? I discovered that this group acts as an umbrella organization for amateur baseball and has become a virtual commissioner's office for all twelve million amateur players in America. USAB, headed by executive director Paul Seiler, claims responsibility for "promoting and developing the game of baseball on the grassroots level." And it does construct the machinery for the formation of a national collegiate team as well as an 18-and-under team, a 16-and-under team, and a 14-and-under team, all of which are male, and (yes!) since 2004 a women's national team as well — separate and unequal, with no children's teams to build from. USA Baseball sponsors no competition for young girls; boys are the focus of its young teams. Girls are evidently not part of America's "grass roots." Perhaps, to USA Baseball, they are merely weeds.

Tom Giffen points out that USA Baseball grooms males for international competition beginning when they are ten years old, but for women the organization merely holds tryouts for adults a month or so before the formation of the national team. As usual, unless the sponsoring organization is one they themselves or their specific supporters have founded, women and girls receive only perfunctory attention when it comes to promotion of their interests.

So to provide chances to play baseball, women ballplayers and their backers must scrape up their own money, form their own organizations, and find their own times and places to compete. That's why we have Justine Siegal's Women's Baseball League, Jim Glennie's American Women's Baseball Federation, Tom Giffen's Roy Hobbs League, Melanie Laspina's California Women's Baseball League, the Pawtucket Slaterettes, Robin Wallace's North American Women's Baseball League, the Eastern Women's Baseball Conference, the Chicago Pioneers Girls Baseball League, and numerous other regional and local leagues like the East Coast Women's Baseball League, the New York WBA, the New York City WBA, the Chicago Women's Baseball League, the Philadelphia WBA, Colorado Women's Baseball, the Great Lakes WBA, Washington (state) WBA, and clubs like the Arizona Cactus Wrens, the South Bend Blue Sox, the Chicago Gems, and the Rochester Rivercats — all of which have an online presence. In fact, if you ask a search engine for a list of women's baseball organizations, you will receive the names of at least forty-five leagues and clubs.

Siegal's extensive WBL has held camps for girls eleven through sixteen; coached women's teams in India; taken a team to an international tournament in Hong Kong; run a baseball camp for girls seven to seventeen at Saint Mary's College in Notre Dame, Indiana; sponsored an adult forum on women's baseball at Springfield College; and brought a young team to play at Cooperstown Dreams Park as the only girls' team among other kid teams from around the world.

It's clear that work like this needs to be done. Such efforts can build a feeder program to construct a ladder that girls and women can climb to professional teams in professional leagues. But it should not have to be done without the help of the big organizations like USA Baseball. And the ladder should be a clear and definable construction encompassing the entire country instead of being limited geographically and financially by whatever a local group can offer.

As Giffen and Glennie both know, USA Baseball's promotion of women's baseball as a whole would encourage the development of the game among girls simply by letting them know that they can play baseball beyond Little League age. But, hold on: not many girls play on Little League baseball teams and other youth baseball teams in the first place, compared with the two million boys who participate. Although the number of girls playing nationally has reached 100,000, girls are thinly distributed across the country's youth leagues — about one per league. Why is that? Because, as Jim Nemerovski points out, even though Little League now accepts qualified girl players, it steers them to its softball branch, usually by simply failing to inform female applicants that they could play baseball instead, as well as by directing them to softball when they show up for baseball tryouts. Nemerovski believes, from evidence he has collected, that a great many more girls would play Little League baseball if they realized that they could. He is in fact pressing LL to make it clear to female applicants that they have a choice.

Nemerovski, whose daughters play baseball, is one of several fathers who assist their daughters in finding access to baseball clubs and leagues in which to play. Although feeling thwarted by bureaucrats and others with vested interests in softball, he promotes girls' baseball in the San Francisco area.

With Justine Siegal's support, Nemerovski says, his daughter Jessica has been able to play baseball for five years. Her experience includes playing on a girls' team in Cooperstown; participating in the World Children's Baseball Fair in Japan in 2005; playing with the Pawtucket Slaterettes in the 2007 Roy Hobbs tournament; participating in the Can-Am (Canadian-American) Women's Baseball Tournament in 2008; and taking part in the Women's Hall of Fame Baseball Classic in Kenosha, Wisconsin, that same year. Through all these and other experiences, Jessica has, says Nemerovski, developed pride and confidence in her ability. Jessica's dad also operates a web site that is part of his proactive stance for girls, and he is working to obtain mainstream coverage for their baseball activities. "Nothing," says Nemerovski, "should stand in their way in pursuit of their playing baseball, or the desire to achieve greatness in any pursuit of their choice." All athletic girls should have a father like Jim Nemerovski. Jim credits Justine Siegal as being "more significant than anyone realizes" because "she has done the most to empower the greatest number of girls in the greatest geographic area."

Another father active in his daughters' efforts to play baseball is John Kovach, a university archivist in Indiana. When Kovach began coaching amateur baseball in 1991, he discovered quickly that "there was a huge segment of the population who were not allowed to dream or follow their dreams of playing baseball because of their gender." His daughters played baseball as children, and one of them managed to get into the Little League. Kovach points out that although virtually all youth baseball organizations belong to USA Baseball, USAB confines itself to picking a national women's team and (as Giffen and Glennie both declare) "makes no effort to try to develop programs for girls through those entities." Kovach says he knows from experience that when children show up for Little League tryouts, boys are directed to the baseball line and girls to the softball line. He has suggested to USA Baseball that it develop a program for girls fourteen and up, but aside from calling his idea "creative," the organization merely "dropped the idea."

Like Nemerovski, Kovach promotes girls' baseball. Most of his promotion takes the form of making presentations about women in baseball, working with the Women's Sports Foundation to convince high schools to stop putting up barriers against girls, and producing a book, *Women's Baseball*, full of joyous images from the earliest days to the present showing girls and women being active in baseball. If anything will convince Americans that females actually do play baseball, this book is it. Kovach also helped his daughter Irina file a discrimination suit against a local youth baseball league when its representatives told her that she could not play baseball because baseball is for boys and softball is for girls.

A third father who became involved in baseball partly because of his daughter's play is Patrick McCauley, president of the Ontario Girls Baseball League and manager of the women's Canadian national baseball team. McCauley explained at a Society for American Baseball Research meeting that he formed a league for girls over twelve expressly because when his own daughter reached that age she no longer had a league in which to play. Several years ago Justine Siegal married McCauley, and what a team they make! Their work immediately expanded internationally and exponentially.

Other fathers have found themselves involved in girls' and women's baseball simply because they want to protect their daughters from discrimination. Gary Sementelli's daughter Marti developed early into an outstanding athlete and successful schoolgirl baseball player, but finding a high school team that would permit her to play baseball instead of softball proved almost impossible until Gary contacted Burbank High. "I would have gone to any length," said Marti's father, to find a school willing to give her a chance, because "baseball is the game she has been playing all her life." Marti has already had the experience of pitching and winning a game for the American women's national team against Australia in the Women's Baseball World Cup. Now her teammates are kids on the high school junior varsity.

Girls like Marti Sementelli need assistance from baseball organizations, but USA Baseball does not involve itself in such cases. Besides USA Baseball, another umbrella organization in the field is the worldwide International Baseball Federation, which governs baseball play between the national teams formed by countries or regions under the auspices of those countries' amateur baseball federations. Adopting the acronym IBAF (from the French version of its name) the International Baseball Federation has supervised baseball play involving the American women's national team, but it does nothing to promote women's baseball, and Jim Glennie complains that "women's tournaments still seem to be an afterthought with the IBAF and other men's organizations we pay homage to." Glennie thus characterizes the big amateur associations as what they really are: men's organizations, where women remain the "second sex."

What do all these women play for? Fat financial rewards in the form of prizes? No. As their organizers point out, they play for "bragging rights." In other words, all they get out of it is the thrill of winning. For them, that's enough. Here, I think, is the true amateur spirit.

How amateur is USA Baseball, which presents itself as an organization for amateurs? Besides the amateur competitions it supervises, USAB also sets up two professional-level championships, a team of minor and major leaguers to play in a World Baseball Classic tournament annually against foreign teams (which often win) and a team of professionals to compete in the Olympic Games. I can't see how selection of professionals for these teams relates to the USAB's goal of promoting amateur baseball. And of course no women have ever been selected to play on those championships.

Yet women and girls still play by the thousands. Why is it that their activity remains mired in obscurity? For the same two reasons women's accomplishments have always remained half-hidden: women follow feminine tradition in failing to promote themselves and publicize their deeds, and men follow masculine tradition in failing to search out women's achievements and consider them important enough to bring to anyone's attention. What women do, therefore, is seldom thought of as on the same level as what men do. Women usually accept men's judgment that their own work deserves less attention than men's. I am guilty of having done that, too.

Moreover, the people who run the women's leagues are too busy — organizing, managing, holding tournaments, looking for backing, and playing the game — to think about promotion. They operate on a shoestring and cannot afford to hire the promotion departments and the outreach representatives that organized baseball uses to publicize its activities. The WBL in particular expends its promotion energies by sending web invitations to girls and women to join its clubs, camps, tournaments, trips abroad, and other activities. Justine Siegal, the WBL's founder and Jill-of-all-trades, is hardly in one place long enough to do much else.

But I am inspired, as all girls and women should be, by the attitude of a girl named Emily McPherson, who plays ball in the East Coast Women's League. Her club's manager, Adriane Adler, says Emily can play any position and "has such a passion for the game" that when asked to play she "will charge out there with a huge smile." Emily, says Adler, "personifies why girls and women should be allowed to play.... They truly love the sport." In the following poignant statement, Emily herself explains what it means to be a female baseball player:

The Hard Way Home

When I was younger, no one told me I couldn't play baseball — no one, that is, until I reached the seventh grade. Being told I could not play on the boys' modified baseball team was like being thrown into a little glass box. I was singled out, told that I could not play a sport I had grown up playing, a sport I had grown up loving.

Looking out through the walls of my box, I could see all the other kids who were allowed to play the sport they loved to play. They laughed with their teammates at practice and shared their sports stories at school. At twelve years old, you don't yet understand why gender matters, but I was forced to understand, because my gender did matter.

The day I learned about the East Coast Women's Baseball League was the day I picked up my baseball bat and shattered my little glass box. I was no longer alone. My heart and soul had been trapped in that box every day for almost four years, but now they soar in New Jersey, with the women who brought me out of my box.

These are women who share my story, who also spent part of their childhood in that little glass box. Discovering women's baseball was like finding a long-lost sister, and when we finally met face-to-face, the emotions that ran through my veins were so overwhelming that to this day I cannot even begin to describe them.

The women I play baseball with are my long-lost sisters, and now that I have found them, I thank God every minute of every day for giving me such a precious gift. It doesn't matter that there is a twenty-year age difference between some of my sisters and me; we are bonded together by a passion to play baseball, a passion we were born with but were told it was wrong for us to have. We are joined in this sisterhood of rejection, one that no one else can possibly understand.

I will never make it to the Major Leagues, I will never win the World Series, but when my team and I won the League Championship last September, there was only a minor difference between Major Leaguers and us. We were women playing in front of twenty people, not men playing in front of fifty thousand.

With two outs in the bottom of the seventh, a game-winning RBI single made our conclusion more dramatic than most World Series endings.

We don't make a million dollars a year, we aren't on TV, we don't even have matching uniforms, but when we won that game, we were Major Leaguers. As I watched that base hit dunk into the right field gap, everything slowed down, the noise disappeared as all eyes watched that scuffed-up baseball that had been knocked around for seven innings.

I could say that it felt like all these sports movies where the home team comes from behind to win in a dramatic fashion, but it didn't. It had a feeling all its own, a feeling that cannot be described, but once you feel it, it stays with you forever. I said I have never won the World Series. That's still true, but I wouldn't trade what we won for anything in the world, because for us, it was OUR World Series.

Everyone has a place in the world. I found my place in Northern New Jersey every Sunday for the past two summers. The most important thing I have learned is that I am not alone fighting this battle. There were women before me who fought the inequities and more women will continue the fight after me. This is such a powerful feeling. It helps me to stay strong and keep facing the inequity in my hometown, where I am still alone.

A new passion has been created in me. I want to keep women's baseball alive so other twelve-year-old girls are not forced to look at the world from inside that little glass box.

— Emily McPherson

12

The Courage of Baseball Women

The International Baseball Federation estimates that between 300,000 and 500,000 women and girls play baseball worldwide. That estimate includes Little League and T-ball players, but it remains an impressive figure.

Despite the many barriers to their participation in baseball, American girls and women who love the national game manage to pursue their passion in several ways. Transcending those barriers, some have not only found places to play, they have risen to the level of stars among their peers and are selected for playing in regional, national, and even international tournaments. And they go right on playing baseball, building their own special baseball culture.

Women who play baseball often remark that they play differently from men. They refer not so much to skill as to attitude. "Women put more heart into the game," says Mariah Brunelle, who plays for the North American Women's Baseball League. "It means more to them." Obviously, it means more because of the blocks they have had to push out of the way in order to reach their goal. Executive director of the NAWBL is pitcher Robin Wallace of Massachusetts. The NAWBL, which averages fifty-five players a season, developed an all-star team that has played other women's baseball clubs in several countries around the world.

An event that reveals the special characteristics of women's ball — because it shows the way baseball women think and act — took place in Kenosha, Wisconsin, for three days over the Fourth of July holiday in 2008. Five highly successful teams traveled there to compete in a twelve-game tournament called the Hall of Fame Classic, organized by the American Women's Baseball Federation (Jim Glennie's organization) and the Kenosha Men's Senior Baseball League.

Four American teams participated: the Nashua (New Hampshire) Pride, the New England Women's Red Sox, the Washington (D.C.) Stars, and the

Chicago Pioneers. A fifth team, the Aussie Hearts, traveled from Australia to take part; the team's manager, Rob Novotny, had grown up in Kenosha, and his wife played on the team. Novotny received an extra thrill when the Hearts won the gold by beating the New England Red Sox, who had been national champions four times. The Aussie Hearts, whose ages range from 17 to 30, were actually an international team, composed of eleven players from Aus-

In 2004 Robin "Bama" Wallace, executive director of the North American Women's Baseball League, was pitching at Fraser Field in Lynn, Massachusetts, for the Seahawks, but she comes from Alabama. That year she also pitched for Team USA and says she was "having a good year." Wallace, a curveball pitcher, likens her style to that of Greg Maddux and continues pitching regularly (courtesy of the photographer, Richard Reddy).

tralia, two from America, and one each from Canada, Korea, and Japan. Novotny believes firmly in the right of women to take part in baseball. "Females," he told a local reporter, "should have the choice to play what they want to play."

But the tournament itself and the return of a hometown boy managing one of its star teams made up only two parts of a rich baseball experience that weekend. The competition was held in a place redolent with women's baseball memories: the home city of the Comets of Kenosha, Wisconsin, a team of the All-American Girls Professional Baseball League of the 1940s. And most tournament games were played on Simmons Field, a park where the AAGPBL had played many games. Kenosha fans who had attended the women's games at Simmons Field had fond memories of the clubs and players; others had heard about them, or at the very least, knew about them from the film that popularized the AAGPBL, *A League of Their Own*.

The Kenosha occasion provided the perfect setting for alumni of the AAGPBL to return to the scene of their younger days, to attend games of the tournament, to observe and have contacts with the youngsters who represent the next generation of stars, and to give the young players the thrill of meeting some of those AAGPBL players they had heard so many stories about. In fact, the whole point of the festivities was to connect the present with the past. Sixteen AAGPBL players attended. Jim Glennie commented aptly on the coming together of the two women's groups, pointing out that the players of the professional women's league "will not be with us forever," so "it's important that a bond be forged between that generation and this generation's young pioneers."

Dolly Brumfield White, who had played for the Kenosha Comets, was one of the AAGPBL women who happily signed baseballs and joined in posing for photographs. White helped unveil a plaque celebrating the AAGPBL and the rededicated Simmons Field. Women and girls ran the games and handled everything, including the Color Guard Ceremony that opened the festivities. Merrie Fidler, the historian of the AAGPBL, snapped many photos to record all this for history. Observing the action were wide-eyed, pigtailed bat girls — part of a baseball generation to follow. Such a significant occasion was certainly newsworthy, but coverage of the tournament came only from Kenosha papers and from nearby Racine, Wisconsin. No other media paid attention to the event.

The celebration and tournament at Kenosha had been set up for one more purpose: to select players for a women's national team to compete in Japan for the Women's World Cup, a competition that has been running since 2001. The 2008 tournament was set for the end of August in Matsuyama, Japan. Eight countries entered women's national teams in the six-day competition

A woman batter, a woman catcher, and a woman umpire take part in a July 2008 tournament. Here the Washington Stars hit against the Nashua Pride in the Women's Hall of Fame Classic, Kenosha, Wisconsin, at Simmons Field, where the famous AAGPBL used to play back in the 1940s and 1950s (courtesy of Merrie Fidler).

for the Women's World's Cup: besides the United States the tournament included teams from Australia, Canada, Japan, Chinese Taipei, and (for the first time) Korea and India. At the tournament Japan took its first gold, while Canada earned the silver and the United States the bronze. Recognized as the top pitcher of the tournament was sixteen-year-old Marti Sementelli of the United States.

While I was wondering how it would be to watch excellent American women players take part in an international tournament against fine women's teams from countries around the world, I read an article by Jennifer Ring, an American college professor, who had traveled to Taipei, Taiwan, in 2005 to see that year's Women's World Cup competition. She found that she was one of only ten Americans to attend, whereas the local Taiwan players and the Japanese women enjoyed "throngs of press and hundreds of fans following them around." ESPN failed to cover the event, and no American press sought interviews with the American players.

The Japanese team consisted of forty women who, like the Canadian team members, play together all year 'round, whereas the American women had played together as a team for only two days. The Americans, who had twice before beaten the best women's teams around the world, won again, but the American press paid no attention.

Ring, who herself grew up wanting to play in the big leagues, found the World Cup tournament thrilling: "I could not imagine a more exciting series, or more inspired play." The American players, coached by Julie Croteau and her assistants, were "impressive." Like Croteau, they had, in Ring's words, "struggled against so much resistance ... that their fundamentals were more highly developed than those of many boys and men." Ring discovered that the women conducted themselves differently from the way males do in tournament play: "no attitude, no superstars — just baseball at its best, like it used to be for the men, too." Moreover, "there was a generosity of spirit shown by players and fans alike that has been lacking in men's baseball on all levels of play." As an example, Ring noticed that when Team Japan lost and a few women on the Japanese team began to cry, the American winners hugged the Japanese players. Of course, according to the character played by Tom Hanks in *A League of Their Own*, "There's no crying in baseball." Wrong. Women are passionate about their love of the game, and if a few tears get spilled, a few empathetic hugs may be in order.

Japanese professional baseball jumped light-years ahead of the American when a sixteen-year-old high school girl, Eri Yoshida, made it in as a member of a Kobe club in a new independent men's professional league. Like many American women players, Yoshida, a knuckleball pitcher signed in 2009, has always played against boys and competed against male professionals that summer, before leaving to attend college. American fans commenting on the Yoshida story at a blogspot made admiring remarks like "How cool is that?"

Women ballplayers from other countries often receive the kind of support and training that American women have to fight for. In Canada, for example, the federal and provincial governments share the costs of supporting Canadian sport. Canadian women's baseball is overseen by one national governing body, not several, and its 400,000 Canadian players are organized into levels by age, beginning at eleven. In the United States, by contrast, as Ann Aronson described it, "women's baseball happens only when a group of extremely motivated people decide to invent a team or league, find players and coaches, fight for field time, raise money, negotiate substantially diverse skill levels among players, and struggle to maintain the interest of women with an infinite number of other commitments and recreational activities."

Australia's seventy women's teams are organized through the club system, in which a baseball club sponsors several teams at different levels, with age groups that span the years from seven to seventy. Perhaps because of this arrangement, about three hundred women play baseball in the state of Victoria alone. The Australian Baseball Association and the Australian states support women's baseball, which has been stimulated by the popular film *A League of Their Own*.

Cuban women, too, play baseball, but the national team is limited to women 24 and younger. A woman umpire, Yanet Moreno, who works in today's Cuban big leagues, suffered her share of difficulty in reaching her goal, beginning with her childhood, when her father punished her for playing baseball with the boys — "but I kept it up anyway." A few individual Cubans played in the All-American Girls Professional Baseball League of the forties. Now a tournament among Cuban women's teams around the country is hosted by the National Sports Institute. In 2004 a Cuban National Women's Team traveled to Edmonton, Alberta, Canada, to compete in a Women's World Championship. Cuban women must have the same passion for the game as American women, for a reviewer of a Cuban documentary film reports noticing that a young woman player being interviewed commented, "I had to choose between baseball or my boyfriend — and I chose baseball."

Looking for financial and promotional support is a perennial problem for American women baseball players, but as long as men believe baseball is theirs alone, women will be blocked from the kind of support that the National Basketball Association gives to women's basketball. Thanks to the NBA, everyone knows that women play high-level basketball. The same isn't true of MLB's relationship to women's baseball. In fact, instead of promoting women's baseball, Major League Baseball promotes women's softball, obviously in the hope that women will stick to that game. MLB and its players and newspaper reporters want to avoid the embarrassment of discovering that some women can play the national game as well as many men.

A lot of people still believe the fiction that softball and baseball are essentially the same game. As one girl put it, "That's like saying ping-pong and tennis are essentially the same game." Not until 1990 did the National College Athletic Association, the supervising organization, reverse its ruling that baseball and softball are the same sport.

Countless girls are quoted in current books and articles saying that they refuse to switch to softball, or they will play it only if they cannot find a baseball team to play on and will leave it as soon as they get a chance to return

to the game they love. Foregoing softball in favor of baseball means foregoing the softball scholarships offered women by some colleges; none offers
baseball scholarships for them. In fact, no college is known to offer a women's
varsity, or even junior varsity, baseball team. What the colleges call their "varsity team" is a men's team, which occasionally — *very* occasionally — may admit
a woman player. For example, in 2008, only three women played on American college baseball teams; yet both Japan and India offer college baseball to
women.

This situation could be remedied with the support of MLB, but it refuses
to recognize American women's baseball. Instead, it has sent tens of millions
of dollars to help the growth of baseball in China! Of course, that money goes
to men's baseball. According to the *New York Times,* MLB does this "because
of the marketing potential of the country's 1.3 billion people." The irony of
MLB's generous financial support of Chinese men's play is that the Chinese
lack the fire in the belly that American women players have. The Chinese are
"just not aggressive people," said their American coach, and after five years'
training their skill has been ranked at about the high school level. Another
coach said they "have no attention to detail." Meanwhile, back here in America are thousands of girls and women pining for the kind of support MLB
gives to Chinese men — a financial boost that would give them more opportunities to improve their skills and play with their peers.

Are the not-very-knowledgeable Chinese more deserving of support than
enthusiastic American women players? In 2000, commissioner of baseball
Bud Selig announced his "Commissioner's Initiative on Women and Baseball," which requests clubowners to find ways to make women "more active
participants in the game." Of course, Selig meant "as spectators only." MLB
fails to realize that the Commissioner's Initiative might best be fulfilled by
backing women's play. Jim Glennie makes the same point; he says, "If they
[the owners] want to add to their marketing strategy, this is the way to do
it." Instead, the clubowners are racking their brains to figure out how to get
more women to watch men play the game. What if MLB started supporting
women players? That would certainly boost women's baseball interest, but it
might result in women fans attending women's games instead of men's games.
Men might attend women's games, too, as they did the games of the AAGPBL.
"Oh, well," must be the MLB reasoning, "send the money to the Chinese and
let American girls and women hold bake sales to support their play. That way
they won't disturb our masculine game."

Owners have displayed other examples of illogical reasoning by respond-
ing to the Commissioner's Initiative by furnishing their parks with play areas
so that women can bring their young children there. That might bring more
women to the parks, but it's unclear to me how women can sit in the grand-

stand and watch the game if they are in a play area supervising their children's play activities. Would you take your four-year-old, or even your eight-year-old, to a new play area and leave him or her there alone, or with a complete stranger, while you go watch a ball game?

In 2008 MLB heard about two young men from Uttar Pradesh, India, who had won a ball-throwing contest by coming closest to throwing at the speed of 90 miles per hour, so their manager is training them to be baseball players. These two young men came to the United States knowing nothing at all about the game of baseball and, according to the sports writer who viewed videos of their "pitching," they appear to have "the worst possible delivery." Their coach states that they have "a 12- to 14-year deficit" in baseball knowledge, but because they can throw a ball fast, the Pirates expect to train them in the Rookie Gulf Coast League, then bring them up to the Show in about a year. Meanwhile, they are reading *Baseball for Dummies.*

These are the rookies that MLB is willing to spend its money on. Meanwhile, young women who have played baseball since before they went to school, and have developed real skill and desire, are languishing in amateur leagues without a chance of upward mobility.

MLB's focus remains upon ways to bring bodies, including women's bodies, into the grandstand. Many women have been baseball fans all their lives, but because of the way women's baseball remains hidden, they haven't been fans of women players. Women cannot relate to excellent players of their own gender if they haven't even heard about them. Without female national idols, women admire those whom the press has helped to build into famous people: male players. Not told about women's stars of the past and unlikely to be informed about today's women players, they have become fans of the stars in the men's leagues. I'm sure that if the AAGPBL had been allowed to continue and spread, it would have developed the generations of stories, traditions, and myths about women's baseball that MLB has fostered for men over the years since the 1870s. Stories about players in the major leagues have become the heritage of American children, passed on from male members of the family to the next generation for a hundred and fifty years. Imagine what it would be like if American girls were able to look back at a hundred and fifty years of women players, hear their stories repeated, read about them over and over, and talk about their accomplishments.

Proof that it can happen is that about a million fans, more than half of them women, bought tickets in one year to see the teams of the AAGPBL. At first spectators came out of curiosity, but they stayed because of the thrills of the game. As a 1950 sports writer named Morris Markey put it, fans, particularly women, were soon "gawking with admiration" at the skill of the players because "women make the game possible. Housewives and cooks, clerks and secretaries, and salesgirls find a delight which they make no effort to conceal in watching members of their own sex play a game just about as well as their brothers can play it. The spectacle feeds their pride and goes a long way toward dispelling the myth of inferiority, the myth of the weaker sex.... The old notions about a girl's structural inability to throw a ball — that she must push it or toss it — were a lot of tosh. The modern girls if properly taught can heave a ball that will put a blister in the palm of most men trying to catch it."

It's clear from those who have studied the AAGPBL that the young women who played for the league in those medium-sized Midwestern cities developed a solid fan base. The players became the town celebrities, welcomed into the family homes, boasted about in ads by local businesses, and swarmed over by local children, who followed them around worshipfully. Fans paid the players' fines, sent them bouquets of paper money, gave them picnics, provided local housing, ran booster clubs, bought season tickets, traveled to away games, and bought Cokes for them. If the league had been allowed to continue, the enthusiasm of female fans for female players would have done more to develop women's confidence in their physical abilities than a thousand token women allowed to enter other male-dominated fields, because baseball is the national game. Given the same support men got for a hundred and fifty years, women could show that they, too, can represent excellence in the sport we have long accepted as thoroughly American. They are already on their way to doing that, but few people know about it. While MLB clubowners of today are scratching their heads over ways to attract women to baseball, the answer lies dormant at their feet waiting to be resuscitated.

Today's women fans enjoy hearing stories about early women players. When I make presentations on this subject, I see appreciative nods, smiles, and even laughter in the audience as I tell, for example, that Lizzie Arlington entertained the crowd at a 1920s ball game by making a show of spitting on her hands and wiping them on her pants. They like learning that Lizzie Murphy boldly walked around the grandstand selling postcards about herself to fans who came to watch her play. They're intrigued to discover that Alta Weiss chewed gum during the game to make saliva for her spitball.

Women fans of baseball and all other pro sports are said to be on the increase as baseball loses its support from middle-aged white males. Many women know as much baseball as their male counterparts. But that may not be a good thing for their relationships with men. Mark Harris dated two such knowledgeable women. One had a head full of figures like Ty Cobb's lifetime batting average; the other carried her baseball glove to the park in her purse in case of the opportunity to catch a ball. Harris indicates that men are turned off by women who play baseball; they may also be confused by women who know as much baseball as they do. Not all men are repelled by women ballplayers: the women in the AAGPBL were besieged for dates, and at least one player married a fan. Two men who later became college professors, John Schultz and Harold Van der Zwaag, told Merrie Fidler, the historian of the AAGPBL, that they, too, had been avid fans of league players.

Meanwhile, without current idols of their own sex, women follow male idols with amazing intensity. Camille Minichino felt so devastated by the departure of "her team," the Boston Braves, for Atlanta that she wept bitterly and never followed baseball again; her story hints that she actually entered a convent on account of her disappointment. For women as well as men, baseball is part of our culture, "one of our natural endowments," as fan Ellen Stolfa puts it. For two others, Sally Mars and Sarah Waddle, it's a warm, nostalgic place full of comforting memories.

One can hardly be a fan without being knowledgeable about the fine points of the game. But women aren't expected to know anything about baseball. A stock scene in many movies shows a couple dating at a ball park, where the woman asks what seems to the man like stupid questions about what's going on. Her lack of knowledge makes the man feel superior, so the woman, used to being considered inferior, thinks she is, and she eventually stops asking. Actually, many women can and do follow the action in detail, keeping score and conversing sensibly about the game. How much more might they be interested in learning if they could follow women's professional baseball?

The women who demonstrate true expertise in baseball knowledge are women umpires. I remember how impressed I was when I met two Canadian women umpires at a conference in 2000; just as umpires should, they exuded confidence and control — what is called "presence." Before that time, I didn't even know that some umpires were women, so their presentation made me realize the way I had been brainwashed to believe that women knew nothing about the finer points of the game. After they had spoken to the group, the two umpires sat at a table having coffee with some of the rest of us when a man seated across the table challenged them to list the seven ways a batter can be put out. It took them only a few moments to come up with the answers, and their questioner admitted smilingly that they were correct. When he had left, an umpire named Lisa Turbitt of Ontario (named Canadian Umpire of the Year for 2004) revealed that they knew other ways a batter could be put out; the ones they had listed were merely the standard ways. Of course, women aren't supposed to know more baseball than men.

Nobody knows more of the fine points than umpires. Beginning with the tall, stately Amanda Clement of the last century, who umpired in South Dakota, American women umpires have often been heckled as brutally as were the early black players in the majors. Fans often shouted remarks questioning Clement's abilities as homemaker and wife; other fans defended her because of her obvious umpiring skill. But Clement's size and demeanor helped her demand respect.

Women of the current era who managed to reach the men's minor leagues, like Bernice Gera in the early seventies, Christine Wren in the mid-seventies, and Pam Postema in the seventies and eighties, were not tall women. They faced meanness above and beyond the usual heckling. Gera was told loudly by a clubowner during the game that she should "be home peeling potatoes"; she could take that, but the death threats she received were difficult to handle. Most discouraging, she found that her colleagues, the other umpires, avoided cooperating with her on the field; her umpiring partner would not even talk to her. Intimidated by the abuse she had to take, she found the stress of it all too great.

Wren, too, faced the claims of male umpires that women "did not belong" in the game as umpires. She said reporters' questions showed they were biased against her, and she stated that the media treated her "like a freak." Pam Postema was told that she'd have to be twice as good as a man to make it to the majors. She remarked that the attitude of the umpires she worked with was "If you have to, work with her, but don't help her. Don't make it easy." After a game that Postema umpired, a player named Bob Knepper stated publicly that "women should not be major league umpires or president of the United States." This sort of stupidity should elicit fines by the club or the commissioner. If a person who graduated from umpire school is hired by organized baseball, that umpire deserves respect.

Respect is something Pam Postema, the longest-lasting female umpire in OB, never got. She said she was "called every name in the book ... sworn at in two languages, blackballed by my own peers, ridiculed by fans, and abused by ballplayers and manager in five countries ... just because I was a woman" who "wanted to be a major league umpire." Postema may be right when she asserts that it's easier for a female to become an astronaut, police officer, fire fighter, or Supreme Court justice than to become a major league umpire. What organized baseball wants, she says, is "big, fat male umpires ... macho, tobacco-chewing sort of borderline alcoholics."

Another recent female umpire, Ria Cortesio, told writer Bruce Weber of the "ugliness" aimed at her during her work in the minors and the way her excellent ratings seemed unable to move her forward in her career. Weber revealed that male umpires, when asked to include women, "behaved like a bunch of brats." Perhaps they should have been told (not asked) to cooperate with her. When Cortesio was finally released, she seemed relieved: "I feel like I just got out of a bad marriage."

The reason for female umpires' difficulties isn't hard to discern. An umpire for Little League teams, Julie Zeller Ware, explains that men still want to put women in a carefully circumscribed position: "Umpiring is considered a power position, and men have been the decision makers for so very long. They want us to be teachers and nurturers. I've never understood that. I can be aggressive and competent and still do the other. I can do both, thank you." Men seem unable to understand that women have more than one facet to their characters.

But the biggest obstacle for women in breaching the baseball wall lies in organized baseball's reflection of the general masculine culture, especially its firm belief that women cannot play baseball. Back in 1911, when Albert Spalding declared that baseball was too strenuous for women, everyone seemed to believe him. Spalding's conviction has never completely died. People treasure their prejudices and refuse to give them up. Even if women do play baseball, men believe they do not and therefore cannot. As historian Marilyn French put it, "Human thought is primarily symbolic: people often cannot see something happening in front of them if it refutes their symbolic vision of a situation." In other words, women may be playing baseball, but men's mindset prevents them from accepting that reality.

One day a reporter for the *New York Times* named Deborah Solomon asked Lou Piniella, manager of the Chicago Cubs, if he thought a woman could manage a professional team. She should have known the answer in advance. Piniella replied that such a woman would need "a good bench coach ... a good hardened baseball man who would help her with the x's and o's during the ballgame. Someone who knew the intricacies in and out of the game." His assumption that not a woman alive knew those intricacies appeared to grate on his interviewer, who replied, "Plenty of women already know the intricacies of the game." Displaying his woeful ignorance, Piniella replied, "I'm not sure of that." I'd like to introduce Piniella to umpire Lisa Turbitt, or league owner, player and coach Justine Siegal, or any of the women who played in the AAPGBL.

At its worst, baseball men's view of women descends to contempt, as revealed in player Jose Canseco's book where he describes players using for sex any women that they consider fat and ugly because doing so might help them get out of a playing slump. This use of "slump busters" goes beyond the phenomenon of "baseball annies"; it's not funny, it's disgusting, because it reveals all too clearly just what some ballplayers think of women. It reminds me too much of the famous quotation from an Oxford professor addressing the female sex in 1884: "Inferior to us God made you, and our inferiors to the end of time you will remain." Not if we can help it.

Author and university professor Bill Marshall is one of those who believe that a woman will eventually reach the majors, asserting that their only problem is building the necessary speed and strength to compete with men; they have everything else, including the determination to rise above the treatment they receive at the hands of male players. Like Ila Borders, Justine Siegal has been spat upon and subjected to vulgar suggestions; Siegal explained that her response and those of others she coaches is to develop coping mechanisms for such abuse. One young player, said Siegal, views herself as a warrior, psyching herself up before each game, in part by applying black reflective shadow under her eyes to make her look and feel ready to fight. This girl asserts that "most of the mean comments just make you want to go out there and show them that you can hit the ball, that you can be a catcher. I guess it adds fuel to the fire."

Women, like blacks, are used to discrimination in baseball. When Jackie Robinson entered the majors in 1947 and the Dodgers were about to travel to St. Louis, some Cardinals thought of going on strike instead of having to play against a black man. Commissioner Ford Frick put a stop to that, reportedly remarking, "I don't care if half the league strikes. This is the United States of America, and one citizen has as much right to play as another." I wonder if any representative of organized baseball today would have the courage to claim the same right for women citizens.

Being used to discrimination does not mean accepting it. Many women play despite the effects of discrimination, even though they must possess inordinate bravery to pursue their joy. They remind me of women of the early suffrage movement, of whom historian Rosalind Miles said, "These women needed every ounce of the courage of their convictions to withstand the rearguard action mounted against them at every turn." Baseball women need the same courage.

In April of 2009 the International Baseball Federation astounded everyone by announcing that its request for baseball to be included in the 2016 Olympics would include a women's component. When asked why, the federation's president, Harvey Schiller, said the main reason was "the growth of the game ... obviously, we have a constituency which makes up women's baseball, and they're asking, 'What about us?'"

Nobody was more surprised by this recognition of baseball women than the president of the International Softball Federation, who has been so abysmally uninformed that he had to admit, "I didn't think many women were playing baseball."

13

What Baseball
Discrimination Is Like

Behind women's failure to attain full participation in baseball lies not only men's view of women but also women's view of themselves. Many girls are still being reared to think of themselves as inferior to males, not as doers but as helpers of doers — capable only of support jobs like assistant, secretary, gal Friday, and second-in-command. One history professor calls the attitude of his female students "polite self-negation" and wonders "how much has been lost" because of the culture in which they were raised.

One thing lost is confidence. In fact, I think women's self-deprecation can lead to a life of servitude. I'm reminded of a recent remark by the director of the Naples Shelter for Abused Women, who declares, "Despite our culture's so-called girl power movement, females continue to be socialized to be caring, accommodating, and passive. Too often there is a high price to pay for learning to be so nice." The price she refers to is acceptance of domestic violence.

Another price is anonymity. One of many examples I could cite is an exhibit of Tiffany lamps at the New-York Historical Society, which revealed that many Tiffany lamps were not even made by Louis Tiffany; they were designed and executed by the anonymous women in his workshop, many of them by a woman finally identified as Clara Driscoll, a gifted artist and craftswoman. Her artistic originality was kept hidden because Louis Tiffany did not want it known.

Those of us inspired by Elizabeth Cady Stanton's famous essay "Solitude of Self" know that for full development of their possibilities in any field, women must cultivate independence rather than passivity. I have met many women my age who profess to be astounded when they learn, for example, that I have traveled to other countries alone; they firmly believed that for traveling they needed a male escort. They have missed a lot by being raised to think that they could not act independently. These women are akin to those of the nineteenth century, who could not speak in public because they knew they would be considered brazen hussies if they stood up in a roomful of people and spoke their minds, so they trained themselves to remain silent. In 2009 a woman who took two baseball trips with Jay Smith Sports Travel & Tours felt she had to reassure other women in her letter to the company, which she signed "Barbara A.": "In case you have other single women who are apprehensive about traveling alone on a tour, please don't hesitate to use me as a reference. I have never felt alone or awkward, and it's easy to fit right in." It's sad that in the year 2009 Barbara felt it necessary to assure other women that traveling "alone"—with a group of other like-minded fans—is not difficult.

Women do take part in Elderhostel trips related to baseball, and a few women have attended fantasy camps. Dennis McCroskey, who has attended many of these occasions, says he has often encountered one or two women at a camp. Sometimes a woman will attend with her husband, and once two couples came on their honeymoons. Another time, along with thirteen father-son combinations, a father-daughter team attended. As for their skill in playing, McCroskey rates most of the women as not very good, but "maybe one in five is a good player, some better than most of the guys." However, women who sign up for a fantasy camp experience might want to steel themselves for the macho atmosphere, in case their coach turns out to be Steve Yeager, former Dodgers catcher, who directed a group of twelve men at the fiftieth, and probably final, fantasy camp at Dodgertown in Vero Beach. Yeager labeled as "pussy" any weak efforts on the part of his charges, and he cheered them on against their opponents by shouting, "Let's cut off their dicks and bury 'em!" Women's style of coaching is rather different.

Women have been more successful at another fantasy activity: forming their own vintage teams and playing by vintage rules. A few have joined men's vintage teams, wearing men's uniforms, but most vintage players form women's teams and play against other women, wearing nineteenth-century costumes, playing by rules of the 1800s, and using nineteenth-century baseball terms in addressing each other and the umpire. Women's appreciation for the fun this sort of activity can engender is shown by the rather tongue-in-cheek name of one New York state team: Priscilla Porter's Astonishing Ladies Base Ball Club. The Porter club celebrates the famous Miss Porter's School, where women played baseball in the 1860s—a truly astonishing activity for the times. Nancy Rhoades, who manages the team, says most of the Porter members "are getting long in the tooth, but a few are still able to run the bases

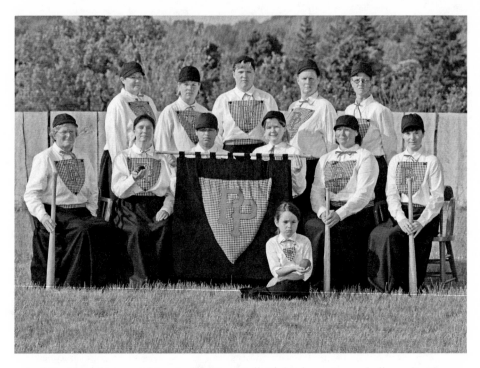

Miss Porter's Astonishing Ladies Base Ball Club plays vintage ball on the Great Meadow at Genesee Country Village and Museum, Mumford, New York, using rules of the 1860s. This photo was taken on the Fourth of July in 2002 (courtesy of the photographer, Grant Taylor).

with their skirts flying." The Porter club represents the school, while another team, the Brooks Grove Belles, is composed of women who play ball casually and for fun. Both teams play in a park-like setting on the Great Meadow of the Genesee Country Village and Museum at Mumford, New York, and occasionally Miss Porter's club plays against men's vintage teams, too.

Proof of the gain in popularity of vintage ball for women is that furnishing uniforms for vintage teams has become a nice business. Paula Weaver, with her husband Ken, manufactures uniforms for women who want authentic nineteenth-century women's uniforms. The Weavers prepare uniforms for people who love the history of women's baseball, for museums, for retired players who want copies of their original uniforms, and even for weddings! They make copies of the original All-American Girls Professional Baseball League uniforms under a license granted by the AAGPBL.

Vintage ball play is more recreation than it is competition. Women can handle either. People like Justine Siegal have inspired many women to realize that they, too, can be strong, can feel independent, and can engage in their pleasurable pastimes without giving up any aspect of their femininity. If you look at photos of these women, you get an inkling of the confidence they have, not only in their skill but in their attractiveness. I believe these players will never look in a mirror and say to themselves, "I wish I were beautiful." They are sure of themselves. Young women of the AAGPBL learned this composure from the older ones who moved fearlessly into their new positions and served as role models for the teenagers on the teams.

Without multi-generational role models like professional women ballplayers who can be held up as examples, most women have been brainwashed to think of themselves as weak and unable to participate in anything as challenging physically as baseball because it might endanger their babymaking equipment. Men, on the other hand, play sports because they are expected to play sports. As Rosalind Miles points out, men have for centuries allowed themselves to engage in sports "without any apparent harm to their organs of generation."

No convincing evidence of danger to women's feminine organs from playing sports has ever been produced. If you check on the post-career lives of the alumni of the All-American Girls Baseball League of the 1940s by studying the books about them, you come away with the understanding that those women, who certainly played intensely, did have children if they wanted children, some as many as five. Does this sound as though playing ball hurt their generative organs?

Biological differences between men and women are not nearly as great as physicians have supposed in the past and certainly do not prevent them from playing baseball. Historian Barbara Ehrenreich, in tallying the specifics of a hundred and fifty years of "the experts' advice to women," showed the so-called experts of the past as completely without knowledge. Their advice led to advantages not for women but for men because it kept women from acting independently, since they thought they could not do so. Crystal Eastman, an early lecturer on women's rights, asserted "women's right to physical equality with men" and pointed out that "when women were expected to be agile, they became agile." Expectation remains a powerful stimulus. We should long since have reached the point where women's success in every field, including the playing of baseball, can be expected.

Perhaps we should recall the ancient Greek women of the city-state of Sparta. These women could boast a measure of freedom that even today seems unusual. Spartan women of the era around 500 B.C. were constantly at the gym, where they removed their restrictive clothing and wrestled naked with the men. Today some women take part in wrestling, boxing, and football, but others have a difficult time penetrating the national game.

The fiction that sports damages women's gynecological organs continued to be accepted almost to the present. When the young women of the Onondaga Nation near Syracuse, New York, started playing lacrosse in 1987, the clan mothers objected, asserting that physical exertion would "affect the girls' ability to procreate," going so far as lying down on the girls' sports field in protest. The girls gave in, but for at least one girl "my heart broke into a thousand pieces.... For me that was my opportunity to go traveling and play the game I loved. We got a taste of it; then it was taken away." Not until twenty years later did the girls of the clan prevail and receive permission to put together another team.

Not only do some people fear for girls' sexual organs; many think women's bodies are so different from men's that they cannot throw a baseball the way men can, in the amazing belief that women's "shoulder joints are hinged differently." As if we were a different species! Even if these people see girls pitching the way men pitch, they fail to believe their eyes. Any person trained in anatomy can assure nonbelievers that no structural reason keeps women from throwing as men do. Women who play baseball by the same rules as men do throw this way every day.

Moreover, research conducted by the Women's Sports Foundation and others has shown that girls involved in physical activities are healthier than others and later in life suffer from fewer physical problems. They even tend to be more successful academically.

Just as women have proven their ability to play baseball, they have proven their ability to do science, although a recent study by the National Academy of Science documents continued "widespread bias against women in science and engineering." Women are no longer prevented from studying these subjects, although they were in the past; yet most people seem to believe that women are innately unable to handle them, as they are innately unable to play baseball. A book on women scientists by Margaret Wertheim shows that women who love math and science continue to evoke "antipathy" inspired by "deep-seated prejudice." Another woman in science, Carol Hanson, who discovered quark jets, says that when women are awarded prizes in the field, they are "often treated worse." All this should sound familiar to baseball women. Girls who become stars on school teams inspire hate and envy on the part of boys, who have been taught to disdain girls.

Women engineers, despite a large rise in those obtaining doctorates in the field, remain a tiny minority on college faculties. Male engineers fear that because the American Institute of Physics is studying the possibility of a bias against hiring women, a quota system might be imposed; in fact, one suggestion to achieve more equality on campuses was to apply Title Nine to science departments in order to create equal opportunities for women. Said one scientist, "In sports, they had to eliminate a lot of male teams to achieve Title

Nine parity. It'll be devastating to American science if every male-dominated field has to be calibrated to women's level of interest." Right now, of course, every male-dominated field is calibrated to men's level of interest, but that seems to be okay with most engineers.

One day I picked up one of the many Christmas gift catalogs I receive through the mail and found it full of gadgets and clothing especially designed to appeal to engineers. All the shirts buttoned from left to right, and attractive ties were pictured, but no women's scarves. I finally found a photo of a woman, but she was there only to model a T-shirt; that was all she had on. Nothing in the catalog was designed to appeal to female engineers; the catalog's editor obviously believed that women didn't enter that field.

Catalogs designed to appeal to baseball players and fans always center upon T-shirts, caps, ties, bottle openers, and cuff links. I once saw a pair of earrings advertised, but they looked like little boxes instead of little baseballs. Luckily, a friend made a pair of metal baseball earrings for me so that I can demonstrate my interest in the national game. One company at Cooperstown offers a beautiful bracelet with a gold baseball, but its price puts it out of reach for a great many female fans. The new MLB.com Shop does offer some women's apparel, notably a bikini suitable only for teenagers.

Baseball discrimination is merely part of the general discrimination that still hampers women. Those just out of college who work full time already earn less than their male colleagues, even when they work in the same field. Males in every field continue throughout their working lives to make more money than women. Why should men stop discriminating against women? Sexism pays. One study proved that "sexist American men" earn an average of almost $12,000 a year more than non-sexist men! In baseball, of course, women's pay is probably non-existent; women pay to play if they cannot get business backing. Those at the top levels of men's baseball receive far more money than our most important government officials.

It should be clear to everyone that discrimination against women in baseball is part of what women have had to cope with ever since early religionists decided that women should be mere chattels of men. Women's attempts to receive equal treatment at golf clubs, as employees, in politics, and in virtually every field continue into the present. In 2008 a champion amateur golfer, Elaine Joyce, sued for and won the right to play in a tournament on her local public course where male members tried to freeze her out. She is like baseball players in desiring to play with those who perform at her level. "In any sport I have ever played," she said, "the only way you get better is if you play with people who are at least as good if not better than you. That is how you get better in basketball ... baseball, any sport." Women have even taken private golf clubs to court in order to get weekend tee times, membership, and access to dining rooms. Overt discrimination still happens in fields other than sports. In 2009 the Sheriff's Office of Sarasota County, Florida, lost a costly gender discrimination suit instituted by a woman who is a 24-year veteran of the office when her attorney showed how the sheriff manipulated the system to promote men over better-qualified women and demoted the women when they complained.

The 2007 U.S. Supreme Court case of *Ledbetter v. Goodyear Tire & Rubber Co.* demonstrates that women and girls often fail to realize that they are the subjects of exploitation. An example from sports is the cheerleading tradition. Some schools concentrate not on forming girls' baseball teams but on creating girls' cheerleading squads designed to support male players. In 2007, after a discrimination complaint surfaced in the New York state high school, the girls' cheerleading squad was dispatched to support girls' basketball games as well as the games of men's teams. The cheerleaders, used to showing off in front of the guys, were taken aback. Half of them quit. A cheerleading captain lamented that interest in cheerleading was declining. My reaction to her dismay is: Get used to it. Women players deserve as much support as the men. I like the approach of Donna Lopiano, head of the Women's Sports Foundation, who refused to permit her daughter to join in cheerleading until "boy cheerleaders were cheering for the girls' teams."

Women aren't expected to enter any aspect of baseball, including management. Lack of access to the top levels of baseball is comparable to lack of access to the top levels of American society in general. In 2008 the United States was ranked twenty-seventh in women's access to executive government and corporate posts — surely the most power-laden positions in our country.

In the past, a few women entered organized baseball as part of the administration of clubs, most of them through inheritance from their husbands or fathers. Probably the most hands-on female clubowner of the past was Effa Manley, who worked closely and effectively with her husband in running the Newark Eagles of the Negro National League and took over the club after her husband's passing. Popular with the players, she fought for the rights of the black leagues both before and after Jackie Robinson left for white baseball. Manley, a true activist, made such an impression on baseball as a whole that in 2006 she became the first woman elected to the National Baseball Hall of Fame in Cooperstown.

One female clubowner, Jamie McCourt, was for a time president of the Los Angeles Dodgers, part of a similar husband-and-wife combination; the McCourts bought the team and operated it together. Jamie said her husband Frank, whose title was "owner and chairman," was the visionary, and that she "actualized the vision." Her work included overseeing all aspects of the business, from leading weekly meetings with senior management to launching new strategies, one of which was to initiate events for women. McCourt knew that "very few women are visible in baseball" and wanted to design programs to bring them closer to the Dodgers. She realized that accepting a woman as leader isn't easy for men, and she admitted that "any woman who's in business has experienced various kinds of biases." Her opinion on how to combat bias was to "focus on your job and do it well." That tactic has not always served her purpose, as Jim Nemerovski found when he watched the 2008 World Series. The camera, says Nemerovski, in panning the audience during the second game in Chicago, focused on Frank McCourt while the sportscaster described him as "president and chairman of the club." Nemerovski found it "enraging" that the camera and voiceover failed to move over and include his wife Jamie, who was sitting next to Frank. Crediting her husband with being in sole charge, says Nemerovski, "did a disservice to all that she and other women have accomplished, especially in the front office of Major League Baseball." All this happened, however, before Frank McCourt, declaring himself sole owner, fired his wife and started divorce proceedings.

When Marge Schott took over her husband's estate, she became an active part-owner of the Cincinnati Reds, but her decisions often proved unpopular, especially because of her money-saving attitude toward employees. Worse, opposition to her use of negative terms for minorities and her other peculiar and offensive actions at the park earned her a year's suspension and eventually forced her out.

Schott acted differently with Cincinnati as a whole. She gave millions to charity and performed other acts of kindness. At her funeral Thomas Turner, who came to Cincinnati from the Negro Leagues, defended her, claiming that OB "gave her a dirty deal ... all over a few words. She was a woman in a man's business, a minority. She was good for the Reds, good for the city. But they looked past all that. They did her wrong." Turner thus saw beyond Schott's faults and realized that if she had been a man, her shortcomings might have been overlooked.

Linda Alvarado became a considerable asset to organized baseball when she joined an ownership group to take charge of the Colorado Rockies. Alvarado, who owns a seventh of the club, is proud of her Hispanic heritage and her status as the first woman to invest in a major league franchise with her own money, earned through her successful construction firm and other ventures, rather than through inheritance or joint ownership with her husband. She credits her success to her mother, who absolved her from housework so that she could "try things" unconventional for girls.

Alvarado, who was once captain of her high school baseball team, believes that "construction and sports are the last bastions of male dominance." She reveals that in her former jobs she experienced a "frosty attitude from co-workers" and became the target of "discriminatory attitudes," especially on job sites, because she failed to fit the "stereotype of women being secretaries and Hispanics being laborers." She asserts that having grown up in a competitive male environment, she is "comfortable working with men." But she knows that women have a long way to go. "What I still hope for and long for," she says, "is the day when people will truly be judged not based on where they came from and their gender but really on their ability."

In recent years women have entered baseball club organizations at an unexpected level. At the Boston Red Sox, the entire legal staff of four is female. Elaine Weddington Steward, like one other woman in that group, bears the title of vice president and club counsel. Steward became the first African American woman to hold such a high post. Kim Ng may move beyond her. After seventeen years in baseball administration, and now working as assistant general manager of the Yankees, Ng is in line to become the first female general manager in MLB. "She knows her job; she's done the work," commented Jeanie Buss, vice president of business operations for the Lakers in the National Basketball Association.

Another reason Ng has a good shot at the job is that she is rated by a former general manager as "smart, tough, and strong." But a current team executive warned that baseball is one of "the most male-dominated, narrow-minded, testosterone-filled, non-feminine-traits places in the world." A female executive for another team brought up the old truism that every woman who works knows: that "women have to be more qualified than the men." Another described the world that Ng has entered as "a good ol' boy business" in which the men demand that a woman "play by their rules." On the credit side, she pointed out that "you don't have to be a player to understand marketing."

Ng's worst moment in her baseball position was the day a former big-league pitcher, Bill Singer, then acting as special assistant to the general manager of the New York Mets, stopped her during meetings in Phoenix, demanding to know who she was, why she was there, and what her heritage was. After her patient responses, he mocked her in gibberish-speak that was supposed to approximate Chinese. The national story that resulted caused Singer to be fired. Ng unaccountably believes that Singer's reaction to her presence stemmed more from gender than from race. But on second thought, she may be right: Singer might not have ridiculed the ethnicity of a man, especially one his own size.

Observers think Ng has only a small chance to make it up to the general manager level because "the knives will be out for her," since "most men are threatened" by a woman who "has some smarts." Ng responds that she has to "ignore a lot" and "just gut it out." She plans to keep going "until it stops being fun."

An aspect of baseball that has long been a closed shop against women is sports journalism. Women weren't admitted to membership in the National Press Club until 1971 (sixteen years after black men finally got in). Women reporters proved to be unwelcome in grandstand press boxes, and male writers often told them so in no uncertain terms. Baseball news and commentary, like the rest of the news and commentary, has long been monopolized by men. As Carol Jenkins, an award-winning journalist, put it, "We're 51 percent of the population and we have only 3 percent of the clout positions [in media] ... so 97 percent of everything you know about who you are, what your country is about, and your place in the world comes from the male perspective."

Even syndicated columnists feel discrimination if they are women. Says Marie Cocco, a political columnist, "What I confronted for the whole time I've been a syndicated columnist is the quota of one. Typically, if an editor is already running [one woman's column], he will not run another woman.... Let me know when you meet the first editor that says, 'Aw gee, I already have a white male, I just can't take another one.'"

Women reporters in sports television still find it difficult to "sit in the big boy's chair" (provide play-by-play rather than commentary), says reporter Mary Carillo. And of course you've noticed that any women who begin to age in front of the television cameras are replaced by youthful ones. What happened to the wise old crone of ancient societies, who engendered the respect of the entire community? Her place was taken by Howard Cosell.

As they have been from the beginning, sports writers and editors remain mostly white and male. In 1949, when I first walked into the all-male newsroom of *The Sporting News*, I thought that the startled members of the staff would either choke on their coffee or swallow their cigars. After I began my research on one of the microfilm machines, however, they seemed to forget that I was there.

The following year, when I first entered the library of the Hall of Fame at Cooperstown to perform research, the library consisted of one room above the hall itself and was presided over by a retired sportswriter named Sid Keener. When I came in, he gazed at me as though I had lost my way and was looking for the department that sold ladies' hats. But after I took down a few boxes of the correspondence of Garry Herrmann, chairman of the National Commission back in the nineteenth century, and began my work, Keener seemed to accept my presence. I learned that once I had gained entry, just going ahead about my business without comment, the way Lizzie Murphy did, worked wonders.

What aspiring women newspaper reporters suffered in their early years is the same kind of discrimination women ballplayers underwent. In the 1940s

I became acquainted with a woman reporter whose later career would include ejection from the press box of a major league park because of her gender. I met her because during college I worked as a gofer (known as a "copy boy") on the *Cleveland News*, where I noticed that only two women ever appeared on the office floor: the one who handled social news and wrote obituaries, and another who had, against all odds, become a beat reporter. Her name was Doris O'Donnell, and she became my idol. As for the sports department, it consisted of a group of men.

In 1967, when I no longer lived in Cleveland, O'Donnell's editor thought of a gimmick: he would assign her to travel with the Indians on an eastern swing. Despite minor problems, all went pretty well until she reached Boston, where the local reporters officially banned her from the press box. It happened again in New York, where Joe Trimble, who had coincidentally been a boyhood friend of my late husband Harold Seymour and was chairman of the New York Baseball Writers Association, kept the discrimination barrier high. Manager Kerby Farrell of the Indians challenged O'Donnell, "Why don't you get married and raise a family instead of bollyfoxing around with ballplayers?" The word "bollyfoxing," I discovered, can be defined as "wasting time" or "fooling around." To Farrell and others, women reporters don't work, they fool around.

O'Donnell hadn't realized how serious the matter had become to male sports writers, who firmly believed that they must protect the press box as a male prerogative. In a piece for *The Sporting News* she described sports writers as "snobbish hermits" who were out of step with the changing world of reporting, which by then included several female sports writers. Back in Cleveland, she was stonewalled by sports writers Hal Lebovitz of the *News* and Frank Gibbons of the *Press*, while writer Gordon Cobbledick of the *Plain Dealer* declared that she had "no place" with the male writers. And she thought they were her friends! Writer Dan Daniels, president of the Baseball Writers Association, announced to the association that "women are not wholly qualified to be baseball writers." These discriminatory words and actions should sully the reputations of well-known writers like Daniels and Cobbledick, but few people know about them because males are in charge of the sports news. Today women make up just over 12 percent of the sports staffs of news media. Linda Robertson, a sports columnist with the *Miami Herald*, put it clearly: "We're still bumping up against the glass ceiling." So when in 2008 a sports reporter from my local paper showed up to interview me, I was truly surprised to find that she was a young woman.

Another aspect of women reporters' relations with baseball is the male assumption that women want to enter sports locker rooms not to search out stories, like their male counterparts, but to look at men's bodies. Women journalists have long since tired of hearing this accusation. Susan Fornoff, a sports journalist who survived harassment and abuse, wrote a book called *Lady in the Locker Room* and co-founded the Association for Women in Sports Media to combat discrimination against women sports journalists.

The most respected woman sports writer is the late Mary Garber, a pioneer who for years was not allowed in the press box; she sat uncomplainingly in the stands to do her job. Garber started to write sports full time in 1946, at a time when coaches often treated her condescendingly and fellow sports writers ignored her. For years the press box tag she wore included the printed note, "Women and children are not allowed in the press box." Garber won more than 40 writing awards. According to Tim Crothers in *Sports Illustrated*, she was "the underdog reporter who developed into a champion of the overlooked." Her greatest achievement may be that she paved the way for other women sports writers.

Garber covered black sports when others neglected them. Over the years she became interested in women's sports, too, and saw a "tremendous" improvement in this field. Women's sports, she pointed out to those who needed reminding, is "not a social event, it's a competition." Garber died in 2008, and today's Association for Women in Sports Media, formed in 1987, often celebrates her accomplishments by describing her with its acronym, AWSM (awesome).

The women who pioneered in the media despite all odds, like the female players who challenged organized baseball by accepting contracts to play in the minors, and like the female children and teenagers who want to play baseball with their peers, deserve recognition and support rather than hostility and backbiting. Their progress since the 1990s has been truly admirable.

One thing women sports writers have been unable to accomplish is coverage of the vast world of women's baseball playing, which remains invisible in the mass media. Too often I have tracked down women's baseball tournaments and other newsworthy events only by searching the internet or by emailing the people involved; nothing appears in the national media about women's national and international baseball, even if the team representing the United States in the World Classic wins the competition. If a mention of an individual girl's or woman's accomplishment appears in the press, as it occasionally does, it's made to seem an exception. That's because men control sports assignments; women reporters cannot make their own decisions on what to cover. Women sports journalists therefore can have little effect on bringing women's high-level baseball into the mainstream of sports journalism. Women who play the game remain frustrated with the lack of media attention and seem to have given up trying to get it.

To the media, women's leagues and clubs and activities are non-existent.

But women are used to being invisible, their accomplishments unrecognized. Historians like Rosalind Miles, in her witty book *The Women's History of the World,* laments not only the "perennial absence [of women] from the history books" but also their absence "from the records of contemporary experience" such as newspapers and magazines, records that could result from the "vigorous and self-renewing contact with each other such as men have always enjoyed through work and public activity." So while men are enjoying these "vigorous contacts" with each other in baseball and being recognized in "the records of contemporary experience," a lot of women are playing their favorite game in obscurity. Future historians trying to piece together what women have been doing with their lives in this period of history are going to have a tough time following the invisible thread leading to the spool of women's "significant activities."

Have you ever read an account of a women's baseball tournament in *Sports Illustrated?* Of course not. Not even the *New York Times* covers these events. For many years I have subscribed to the *Times,* and I have yet to see any news of the women's baseball leagues, their tournaments, games, baseball camps for girls, trips to play in New Zealand or Japan or Australia or India — nothing. Thinking that perhaps I was just missing the stories, I registered for the paper's service called Times Direct, through which subscribers with interest in a particular subject can be alerted to articles about that subject in the current issue of the paper. Hoping to receive frequent heads-up emails about articles that interest me, I listed my email address with the key words "women" and "baseball." As a result, I have often received emails directing me to articles in the current issue. Guess how many of these articles have actually contained a story about a women's baseball league or club event. None. If the article I was directed to did mention a woman, its subject was something other than baseball. Once in 2009 I received an email pointing me to a story that actually told about a high school girl who played baseball, but her story was made to seem exceptional.

As Professor Anne Aronson put it, baseball women are merely occasional and "token" celebrities in the media. Aronson wonders when women's baseball will be covered not in the lifestyle section of the paper but in the sports section, where it belongs. Even Hollywood is moving ahead of the media and beginning to pay some attention to women who love sports. *Bend It Like Beckham* isn't an American story, but it might as well be, since it shows how men raise barriers to keep out the girls and young women who love to play sports. Those who stick to the sport they love and succeed deserve encouragement rather than shrugs or sneers. Media attention would help.

Although I subscribe to *Sports Illustrated,* the magazine's emphasis on hard-driving professional men and those expected to join their ranks leaves me cold. What about those Americans who play for enjoyment? Where is their national magazine? For a while Time Inc. published a magazine called *S.I. Women,* patterned after *Sports Illustrated,* but it hardly lasted long enough to get going. The idea behind the magazine was to cover "women for whom sport is not a means to an end — an ab or a biceps — but a way of living one's life." I guess that ideal proved too distant from the usual professional goals of fame and fortune for *S.I. Women* to become viable financially. Women who play baseball think not of abs and biceps, or even of fame and fortune, but of pleasure in competing with others as skilled as they are at playing the national game.

I never truly understood the assertion that women are "the second sex" until I began to study women in baseball and saw how their experience fits in with the history of discrimination against women in general. This discrimination is real and multifaceted, and it presents a huge barrier to the pursuit of their passion for the national game.

14

Women Fans Follow
Their Passion

Many women see themselves as devoted fans of the national game. Even if they never played baseball themselves, they love to watch their favorite male players in action and see exciting games. They get caught up in pennant races and thrill to the World Series. Women don't generally watch as much TV sports as men do — except for the Olympics, which has a huge female audience — but women baseball fans can be as intense as men.

These women never thought of taking part on the field, or if they did, it was only casually, at a Fourth of July picnic or a family get-together. Instead, they enjoy attending as many baseball events as they can, watching games on television, visiting baseball exhibits, even reading about baseball and playing various board games.

Women collect baseball cards, too, sometimes as an income-earning hobby. Barbara Ann Artusa and her husband buy boxes of baseball cards for as much as $1,800, then look through them for something special. Once Barbara Ann found a baseball card in which the maker had inserted a hair from the head of Abraham Lincoln, along with his signature. She sold the card for $24,000, planning to donate some of the money to cancer research, but she thought she would buy more cards with the rest.

Some women take part in fantasy baseball. Carol Bengle Gilbert, who writes for the web, once worked in an office where fantasy baseball remained the prime topic of conversation from April to October. She selected a team and entered it into the competition, but she was rejected from the men's fantasy league because the men disapproved of her selecting players for her team randomly instead of composing her team carefully and deliberately, as they did. She points out that her method is more logical than theirs; since players in MLB are forever being traded, chance is apt to dictate who plays on a team. Gilbert thinks the rules of fantasy baseball are too stringent. Besides, she says, she would also like to add the rule that "any player who spits on the field gets a three-inning time out," but that seems to be a bit of humbug. Still, she may be right in believing that tightly controlled games stifle creativity. But they do offer opportunities for competition, and some women enjoy being competitive.

Women play fantasy baseball with boyfriends or husbands; others have joined leagues that consist mostly of men. For their skill at playing fantasy baseball, a few have garnered praise through comments on a web site called Fantasy Baseball Café. Women's presence also alters the tone of league interactions. One man thought that having a woman on the message board contributed a different dynamic to the game: "I have noticed that I swear less on the board."

Women sometimes take part in games like those played with the popular dice-and-baseball card game called APBA, the initials standing for "American Professional Baseball Association." Now fans of the APBA game have something new to try: a version of the game featuring cards for some of the stars of the All-American Girls Professional Baseball League. This version centers on women's professional clubs that played during the two years 1952 (Fort Wayne, Rockford, Kalamazoo, South Bend, Grand Rapids, and Battle Creek) and 1954 (Fort Wayne, Rockford, Kalamazoo, South Bend, and Grand Rapids). The player cards included in this set therefore include the records of such players as the three famous Dorothys (Kamenshek, Schroeder, and Wiltse Collins), along with other names that were well known among fans of these clubs, like Rose Gacioch, Dolly Brumfield, Jean Faut, June Peppas, Bonnie Baker, Doris Sams, Jean Cione, Sophie Kurys, Lois Youngen — two hundred nine cards in all, but for some players you'll find two or even three cards.

These baseball cards omit the likenesses of the chosen players but do give their positions and playing records, along with numbers used in the game in order to earn scores. A spare pack of player cards that came to me with this set represent the male players who took part in organized baseball's 1953 World Series, the New York Yankees and the Brooklyn Dodgers, so those cards include players like Campanella, Erskine, Furillo, Hodges, Podres, Reese, Robinson, Roe, and Snider for the Dodgers, along with players like Berra, Ford, Lopat, Mize, Raschi, and Rizzuto for the Yankees. Notice how much more familiar those names are? I'm not sure why I need this additional men's set if I want to play APBA with cards describing the women of the AAGPBL, but perhaps the makers thought I might get bored with the women's cards. I won't. Besides, looking at their records and deciding which players to put on my two teams helps me learn more about these talented women and their skills.

The president of APBA International reports, however, that the APBA set for the women's league, which was inspired by a customer, "has not been a fast mover and has been received with minimal interest." Here is where the women's league alumni could use some promotional help: how about starting women's APBA leagues with the set featuring AABPBL women? The stars of the league could become better known if groups of women formed organizations to play the APBA game.

Like men, women fans engage in many other baseball activities — attending baseball exhibits, going to lectures, showing up at SABR conventions, traveling to Elderhostel events, and scheduling trips to baseball museums, often with their entire families, because as polls have often revealed, women usually make the entertainment selections for their families.

Doubtless the most important exhibit for their gender has become the one celebrating baseball women at the Baseball Hall of Fame at Cooperstown. Women fans find this exhibit intriguing. The Hall of Fame's display on women in baseball would not have come into being without the hard work and promotion by alumni of the All-American Girls Professional Baseball League.

At periodic reunions of AAGPBL players, certain members like Dottie Wiltse Collins often spoke of their desire to preserve and promote the league's history by finding a place for league archives to be preserved. Player Sharon Roepke visited the Hall of Fame in 1976 and found "virtually nothing on women" or the league and wondered why women were considerably less visible in the Hall of Fame than were players of the Negro Leagues. Another alumna of the women's league wanted to know, "Where [in the name of this institution] does it say 'Men's Baseball Hall of Fame'?" Nowhere, of course.

When Roepke and Rita Meyer came to the Hall in 1984 to contribute a set of the AAGPBL baseball cards, Sharon asked the Hall's curator, Ted Spencer, if he would consider mounting an exhibit on women's baseball that would feature the AAGPBL. Spencer had to admit that he knew little about the league, so the women gave him information. Eventually, Spencer realized that one of his schoolteachers, Mary Pratt, must have played for the league, and he became interested in the exhibit idea. But nothing happened; not until a couple of years later, when Spencer was queried by a woman reporter for the *Los Angeles Times,* did he say that Cooperstown would like to present a woman's exhibit. The AAGPBL then selected a committee that began work on supplying what the Hall of Fame would need for an exhibit.

But some league members began insisting that the Hall of Fame induct all the players of the AAGPBL and install individual plaques for them, as it did for star male players; others wanted only the league's best players honored with induction into the Hall of Fame. Spencer couldn't see either of those events happening; he said Major League Baseball "wouldn't stand for it." And of course Major League Baseball thought of itself as owning the Hall of Fame. So the league's individual players were never honored with regular Hall of Fame plaques, but the exhibit eventually included one plaque bearing the names of 555 of the women who played in the league (although there may have been as many as 600 who played).

Sensibly, Spencer told the league members that the Hall saw the women's league as only part of the "landscape" of all American women who played from the mid–1880s and said he wanted to honor those earlier pioneers as well, those who played in the face of great social opposition. He admitted that the AAGPBL represented "the apex of the story" of women's baseball but refused to budge from the goal of including all women players, not just the league, in the exhibit. Spencer, to his credit, thus exhibited a view of women's baseball broader than either MLB's or the AAGPBL's.

The holdouts from the women's league gave in, and the Hall agreed to an exhibit of about eight feet by eight feet. The league alumni sent appropriate memorabilia, and when the exhibit had been mounted, a hundred and fifty of them, with families and well-wishers, arrived for its unveiling in early November of 1988.

Ted Spencer expected four hundred visitors to the unveiling, but twelve hundred interested people arrived. The women who had played in the AAGPBL and came to the unveiling, overwhelmed with joy at their public recognition, hugged and laughed and cried and sang their league song several times. For them, the acknowledgment of their contribution to baseball represented the thrill of a lifetime. "The emotion that day," said Spencer in 2007, "was incredible. I'll never forget it." Merrie Fidler, the historian of the AAGPBL, who attended, saw the players' delight and wrote that they could finally "revel in the honor of being recognized as a part of baseball's history," and they could realize that future generations of girls might be inspired by their accomplishments to know that they, too, could play the game.

What struck player Dottie Collins about the occasion was the reaction of the players' children, many of whom had no idea of their mothers' important contribution to the world of baseball. Collins said she found the moment immensely gratifying because many kids assumed that their moms had played softball. They could hardly believe what they were experiencing on that exciting weekend when their mothers were honored for their contribution to baseball during what Collins termed "the most meaningful days of our lives."

The exhibit demonstrating the extent of women's baseball became hugely attractive to fans of both sexes. In 2004 Ted Spencer admitted that the Hall of Fame's exhibit on women had become the most popular one ever, "by a thousand percent." I believe that's because earlier exhibits merely reviewed what fans already knew; the women's exhibit taught them something entirely new about baseball. Moreover, Spencer knew he had done the right thing. "I realized then," he said, "that we had changed the whole direction of the museum. Because it really brought home to me how important the game is culturally. We always knew how important it was, but this really drove it home." What he meant was that including attention to women showed baseball's importance in the general culture and not just the masculine part of that culture. Visitors to the exhibit have abounded, and in twenty-two years of working at the Hall, Spencer never received so many letters about anything as he did about the women's exhibit. Jeff Idelson, president of the Hall of Fame and Museum, wrote in 2007 that "not even in their wildest dreams could the administration have known the type of impact" the 1988 exhibit inspired.

Dottie Collins truly appreciated the Cooperstown tribute to the women's league. To her, the film *A League of Their Own* was secondary in importance to the exhibit: "Being accepted by Cooperstown was the greatest thing that happened to any of us." But not everyone appreciated the women's exhibit. The umpire Pam Postema, whose picture and brief biography was eventually included, thought the exhibit merely perpetuated the myth that baseball is open-minded and willing to include women in its power structure. "Baseball and the men who run it," she declared, "couldn't care less about equal rights." I'm sure they don't, but I believe that including the exhibit has educational value for those who until then had no idea of women's contribution to the national game.

After the appearance of the film *A League of Their Own* in 1992, the surge of interest in women made it clear to Hall administrators that they couldn't ignore women's baseball, and they started a collection of library files about the women and girls who played the game, or even those who wanted to play and were unable to gain access to teams. The Hall now owns AAGPBL clippings, scrapbooks, photo files, and artifacts like schedules and even jewelry, which players had designed for themselves to symbolize their special experience. Male players of organized baseball could show off baseball rings; the women had special charm bracelets, pendants, watches, and even players' rings. Merrie Fidler states that the few items relating to women that the Hall owned in the 1950s were "rather well buried" until the league's recognition by the Hall in 1988. It was the work of the AAGPBL that opened the tomb so that they could rise again.

The AAGPBL finally established its permanent archives at the Northern Indiana Historical Society Museum. Most of the work in gaining a place for women at the Hall of Fame and establishing an archival site in Indiana was accomplished by the women themselves, as alumnae of the league, and the members managed it by networking and through the circulation of newsletters among the alumnae. Any time a newspaper picked up a story about the league or a league player, it was mentioned or republished in a newsletter.

Inevitably, modern media became intrigued with the league. About the same time as the Hall of Fame's first women's exhibit opened, a doctoral student at Northwestern University, Janis Taylor, produced a documentary about the women's league called *When Diamonds Were a Girl's Best Friend,* containing clips from the National Archives and home movies as well as interviews with AAGPBL players and scenes from an alumnae game. And Kelly Candaele, a filmmaker whose mother, Helen Callahan, had played with the Fort Wayne Daisies of the AAGPBL, became seriously interested in the league. Candaele, along with his girlfriend, Kim, produced a documentary, which they called *A League of Their Own,* based primarily on the events of the AAGPBL's reunion of 1986 in Fort Wayne, Indiana.

Candaele's documentary led to interest by Hollywood film director Penny Marshall, who had also been inspired by attending the unveiling of the women's exhibit at the Hall of Fame. For Marshall, Candaele wrote a story outline about two sisters, both playing in the league, whose sports rivalry with each other nearly led to a permanent split. He got the idea from his mother's life, because she and her sister Margaret participated together in every high school sport and then became the first sister combination in the women's league. Candaele's script about the sisters' rivalry became the basis for Marshall's Hollywood movie of the same name, produced by Columbia Pictures and released in 1992.

Of course a big, expensive, Hollywood-sponsored movie featuring well-known actors can attract a lot more attention to women's baseball than can a documentary. And it did. Marshall's film has become a classic. Watching it was the way most Americans discovered that women actually played baseball in the past. The film even persuaded Coors Brewing Company to sponsor the Colorado Bullets for three seasons as the first professional women's team since the days of the AAGPBL.

The release of the movie in 1992 caused another flurry of interest in the women's league. It revealed for the American public something that had remained below the radar for half a century. Newspapers contacted local players and wrote features about them as well about the league and its history. Players received honors from their cities and their states. Player Terry Donahue credits the film with opening women's baseball history for posterity: "If it hadn't been for that movie, we all would've been dead and gone and no one would have ever known about us." That would certainly have been a shame.

The Hall of Fame has continued to develop its interest in the history of women's baseball. In 2006 the Hall expanded its exhibit about women in baseball into three main segments: one about players on the field, from the AAGPBL to Ila Borders; a second about female owners and those in other executive positions; and a third, which included female fans and women broadcasters, along with items dealing with "the cultural impact of *A League of Their Own.*"

This film was doubtless the single most effective promoter of women's baseball history. But that doesn't mean that documentaries are ineffective. More female players should watch *Girls of Summer* (2008), a video by Max Tash, which opens with scenes about the WBL Sparks, the first team of girls to play in Cooperstown against boys. Justine Siegal brought the girls to Cooperstown because, as she said in the film, "I want them to have the time of their lives!" Even in the trailer you can see how enthusiastically the girls played. One girl says mischievously for the camera, "We're gonna beat the boys!" Tash says that after talking with Justine and getting permission to follow her and the team around town, he "developed a fondness for the girls and Justine's dreams." His admiration shows, and the resulting video deserves wider distribution.

Justine Siegal, shown here with her daughter Jasmine of the Cooperstown Sparks, fills multiple roles in women's baseball. She has helped many girls and women find or develop teams so that they can enjoy playing the national game. This photo was taken August 14, 2009, at the Cooperstown Dreams Park, where Jasmine's team played (courtesy of the photographer, Bob Devlin).

Another lively and informative source is *Baseball Girls*, produced in 1995 by the National Film Board of Canada under the direction of filmmaker Lois Siegel. The videotape presents a great show for both girls and women. Its coverage of softball as well as baseball is its only drawback for baseball players, many of whom resent the relentless emphasis on softball by sports organizations. Baseball players believe that kind of attention belongs to women who play the national game. Mixing the two different games on this video can also prove confusing to viewers.

The Hall of Fame itself has gone into what looks surprisingly like promotion of women's baseball by producing *Dirt on Their Skirts: 150 Years of Pioneers in Women's Baseball,* and releasing it for television while also preparing a detailed lesson plan for teachers about the history of women's baseball. The lesson plan's bibliography includes some adult histories and some children's books about women's baseball, along with web sources of information and photos. This plan could make a nice start for high school students, as does one prepared by James Percoco, an author and award-winning teacher, for the Organization of American Historians and published in 1992. The OAH plan emphasizes the place of women's baseball in World War II, and it lists additional sources, including the third book in the Oxford University Press series I wrote with Harold Seymour, *Baseball: The People's Game* (1990).

Some women love Ken Burns's monumental documentary, *Baseball,* with its many hours of warm and sentimental treatment of the national game's history, but showing us what many fans characterize as "feel-good drama" meant depicting male players in their best light and including historical inaccuracies. The series does include the beginnings of women in professional baseball but really features the Negro Leagues. One male fan made the following criticism in his review: "If you really want to puke, just try to get through Burns's attempt to make baseball a struggle for gender equality!" Burns hardly makes such an attempt, of course; his film series represents a patriotic, sentimental effort to depict those aspects of baseball history that interest him.

People who deeply appreciate women's baseball are the ones that women need to go to in order to learn about the history of their gender in baseball. That group includes librarians and curators. Chances are that if you visit any libraries and museums featuring recent American history, you'll run across exhibits about women's baseball, particularly about the All-American Girls Professional Baseball League of the 1940s–50s. Cities in which AAGPBL teams played, like South Bend, Racine, and Kenosha, have mounted permanent exhibits featuring the league. In 2007 the library of the Blackwood Campus at Camden County College, New Jersey, combined a display representing events of the AAGPBL with action photos from the 2006 season of two women's teams, as well as photos from Team USA's triumph over Japan to clinch the 2006 World Cup. On this occasion, Sheila Sikorski, who is both a ballplayer and a local adjunct professor, made a presentation called "Women Playing Baseball," based on a master's thesis she was preparing at the time.

Mainstream museums, too, have shown interest in women's baseball. Joyce Westerman, who played for several teams in the AAGPBL, contributed one of her uniforms, an autographed baseball, and photographs to the Smithsonian's National Museum of American History as a permanent exhibit. Other museums mount occasional displays, like the Fullerton (California) Museum

Center, which is among those that have presented "Line Drives and Lipstick, the Untold Story of Women's Baseball," curated by John Kovach, the archivist of St. Mary's College and author of a charming set of images collected in a book called *Women's Baseball*. The "Untold Story" exhibit includes displays from as far back as the 1860s. Curators and library officials are becoming truly knowledgeable about this branch of American history, and the untold story is beginning to be told.

Other organizations celebrate women's baseball achievements in their own way. The Shrine of the Eternals has even elected Pam Postema to its Virtual Hall of Fame. Two women's leagues have established their own Halls of Fame: the Eastern Women's Baseball Conference, which has selected mostly the top achievers in its own league (although the list includes Maud Nelson, Babe Didrikson Zaharias, and Faye Dancer), and Justine Siegal's Women's Baseball League, which looks even beyond excellent players and selected me as its first honoree, for my work in the history of women's baseball. Although not bricks-and-mortar Halls of Fame, these honor lists of contributors to the sport nonetheless recognize women's special achievement in baseball. In 1998, the Canadian Baseball Hall of Fame bested its Cooperstown counterpart by inducting into its organization as honorary members all sixty-four of the Canadian women who played in the AAGPBL.

Teachers, too, realize that women's baseball represents a colorful part of our history that can serve as a magnet for learners. Once while attending the annual convention of the Society for American Baseball Research in Toronto I took a cab to the University of Toronto's Robards Library, where a free visiting scholar's pass enabled me to examine material in the sports section of the stacks. There I noticed many sources on women's baseball obviously used in classrooms as texts or supplementary readers. That's because college history professors, including women professors, now give courses in sports history. Dr. Leslie Heaphy, a woman who teaches at Kent State, is among those who have both written and taught baseball history. Once when an Ohio reporter emailed me to ask for a local historian he could interview on women's baseball, I referred him to Heaphy, and when he later thanked me bountifully for the reference, I detected considerable surprise in his wording. Yes, women professors of history can actually become experts on women's baseball history. Is there anything relating to baseball that women can't do?

Women not only teach about women's baseball history, they write about it. An enthusiastic fan, writer Sue Macy, published an excellent history of the AAGPBL for young people called *A Whole New Ball Game*. It's a fine introduction to the subject. Serious scholars and devotees should advance to Merrie Fidler's *The Origins and History of the All-American Girls Professional Baseball League* (2006) as well as histories describing women's much-earlier baseball participation. Barbara Gregorich's *Women at Play: The Story of Women in Baseball* (1993) and Gai Ingham Berlage's *Women in Baseball: The Forgotten History* (1994) cover early players like Lizzie Murphy, Margaret Nabel, and others who deserve much more attention in American history as pioneers. These two important books came out just after *Baseball: The People's Game* (1990), in which Harold Seymour and I presented five chapters describing women's play in America before the onset of World War II.

Who better to write the history of women in baseball than women deeply interested in the national game? If you have encountered males who scoff at the idea of women playing baseball, refer them to the two excellent efforts by Berlage and Gregorich, which demonstrate the level of excellence some women players reached in the past. Gregorich selects outstanding people like Jackie Mitchell and teams like the Rockford Peaches to feature. As a child Gregorich played baseball (never softball), and she loves the game. She has also published a baseball novel, *She's on First* (1987), which Peter Bjarkman singles out from others of its type as depicting "a real flesh-and-blood player." Berlage, a professor of sociology, gives us solid and footnoted research starting with early women players and especially outstanding individuals like Alta Weiss and Amanda Clement. Another sociologist, Susan E. Johnson, presents a history of the women's league from the point of view of a devoted fan of the Rockford Peaches: herself. Full of quotations from the players, Johnson's book, *When Women Played Hardball* (1994), is warmly evocative of the years when girls and women players of the pro league thrilled audiences and exulted in the excitement of playing their game on a high level. These books are treasuries of memories and belong in every library that purports to collect books that explain American history.

Scholars have become interested in creating oral history by preserving the voices and stories of individual professional women players, just as some men have done with the professional men players. One such valuable production, prepared by Janis Taylor, a filmmaker and retired college teacher, features interviews with forty AAGPBL players.

The next important work on baseball to appear after those of the nineties is Jean Ardell's comprehensive history revealing women's extensive and varied participation in baseball, including the phenomenon of baseball annies. Her book, *Breaking into Baseball* (2005), is deeply thought through, for she loves the game as a fan as well as an observer of women's contribution to baseball in all its ramifications.

In addition to these standard works, we have two newer books on women in baseball, both of them carefully documented, written by women who center on different but related themes. Marilyn Cohen's treatise, *No Girls in the Clubhouse* (2009), explains to us how girls came to be excluded from baseball, while Jennifer Ring's *Stolen Bases* (also 2009) tells us why. Ring brings a more personal perspective to her work, beginning with her daughter's experiences in trying to play baseball, experiences that opened Ring's eyes to the reasons girls have been shut out of the national game. Don't miss the chapter called "How Baseball Became Manly and White." These two cultural studies deserve the attention of every woman who ever wanted to take part in sports by playing baseball.

AAGPBL players, too, have written books about their experiences. What could give us a closer look of what it was like to play in the first pro women's league? Patricia "Pat" Brown played for the Chicago Colleens and two other teams, afterwards becoming an attorney and law librarian. In *A League of My Own* (2003), Brown tells her own poignant story, beginning with being cut out of the boys' sandlot games until she proved herself. Then came her unsuccessful attempts to play Little League ball, being pushed into softball, and finally the triumph of pitching for the All-Americans. Reading her book makes you want to live her life.

Close in flavor to an autobiography is an effective book published in 2005 by writer Carolyn Trombe about the pro league's "strikeout queen," Dottie Wiltse Collins. If you're a woman, I guarantee that you'll find her book a lot more interesting than a bio of a male player written by a male sports writer.

But women writers on baseball history don't confine themselves to writing only about women; they can take on other subjects. Some become interested in writing about the game through family connections — remembering family members who played ball, the way Catherine Petroski, a prize-winning poet, decided to write about her father, the pitcher Bob Groom, and Susan Dellinger, a psychologist and inspirational speaker, wrote about her well-known grandfather, Edd Roush. Bonnie Crosby, a dance specialist, prepared a book made up of striking images of the Brooklyn Dodgers created by her father, Barney Stein, the team's official photographer. Cindy Thomson, a writer, working with a cousin, provided a biography of her distant relative, Mordecai "Three-Finger" Brown. Cindy says she got her love of the game not from her father but from her mother, a great fan and the family member who is related to Mordecai. Judith Testa, although unrelated to Sal Maglie, prepared a strong and complete biography of the player simply because she became interested in him as a person. Priscilla Astifan, an archivist, entered baseball studies by approaching them through local history — baseball as played in Rochester, New York. Wendy Knickerbocker, an academic librarian, wrote a book about the colorful Billy Sunday, and Monica Nucciarone, who teaches the social sciences, has studied and clarified for us the role of the Knickerbockers' Alexander Cartwright with her striking new book. Other women are engaged in similar projects that will open our eyes to still more aspects of baseball history.

Regional chapters of SABR often invite speakers to share their special baseball knowledge. Susan Dellinger, author of *Red Legs and Black Sox: Edd Roush and the Untold Story of the 1919 World Series*, spoke about her grandfather Edd at a SABR chapter meeting in Naples, Florida, in March of 2009. Dellinger (center) was photographed with the chapter president, Mel Poplock, and Dorothy Mills, for whom this SABR chapter is named (courtesy of the photographer, Bonnie Crosby).

As examples of work in the pipeline, I can cite a book about the early Ohio player, Alta Weiss, being planned by her family, and another about Helene Robison Britton, who inherited and ran the St. Louis Cardinals for several years, being written by Joan Thomas, a journalist. Martha Ackmann, who is a journalist, teacher, and speaker, is working on a book called *Curveball* about the noted black player Toni Stone, and Kelly Boyer Sagert, who authored a biography of Shoeless Joe Jackson, plans to write about the well-known black player Mamie "Peanut" Johnson. Moreover, Penny Marshall has another film in store for us, this one about Effa Manley, the woman who became the best-known owner of the Negro Leagues. Manley, commented Leslie Heaphy, "learned early not to be overlooked." Those of us who have done research on baseball in Manley's era recall her photos in newspapers of the thirties and forties, sitting erect in the stands, wearing a stylish hat and smiling confidently, as if knowing that her work was important. Projects like those I have described are worth waiting for.

All these writers are not only perfectly capable of writing baseball history, they do it very well. Perhaps they are fulfilling the old saying that, in order to compete with men in any job, women must be twice as good. These books are certainly better than many team and league "histories" and worshipful player bios produced in the past. One big improvement is that they avoid descending to sports writers' jargon.

Women's serious interest in baseball means that it may even come to dominate their professional lives, as it has the work of Leslie Heaphy, who has produced an award-winning book on Negro League history, manages the production of a Negro Leagues journal, teaches a university course on baseball literature and history, and has been editing a huge and ongoing project, the *Encyclopedia of Women and Baseball.* Even though I contributed to the *Encyclopedia* myself, just browsing this volume startled and amazed me with the sheer number of people, clubs, leagues, and other new information about women that it offers. Heaphy juggles many baseball projects at the same time, but she is not the only woman teaching about baseball at the college level. At Rutgers, for example, Theresa Collins uses her course about the New York Yankees as an opportunity to "open up the minds of these students to the joys of research."

Knowledgeable women like Heaphy obtain recognition for their accomplishments from the professional groups in which they participate by sharing their knowledge and learning about others' discoveries — just as in any professional group. Jean Ardell, for example, gives many speeches, particularly at the NINE Conference, an outgrowth of the baseball journal of the same name, and at the annual meetings called the Cooperstown Symposium on Baseball and American Culture, held at the Otesaga Hotel in that baseball mecca, Cooperstown. Once Harold Seymour received an invitation to speak at the symposium; he could, however, no longer make such presentations, so I stood in for him.

Women also attend the various meetings set up by the Society for American Baseball Research. Although women make up only a small percentage of SABR's membership of nearly seven thousand, they have become actively engaged in making presentations as well as sharing information in SABR's committee meetings, particularly the Women in Baseball Committee, that are scheduled during the society's annual conventions.

Women have therefore discovered that one way they can participate fully in baseball is through scholarship. Although I still see tiny smiles ("Is she kidding?") when I explain that I'm a baseball historian, once I begin to discuss my work, my listeners start to believe me. Studying baseball, although still unusual for women, provides an acceptable outlet for those deeply interested in the national game and its place in our culture.

One of the most effective pieces of work on baseball history produced recently by a woman comes in the form not of print media but of film. Sam Marchiano, a female filmmaker, produced a dramatic and scholarly study of baseball's origin with her documentary *Base Ball Discovered*, which won the award for excellence in research and accuracy at the third annual Baseball Film Festival held by the National Baseball Hall of Fame and Museum.

David Block, author of a book on the origins of baseball, here pictured with Dorothy Mills, receives the Seymour Medal at SABR's Seymour Conference in Cleveland, Ohio, in 2006. Block's research indicates that British women may be the ultimate source of the American game of baseball (courtesy of the photographer, Barry Evans).

Marchiano's film pursues one of the central questions in baseball history: how did the game begin? It explores the game's relation to rounders and other very old games, many of them still played in the United Kingdom, where baseball was surely enjoyed much earlier than in the United States — probably as early as the fourteenth century, in fact. This highly professional film, shown at a recent SABR convention, is full of wonderful images and carries viewers along with surprising stories and intriguing events. Moreover, it supports the research of David Block in his important book *Baseball Before We Knew It*, demonstrating that the game of baseball grew out of early women's play.

Because of women's participation in studying and sharing information about baseball, the next generation of young women will be able to pursue baseball more easily and naturally in a multitude of ways, assisted by the contribution of writers who now produce not only adult but also children's books about baseball, including books about the All-American Girls Professional Baseball League. Children can pick up and become absorbed in a book bearing the same primary title as a film; it's called *Dirt on Their Skirts: The Story of the Young Women Who Won the World Championship*, about the exciting 1946 championship game between two skillful teams, the Racine Belles and the Rockford Peaches of the AAGPBL. The story, based on what really happened, is told from the point of view of a young fan, and the authors dedicate the book to "all those playground heroines and sandlot sluggers whose hearts beat a little faster whenever they hear the words ... 'Play ball!'" I bought a copy of this book secondhand, though it was in excellent condition, and was shocked to find it stamped "DISCARD" by the library that no longer wanted to share this piece of authentic history with its readers. Librarians need to help girls realize that they, too, can aspire to play baseball, and explaining the truth behind this book is one way.

Children can also read another charming book of historical fiction, Shana Corey's *Players in Pigtails* (2003), about a girl who loves to play baseball and gets the chance to join the women's league. Corey, who has studied women's history and written children's stories about other women of achievement, was inspired to write this book after seeing the film *A League of Their Own*. In an author's note she comments on how amazed she was to learn about the league: "Was it all true? I wondered, and why didn't I know about it until now?" Girls of the twenty-first century won't have Corey's problem if librarians steer them to these and other books about women players.

Baseball literature for boys, beginning with the 1880s, has never stopped flooding the market, while girls have been subsisting on weaker fare like *Nurse Nancy*. That's because adults of earlier generations set low expectations for their daughters, assuming that as adults they would lead lives not as achievers themselves but as helpers to male achievers. Even when women were finally permitted to pursue higher education, the president of a women's college told the students, "This education should tend to make you more serviceable as wives and mothers." Girls no longer attend college in order to become "serviceable"; they seek schooling in order to become educated and independent persons. Reading about the exploits of women who pioneered in the national game should be part of every girl's education.

15

Baseball Women of the Future

Women of today act under a lighter load of historical baggage than I was encumbered with during my growing-up years and in my active working life. Many more of them see themselves as independent persons, and they assume that they are free to pursue their happiness through a life of interesting work and play, to form whatever relationships they desire, and to achieve their goals no matter how high.

That doesn't always work out for them, especially if they are trying to break into a field traditionally dominated by men. But the barriers between women and success are lower now, thanks to the pioneering women who have chopped at and weakened those obstructions of the type faced by women of my era.

I grew up with traditional lower-middle-class parents who thought my highest goal in life should be to become a secretary. They saw "acting lady-like" as the embodiment of femininity. Because they assumed that sports were for boys, I made the same assumption; bicycling, not competitive sports, became my favorite playtime activity.

By the time I reached high school, my parents realized that my educational goals were loftier than any in our extended family, and although they seemed nonplussed by my desire to attend college, they accepted it, managing to supplement my own part-time earnings to an extent that enabled me to study at a local institution, where I could gratify my desire to learn more and more, especially about English and history. School sports were never made to seem appealing to me. Although I managed to pass the swimming test in the college pool, I never enjoyed anything more active than dancing.

Although studying history broadened me, I absorbed and accepted the standards for women that were part of the middle-class mores of my time. When Harold Seymour, first my history professor and later my husband, interested me in using my skills in research and writing on his own work, I never thought of declining the suggestion. Although later, in my lifetime of teaching, researching, writing, and speaking, I published many articles and books of my own, I expended most of my lifetime energy on the baseball work that was attributed wholly to Harold Seymour. I know now that I accepted much too easily the roles of helper, assistant, clerk, secretary, muse, researcher, editor, typist, and ghost writer, as well as the role of wife and homemaker. It was not until many years of keeping silent about my lack of appropriate recognition that I began to chafe under this regime. Meanwhile, I continued to enjoy the work.

Not the least of what I enjoyed discovering in my baseball research and writing was the depth of feeling for baseball among those who played the national game simply for fun. Our third book together, *Baseball: The People's Game* (1990), can be considered more mine than Harold Seymour's, since I found working on it much more intriguing than researching and writing about the professionals. I loved finding out about, and describing, the surprising number of Americans who took every opportunity to play the game they loved, pushing for the right to do so until the persons to whom they had to answer (like employers, college administrators, military officers, prison supervisors) finally gave in ... and eventually, caught up in the game, began to take charge of that play themselves, promoting it, making money from it, and creating reputations on the skill displayed by their charges.

To me, the most intriguing evidence of the strong hold that amateur baseball retained on the population came from bits and pieces of information I had collected over the years, and continued to collect in the 1980s and 1990s, about women desiring to play baseball and, like the men, finding ways to fit it into their lives for play and even as a way of earning money. I reveled in the material I was locating about women's little-known participation in the national game, and together Harold Seymour and I created five lively chapters revealing the place of women in baseball before World War Two. For me, the story of early baseball women became the high point of the book, for with the beginnings of women's involvement, baseball was truly becoming the people's game.

Moreover, women's obvious delight in physical activity, proven by their determined pursuit of opportunities to play baseball and sometimes supported by quotations I found about the fun they were having, made it clear that I had missed a lot by failing to challenge myself in competitive games. By then I had learned about the All-American Girls Professional Baseball League, an amazing piece of American history. I admired the gumption of the participants, and I wished that the third book in our series — which was already too long — could have been longer so that we might have included the era of the 1940s.

With the publication of *Baseball: The People's Game*, reviewers, not knowing of my heavy contribution to the work, lavished praise on Harold Seymour for his "exhaustive research," with historians, for example, lauding the book for linking baseball developments to larger social and cultural contexts, for displaying "remarkable breadth and richness of detail," and for making "precisely the kind of connection often overlooked by sports historians."

Two years after publication of *Baseball: The People's Game*, when the delightful film *A League of Their Own* appeared, I realized that it was historically authentic and thought, "What a wonderful way to present this beguiling success story to the American people!"

After I finally revealed to the world of scholarship, in an article published in 2000, that I was Harold Seymour's co-author, I discovered that I hardly stood alone in the position where I had placed myself. By then I was noticing — and people were sending me — evidence of other women's exploitation by their husband-colleagues. I learned, first in a television documentary and then in a biography, that the explorer John Frémont's famous reports on the Oregon trail were written not by him but by his wife, Jesse. I found out from an email correspondent that the plays attributed to Berthold Brecht had been written by a group of women, especially his secretary and collaborator. I heard from several people that Lafcadio Hearn, who did not speak Japanese, assigned his wife, Setsuko, to perform research in ancient Japanese tales, which he then rewrote, embellished, and published, never mentioning her contribution. I received an email from a stranger who pointed out that Zelda Fitzgerald's famous husband Scott "pilfered shamelessly from her letters and diaries"; another person declared that T.S. Eliot and Henry James are also indebted to female collaborators whose contributions those writers kept secret. Several people pointed out to me that Dick Francis's wife wrote some of his bestsellers about horse racing and that only after her passing did he recognize her contribution to his work. Another correspondent, who had just finished reading the biography of Vladimir Nabokov's wife, commented that "the degree to which she edited his work is extraordinary, both on paper and on their ruminative walks together. And then," he added, "there are de Beauvoir and Sartre, a literary nightmare for the female of the pair if ever there was one." In 2006 I learned, from the *New York Times Book Review*, that Alvin Toffler had just begun admitting that he and his wife "have always written and spoken as a team" but that he had never included her name as co-author of his books until publication of his latest one, called *Revolutionary Wealth*. Perhaps the most disturbing information I received lies in the story of V.S. Naipaul, whose wife had "sacrificed everything to help him both as a person and as a writer.... [She was] consecrated to his work and his success. He used her as an unpaid editor and amanuensis, and then spurned her."

This sort of highway robbery happened in other fields, too: in describing female anthropologists, Marilyn French asserts that "male bias kept female anthropologists from prominence," explaining that "Daisy Bates worked for fifty years among Australian aborigines only to have her material appropriated by [British social anthropologist] A. Radcliffe Brown." French added that "husbands often appropriate their wives' research: classic works of the period by men acknowledge such contribution in a preface, not on the title page." And that's where my name always appeared: in the prefaces of the Oxford books, in the company of people who might have contributed an hour's work or translated a page from a foreign language for us.

In some ways, all this proof that writing husbands commonly took advantage of women's low position in society, as well as their low expectations for themselves, should have made me angrier about my experience, but I found it strangely comforting to learn that I was not the only exploited colleague-wife. Besides, I knew that I had learned a great deal by the experience.

After the publication of the third volume in the series I wrote with Harold Seymour, I became sidetracked into historical fiction, but I remained interested in baseball history. When a McFarland editor invited me to write my autobiography, I took advantage of the opportunity to explain exactly how the books attributed to Harold Seymour were really produced.

After the publication of my autobiography, *A Woman's Work*, in 2004, reviews showed that readers appreciated my "upbeat attitude," my "restraint" in avoiding the pitfall of writing a "whining rant" or picturing myself as a martyr; instead they saw that I emphasized the great value I had received in having the world of research and scholarship opened up for me, as well as the thrill and satisfaction of contributing heavily to an entirely new field as it was being established, with my work in baseball history subsequently recognized and praised by scholars.

With recognition for *A Woman's Work*, despite being sidetracked by my interest in historical fiction and other writing, I found myself increasingly involved with the work of other women who wrote about baseball, especially members of the Society for American Baseball Research. I became impressed with their creativity, skills, and determination to open the field of baseball writing to talented women. For although the number of women members of SABR remained much smaller than those of the men, women seemed to be contributing to baseball scholarship out of proportion to their number, making scholarly presentations, becoming active in committees, and even producing books of such high quality that they were nominated for SABR's literary prizes. Moreover, these women, having read my autobiography, understood the contribution I had made to baseball history.

It was Jean Ardell, then in the midst of writing her excellent book *Break-

ing into Baseball, who asked me if Oxford University Press planned to add my name to the title page of future editions of the three books the company had published as written by Harold Seymour. That opened a new issue.

While preparing the Oxford series, Seymour and I had worked for more than thirty years with Oxford's prominent editor, Sheldon Meyer, who considered publication of the baseball series one of his finest achievements. Meyer was proud to be the first editor ever to bring into print a scholarly book on baseball. So when *A Woman's Work* was published by McFarland in 2004, I sent Meyer a copy. He responded with embarrassment and dismay, surprised to learn that I had "played a central role in the whole enterprise," and he apologized for his failure to recognize that I was actually co-author of these books. He called *A Woman's Work* "instructive," said that I "write with grace," and admitted that the lack of recognition for my work was "certainly an injustice."

Not until Jean Ardell queried me did I finally ask Meyer if Oxford would be willing to rectify this injustice in future editions by placing my name on the title pages of the three books, along with Harold Seymour's name, where it belonged. By then Meyer had retired, so he had no power to make that decision, but he did pass my query on to the Oxford management, which replied, "No, not at this late date."

Lily Ledbetter knew all about this kind of reasoning! Because the "injustice" didn't happen yesterday, and because I omitted to reveal it while Seymour lived, that injustice will never be rectified. Evidently, Oxford has adopted a self-imposed statute of limitations on injustices that occurred in the past. So the Cold Case File of "Who Really Wrote the Seymour Books?" despite overwhelming evidence that other researchers can attest to, will forever remain cold. And most people who today buy the three seminal Oxford volumes believe that Harold Seymour was the sole author of the first scholarly books of baseball history.

But the scholars of SABR today, particularly the women scholars, have begun taking the matter of correcting the record into their own hands. Text references to the Oxford books in serious work about baseball now refer to these books as having been written by "the Seymours," and writers like Jean Ardell are citing the books in footnotes and bibliographies in a way that reflects an authorship team. I have adopted the same habit. Librarian Mary Ellen Kollar, a specialist in baseball history, saw to it that the Cleveland Public Library's pamphlet on its baseball collection lists both Harold Seymour and Dorothy Seymour Mills as authors of the Oxford series. Why shouldn't these knowledgeable persons use citations that reflect reality? They know their business, and for them to continue citing these three books as though one person did all the work on them would be inaccurate as well as unfair, despite Oxford's persisting in presenting them that way.

From some women readers of my autobiography, and some audiences of my speeches, I still receive expressions of their indignation at my treatment and their emphatic assurance that they would never, but never, allow their husbands to attempt taking credit for work that the wives had performed. And I'm pretty sure that what happened to me will not happen in the future. Today's young women would hardly be able to grasp that in the 1940s it was expected that a young woman might contribute heavily and anonymously to her husband's work. The new generation of women studying baseball will not let themselves be exploited.

Another query I still receive is the question of why I continued to work on the Oxford project even after it became clear that I would never, in Harold Seymour's lifetime, receive appropriate recognition for my substantial contribution to it. The reason is that halting my work would have seriously endangered the project, for with time Seymour became less and less able to contribute to it, and in the end I was the only one working on it. I could not leave the third book incomplete; it is by far my favorite, for it opened new fields that are now being developed extensively by other scholars, thus greatly increasing our knowledge of the American past. One of those fields is the topic of women in baseball; the proliferation of valuable studies in this field is deeply gratifying to me. Even *Who's Who,* which at first entirely omitted any mention of my baseball work in entries for me, now correctly lists me as co-author of the three books in the Oxford trilogy.

The Society for American Baseball Research, too, recognizes my contribution to baseball history, especially with its annual literary award, named after both Seymour and me. I'm happy to attend the presentation each year of SABR's Dr. Harold and Dorothy Seymour Award to the author of the best history or biography published in the previous year, as well as to comment on the book itself. Since my move to Naples, Florida, the local SABR chapter has even been named after me.

Women in every field find themselves faced with special hurdles to recognition and success to be surmounted — or circumvented, whatever it takes! Susan Johnson, author of *When Women Played Hardball,* believes that women are deliberately taught the "damaged view" that they are weak, timid, afraid of being hurt, and in need of protection from the rigors of adult life, including sports. One result of this teaching, says Lourdes Beneria, who studies gender economics, is the passivity of the "dutiful daughter," acceptance of which prevented women from taking the initiative or thinking critically; they learned to follow and not lead, to accept rather than to ask difficult questions.

Johnson explains that the women of the AAGPBL proved that women can, if they desire, be "powerful, combative, fierce, relentless, sure of their own capabilities, and focused on the prize." Johnson's description reminds me of the way girls and women played in reformatories and prisons in the 1920s and 1930s. Nobody told them they couldn't play baseball, and in fact administrators introduced and promoted baseball to inmates for its health and socializing benefits. As a result, those who watched them enjoying the game saw girls who learned teamwork and developed what one observer called "a commendable competitive spirit."

Too bad all girls weren't encouraged to develop this same spirit, which they could have learned in the AAGPBL. Pat Brown, for example, said playing ball in the league gave her confidence and the ability to cope with difficult tasks; she also learned "discipline, hard work, and caring," and from her teammates she drew upon "friendship and loyalty." Many young women of the past received no encouragement to develop qualities that would make them more well-rounded persons. To develop drive and determination, women needed opportunities to show what they could do.

Nowadays, women receive scoldings for standing back and "making nice" instead of asserting themselves. Females, says journalist Lyn Chamberlin, are "notorious for not taking credit for the things they do." She reproaches women for "leaving perceptions to the randomness of the universe," explaining that being good at what they do "is not enough"; women must also "tell people you're good — and do it in a way that [people] remember."

One way the women of SABR have displayed their abilities related to baseball is their presentation of a stimulating panel discussion at the SABR convention in St. Louis in 2007. Nobody who was there will forget AAGPBL player Emma Bergmann's answer to a question about how true-to-life the film *A League of Their Own* was: Bergmann, who played for four different teams in the women's league, elicited roars of laughter when she asserted, "Well, I never had a manager as drunk as the one played by Tom Hanks!" Bergmann thus avoided stating just how drunk her managers were, but we all got the idea.

On this occasion, the roomful of about three hundred rapt listeners, most of them men, appeared to be learning for the first time about the many forms of women's participation in the national game, as six women representing various baseball interests spoke and answered questions. The audience heard, for example, remarks by Cecilia Tan, who is both a writer and a ballplayer (with the Slaterettes), explaining how to start a women's league; she surprised listeners by urging them to start their own leagues! Judith Testa, author of the well-received biography of Sal Maglie, recounted to gales of laughter Hank Greenberg's attempt to buy Maglie for Cleveland at a bargain-basement price.

One of the most significant questions asked of the panel was why, in the 1920s and 1930s, women stopped playing baseball in college and amateur

At the 2009 SABR Convention in St. Louis, SABR women presented a ground-breaking event, a women's panel called "Our Mothers' Game — and Our Own: Tales from the Women's Side of Baseball." Left to right are Cecilia Tan, a writer as well as a player for the Pawtucket Slaterettes; Dorothy Mills, speaking about *A Woman's Work: Writing Baseball History with Harold Seymour*; Melody Yount, assistant director of media relations, St. Louis Cardinals; Judith Testa, author of *Sal Maglie: Baseball's Demon Barber*; Sara Blasingame, daughter of major leaguer Walker Cooper and widow of major leaguer Don Blasingame; and Emma Bergmann, former player in the AAGPBL. Panel members are looking to their left because invisible, at right, is the organizer and moderator of the panel, Jean Ardell, author of *Breaking into Baseball: Women and the National Pastime* (courtesy of Monica Nucciarone).

leagues, turning to softball instead. Cecilia Tan and I took turns explaining that it was female college athletic directors, influenced by physicians (then almost entirely men), who believed that women were not strong enough to play the game they had already been playing for decades. Those athletic directors banned sponsorship of baseball and saw to it that softball was substituted; the Amateur Athletic Union, which then controlled women's amateur play, supported their decision.

Only in 2009 did the National Collegiate Athletic Association, an important umbrella organization, decide that this ruling on women was a mistake. It acknowledged that women might play both baseball and softball, or either one. Now perhaps women who want to play baseball in college and in amateur leagues will no longer have to contend with administrators who try to confine them to softball. Future opportunities of women ballplayers, especially in college, should improve as a result.

The men who attended the 2007 panel discussion seemed unprepared for the abilities and knowledge displayed by the women they were listening to. Comments heard afterwards included the remarks, "You women sure know your stuff!" "That was simply fascinating!" and "That was the best session I've ever attended at any SABR convention." Obviously, some men had harbored low expectations for the panel; perhaps they attended the session only out of curiosity. The results of our work that afternoon would have pleased Lyn Chamberlin, for we were certainly showing our audience what we knew — and doing it "in a way that they would remember." By celebrating what pioneering baseball women had done and were still doing, we demonstrated women's deep connection to baseball.

This panel, chaired by the redoubtable Jean Ardell, proved that women today embrace baseball as their own, whether in watching, playing, or studying it, and that they are unafraid of showing their special knowledge of the national game. Even the title that Ardell gave the presentation makes bold assertions: "Our Mothers' Game — and Our Own: Tales from the Women's Side of Baseball." I believe that some men are slowly beginning to realize that baseball can be a womanly pursuit.

Another development boding well for the future of baseball women is the revelation by some male players that their mothers, not their fathers, were their baseball coaches. Jimmy Rollins of the Philadelphia Phillies admitted that his mom, a star church league player, taught him how to play. Casey Candaele, who played for the Houston Astros, is the son of Helen Callaghan, who took the 1945 batting crown in the AAGPBL and taught Casey how to go after ground balls. These experiences teach boys that women can do much more than transport their children to games and furnish post-game snacks.

The future of women in baseball depends on several factors. Changes in attitudes, both men's and women's, lie at the basis of any future. Those who have studied children playing organized games have discovered that girls' success in play is called "luck" and failure is attributed to "lack of skill"; boys' success is laid to "skill" while failure is called "bad luck." That kind of judgment demonstrates once more that we have different expectations for each sex, and we must start expecting females to do as well as males in every endeavor.

Changing attitudes would include relieving men from what they assume is the necessity for constantly proving their masculinity by setting aside certain activities for themselves alone. Tennis pro Bobby Riggs, when (in 1973) he was beaten soundly by Billie Jean King in a game he assumed men would always dominate, must have realized afterward that his loss merely encouraged more women to play tennis. Men do not really need to prove anything, and trying to set up private bailiwicks for males merely challenges competitive women to infiltrate them.

That's why the rule preventing women from signing professional contracts with teams in men's professional baseball leagues must be struck down. Peter Bjarkman points out that no other professional sport supports a written stricture preventing women from signing contracts offered to them by men's teams. Should our national game discriminate against half the American population?

For women as for men, all options should be open. There will always be a few women, like Lizzie Murphy and Ila Borders, who believe they can play on the same level as men with a men's team and want to make the effort; those who can meet the same standards as male rookies should be permitted to enter the men's leagues and given as much encouragement as the men.

That other minority, made up of black men, finally got a chance to shine in the pro leagues; why shouldn't white and black women? Everything I have read about the requirements for playing baseball at the highest level indicates that the only qualities needed are the skill and the passion to excel in a strong and athletic body. I have seen women with those qualities playing baseball.

Since most female players prefer to play against other women, their female teams and leagues should receive as much backing as men's amateur teams. And why should they not aspire to set up women's professional leagues as exciting as the All-Americans of the 1940s and 1950s? I think women fans are ready to become fans of women players.

Alumni of the AAGPBL already support and promote emerging women's baseball programs. Proposals for women's national leagues are being made. Current players from various locations — Michigan, New Jersey, Long Island, North Carolina, Spokane — have kicked this topic around in a series of blogs posted in 2008 to a site called *Baseball Fever* in answer to the posed question, "What would a Women's MLB look like?" In their creative and informed replies to this question these players proposed cities for each league and gave the reasons for their choices; they explained the necessity for shaping a league with team rivalries; they mentioned the importance of developing baseball at the lowest levels, through high school and college, so that the league could boast "solid pro players" with a base of talent behind them. The women players who contributed to this discussion, known to each other and readers only by their "net names," sound so knowledgeable that I believe they could form a committee to make a formal proposal for a new professional women's league.

But who, or what organization, would back a women's pro league? Is there any forward-looking entity available today like Wrigley and his gum company? I may have the answer.

My suggestion is to form a consortium by asking all of the women's leagues who aspire to become big-league organizations, or want to send players to a league, to send representatives to a regional group that will plan a major women's league or leagues. As for financial support, it will come from the companies that have received from Major League Baseball a license to sell their products as official MLB items. Half of the money MLB receives from companies who pay for the right to put the MLB logo on their products would go to finance MLWB, Major League Women's Baseball. There must be hundreds of such companies now paying MLB very well for the right to put that logo on their clothing, souvenirs, and all kinds of other items. Thus might MLB find itself actually supporting women's baseball! And it's about time.

Team names could come from those approved companies, too. I'm sure some team would like to use the name "Cooperstown Cookies," after a small company that holds an MLB license, but in order to be viewed as tasteful the clubs might have to turn down the name of another licensed product, "Belly Button Navel Rings." Besides, that name sounds redundant.

I thought MLB had suddenly decided to support women's baseball when I opened the MLB.com web site and found a photo of a young woman in pink T-shirt and cap standing in batting position and wielding a pink bat, but the picture merely signaled that MLB supported the fight to end breast cancer with a contest inviting fans to write an essay describing their own connection with this fight. The reward was not a chance to go up to the plate and hit but to act as "honorary bat girl or boy" in a Mothers' Day Game. MLB has not yet awakened to the possibilities of women's baseball.

One of the biggest obstacles to women's integration into baseball today is continued lack of knowledge about the long history of women who played baseball and women's continued play in the present. Despite the proliferation in recent years of books, films, and exhibits on women ballplayers, most Americans remain unaware of women's contribution to this part of American history. Their lack of knowledge is part of what Susan Johnson called "the silence that blankets much of women's experience." Patricia Brown, a career librarian as well as former AAGPBL player, states categorically that important books covering the history of women still fail to mention the women's league and its place in World War II history.

Women historians have been trying to rectify the problem of knowledge, but a lot remains to be done with promotion, especially through the mass media, where, as of 2008, 90 percent of sports editors, sports columnists, and sports reporters are male and seem to know and care little about women's baseball. During a book tour for her recent history, *Breaking into Baseball: Women and the National Pastime*, Jean Ardell met people who simply did not believe that women have a history in baseball and still play the game.

Perhaps women need to adopt the assertive attitude of Justine Siegal, ballplayer and promoter, when she says, "Believe! Girls do play ball!" Then they must back it up by going out and taking part in the national game themselves.

Conclusion

The national game is not dead or even dying. It's just changing, and change is a sign of life and progress, as John Ruskin told us back in the 1850s when writing about Venetian architecture. Baseball is like the fine buildings Ruskin described as full of "wolfish life" and "sturdy power."

Even when fans become temporarily annoyed at events in organized baseball and when attendance at baseball parks wavers, those fans continue to engage in myriad outside-the-park activities that hold their interest in baseball and can bring them back to the park.

American boys, even if they enjoy other entertainment, can still find ways to play ball at every stage of their lives, even preparing to enter organized baseball if their skills warrant. They know that professional players' feats are celebrated every day on the sports pages written by men and that the best players can demand huge salaries, so becoming a pro ballplayer can be a lucrative goal.

Men, if the level of their baseball ability remains too low for professional play, can easily find opportunities to reinforce their boyhood playing skills by taking part as amateurs, even at retirement age. They are willing to pay well, if necessary, for the chance to recapture their memories of youth. Men also confirm their delight in the game with myriad outside-the-park activities through which they utilize and further develop their knowledge of baseball's nuances.

Girls and women, unlike the men, find many blocks to their full participation in the national game. They can take part in fantasy ball and collecting, for example, but if they want to enjoy the game by playing it, they discover that they may need legal remedies for helping them surmount the barriers erected along every step of the path to their entrance into the highest ranks of play. As adults, they are edging ever closer to conquering those barriers by forming their own clubs and leagues, even traveling abroad to compete against other excellent teams, while a few talented women — as women have always done — keep before them the goal of participating in the baseball leagues set up by and for men.

Women baseball historians, stimulated by the striking evidence of women's long history in baseball and the apparent surge in the desire for equality in pursuing the national game, are publishing books revealing the close association of girls and women with baseball for more than a century and their continued determination to play the game they love.

I predict that women will become an increasing influence — even a force — in the national game, and that men will find it advisable to loosen their hold on organized baseball as the game changes even further in the future.

Is there something bad — or anything good! — about pursuing baseball as fervently as we have been doing for more than a century and a half? At the minimum, baseball has shaped our character. We have become a games-oriented society. Even if we don't play baseball, we know it well. It's part of our conversation, our view of American life, and often part of our regular activities, either in work or in play. It's become ingrained in us. What has it done to us?

First, it has given us joy. Play is joyful, and outdoor play is stimulating both physically and mentally. Second, watching it played well has given us entertainment, sometimes of amazing beauty and excitement. Third, it has given us something in common, something we can all talk about and appreciate, something that we think of when we describe ourselves as Americans.

Has baseball hurt us? Sometimes it does, when the athletes whose skill we admire disappoint us by churlish actions or illegal behavior, or when club owners fail to act in ways that help baseball more than themselves. At those times we feel our national character being impugned, for when baseball is injured, so are we.

Perhaps baseball hurts us in more subtle ways. We have become so enamored of professionalism that we sometimes lack appreciation for amateur play and its joyous spirit. We shrug off flaws we notice in the way baseball is presented to us. We would rather not think, for example, of our top athletes as millionaires who can afford every luxury while many fans need to save carefully in order to attend a game displaying their heroes' abilities. We brush aside with jokes the stories of players who break the rules of behavior they agreed to uphold and who use as an excuse their desire to perform better. We have developed the character blemish of self-congratulation for finally having become liberal enough to accept men of color in the professional leagues after having denied them their chance for nearly a century. We forget that many women aspire to the same chance; we scoff at their aspirations as we once scoffed at the desire of African American men to play in the white leagues.

Despite these problems in our celebration of the national game, it has given us much. We owe it to baseball to push it, and ourselves, to a higher level of conduct.

For a great many Americans, the pursuit of baseball equals the pursuit of happiness. We have discovered that sitting in baseball parks to watch others play is only one way we can delight in baseball. Happiness is pursuing the national game at home and around the country in an amazing variety of enjoyable activities. Our eager embrace of baseball has made it part of us.

Bibliography

Books and Book Chapters

Ardell, Jean Hastings. *Breaking into Baseball: Women and the National Pastime.* Carbondale: Southern Illinois University Press, 2005.

_____. "Cuba Libre Versus Women's Lib: A Comparison of the Feminine Side of Baseball in Cuba and in the United States." *The Cooperstown Symposium on Baseball and American Culture, 2003–2004.* William M. Simons, ed. Jefferson, NC: McFarland, 2005.

Asinof, Eliot. *Eight Men Out.* New York: Holt, Rinehart & Winston, 1963.

Baseball and the American Dream: Race, Class, Gender and the National Pastime. Robert Elias, ed. Armonk, N.Y: M.E. Sharpe, 2001, pp. 170–186.

Bean, Billy, with Chris Bull. *Going the Other Way: Lessons from a Life in and out of Major-League Baseball.* New York: Barnes & Noble, 2003.

Beneria, Lourdes. "In the Wilderness of One's Inner Self: Living Feminism." *The Feminist Memoir Project: Voices from Women's Liberation.* Rachel Blau DuPlessis and Ann Snitow, eds. New York: Three Rivers, 1998, pp. 249–267.

Berlage, Gai. *Women in Baseball: The Forgotten History.* Westport, CT: Praeger, 1994.

Block, David. *Baseball Before We Knew It: A Search for the Roots of the Game.* Lincoln: University of Nebraska Press, 2005.

Blumenthal, Karen. *Let Me Play: The Story of Title IX, the Law That Changed the Future of Girls in America.* New York: Atheneum, 2005.

Briley, Ron. "Ambiguous Patriotism: Baseball and the Vietnam War." *The Cooperstown Symposium on Baseball and American Culture, 2005–2006.* William M. Simons, ed. Jefferson, NC: McFarland, 2007, pp. 165–178.

Brown, Patricia L. *A League of My Own: Memoir of a Pitcher for the All-American Girls Professional Baseball League.* Jefferson, NC: McFarland, 2003.

Budig, Gene A. *The Inside Pitch ... and More: Baseball's Business and the Public Trust.* Morgantown: West Virginia University Press, 2004.

Carney, Gene. *Burying the Black Sox: How Baseball's Cover-Up of the 1919 World Series Fix Almost Succeeded.* Dulles, VA: Potomac, 2007.

Christensen, Karen, Allen Guttman, and Gertrud Pfister, eds. *The International Encyclopedia of Women and Sports.* Great Barrington, MA: Berkshire and Macmillan, 2001.

Clark, Joe. *A History of Australian Baseball: Time and Game.* Lincoln: University of Nebraska Press, 2003.

Cohen, Marilyn. *No Girls in the Clubhouse: The Exclusion of Women from Baseball.* Jefferson, NC: McFarland, 2009.

Coover, Robert. *The Universal Baseball Association, Inc., J. Henry Waugh, Prop.* New York: Penguin, 1968.

Corey, Shana. *Players in Pigtails.* New York: Scholastic, 2003.

Dailey, Thomas F. "Believing in Baseball: The Religious Power of Our National Pastime." *The Cooperstown Symposium on Baseball and American Culture, 2002.* Jefferson, NC: McFarland, 2003, pp. 339–356.

Deadball Committee of SABR. *Deadball Stars of the American League.* David Jones, ed. Dulles, VA: Potomac, 2006.

Dellinger, Susan. *Red Legs and Black Sox: Edd Roush and the Untold Story of the 1919 World Series.* Cincinnati: Ennis, 2006.

Eastman, Crystal. *Crystal Eastman, On Women and Revolution.* Blanche Wiesen Cook, ed. New York: Oxford University Press, 1978.

Egan, James M., Jr. *Base Ball on the Western Reserve: The Early Game in Cleveland and Northeast Ohio, Year by Year and Town by Town, 1865–1900.* Jefferson, NC: McFarland, 2008.

Ehrenreich, Barbara, and Dierdre English. *For Her Own Good: 150 Years of the Experts' Advice to Women.* New York: Anchor Doubleday, 1978.

Encyclopedia of Women and Baseball. Leslie A. Heaphy and Mel Anthony May, eds. Jefferson, NC: McFarland, 2006.

Fasteau, Brenda F. "Giving Women a Sporting Chance." *Out of the Bleachers: Writings on Women and Sport.* Stephanie L. Twin, ed. New York: Feminist, 1979, pp. 165–174.

Fidler, Merrie. *The Origins and History of the All-American Girls Professional Baseball League.* Jefferson, NC: McFarland, 2006.

Fields, Sarah K. "Cultural Identity, Law, and Baseball." *Sport and Memory in North America.* Stephen G. Wieting, ed. London: Frank Cass, 2001, pp. 23–42.

___. *Female Gladiators: Gender, Law, and Contact Sport in America.* Champaign: University of Illinois Press, 2005.

French, Marilyn. *A History of Women in the World. Vol. I, From Eve to Dawn.* New York: Feminist, 2008.

González Echevarría, Roberto. *The Pride of Havana: A History of Cuban Baseball.* New York: Oxford University Press, 1999.

Greenberg, Eric Rolfe. *The Celebrant.* Lincoln: University of Nebraska Press, 1983.

Gregorich, Barbara. *Women at Play: The Story of Women in Baseball.* New York: Harcourt Brace, 1993.

Harris, Mark. "Ladies' Day at the Game." *Diamond: Baseball Writings of Mark Harris.* New York: Donald I. Fine, 1994, pp. 148–154.

_____. "Recalling the Joy of Watching Baseball on the Radio." *Diamond: Baseball Writings of Mark Harris.* New York: Donald I. Fine, 1994, pp. 144–147.

Hauerwas, Stanley M. "Foreword." *The Faith of 50 Million: Baseball, Religion, and American Culture.* Christopher H. Evans and William R. Herzog II, eds. Louisville, KY: Westminster John Knox, 2002.

Hitler, Adolf. *Mein Kampf.* (1925–1926.) Boston: Houghton Mifflin, 1971.

Holbrook, David. *Children's Games.* London: Gordon Fraser, 1957.

Hollander, Russell. "On Being Gay in Major League Baseball." *Cooperstown Symposium on Baseball and the American Culture, 2002.* Jefferson, NC: McFarland, 2003, pp. 287–299.

Humber, William. "It's Our Game Too, Neighbour." *Dominionball: Baseball Above the 49th.* Jane Finnan Dorward, ed. Cleveland: SABR, 2005, pp. 3–9.

Johnson, Hody. *The Rise and Fall of Dodgertown: 60 Years of Baseball in Vero Beach.* Gainesville: University Press of Florida, 2008.

Johnson, Susan E. *When Women Played Hardball.* Seattle, WA: Seal, 1994.

Jozsa, Frank P., Jr. *Baseball in Crisis: Spiraling Costs, Bad Behavior, Uncertain Future.* Jefferson, NC: McFarland, 2008.

Katz, Marc. "I Didn't Think Baseball Players Were Real People: An Interview with Richie Scheinblum." *Batting Four Thousand: Baseball in the Western Reserve.* Brad Sullivan, ed. Cleveland: SABR, 2008.

Kern, Herman. *Through the Labyrinth: Designs and Meanings over 5,000 Years.* Munich: Prestel, 2000.

Kinsella, W.P. *Shoeless Joe.* Boston: Houghton Mifflin, 1982.

Kovach, John M. *Women's Baseball: Images of Baseball.* Charleston, SC: Arcadia, 2005.

Krieger, Kit. "My PCL Career." *Dominionball: Baseball Above the 49th.* Jane Finnan Dorward, ed. Cleveland: SABR, 2005, pp. 25–39.

Layden, Joe. *Women in Sports: The Complete Book on the World's Greatest Female Athletes.* Santa Monica, CA: W. Quay Hays, 1997.

Lowenfish, Lee. *Branch Rickey: Baseball's Ferocious Gentleman.* Lincoln: University of Nebraska Press, 2007.

Macy, Sue. *A Whole New Ball Game: The Story of the All-American Girls Professional Baseball League.* New York: Puffin Penguin, 1993.

McDonagh, Eileen, and Laura Pappano. *Playing with the Boys: Why Separate Is Not Equal in Sports.* New York: Oxford University Press, 2008.

Miles, Rosalind. *The Women's History of the World.* New York: HarperCollins, 1993.

Mills, Dorothy Jane. *A Woman's Work: Writing Baseball History with Harold Seymour.* Jefferson, NC: McFarland, 2004.

Moolman, Valerie, et al. *Women Aloft: The Epic of Flight.* New York: Time-Life, 1981.

Morris, Peter. *But Didn't We Have Fun? Baseball's Pioneer Era, 1843–1870.* Chicago: Ivan R. Dee, 2008.

_____. *A Game of Inches: The Stories Behind the Innovations That Shaped Baseball. Vol. I: The Game on the Field. Vol. II: The Game Behind the Scenes.* Chicago: Ivan R. Dee, 2006.

Murphy, Cait. *Crazy '08: How a Cast of Cranks, Rogues, Boneheads, and Magnates Created the Greatest Year in Baseball History.* New York: Smithsonian Books of HarperCollins, 2007.

Nathan, Daniel A. *Saying It's So: A Cultural History of the Black Sox Scandal: Sport and Society.* Champaign: University of Illinois Press, 2003.

O'Donnell, Doris. *Front-Page Girl.* Kent, OH: Kent State University Press, 2006.

Owen, Carol. *Crafting Personal Shrines.* New York: Lark, 2004.

Palmer, Gladys E. *Baseball for Girls and Women.* New York: A.S. Barnes, 1936.

Perrottet, Tony. *The Naked Olympics: The True Story of the Ancient Games.* New York: Random, 2004.

Postema, Pam, and Gene Wojciechowski. *You've Got to Have Balls to Make It in This League: My Life as an Umpire.* Lincoln: University of Nebraska Press, 2003.

Rappaport, Doreen, and Lyndall Callan. *Dirt on Their Skirts: The Story of the Young Women Who Won the World Championship.* New York: Dial, 2000.

Reaves, Joseph A. *Taking in a Game: A History of Baseball in Asia.* Lincoln: University of Nebraska Press, 2002.

Ring, Jennifer. *Stolen Bases: Why American Girls Don't Play Baseball.* Champaign: University of Illinois Press, 2009.

Rosen, Joel Nathan. *The Erosion of the American Sporting Ethos: Shifting Attitudes Toward Competition.* Jefferson, NC: McFarland, 2007.

Rudd, Robert, and Marshall G. Most. "American Values: The Oppositional Discourse of Baseball Films." *The Cooperstown Symposium on Baseball and American Culture, 2005–2006.* William M. Simons, ed. Jefferson, NC: McFarland, 2007.

Ruskin, John. *The Stones of Venice*. New York: Barnes & Noble, 2008.

Schubert, Arline, and George W. Schubert. "The Changing Language of Baseball Writers in Historical Context, 1900–2001." *The Cooperstown Symposium on Baseball and American Culture, 2002*. Alvin L. Hall, ed. Jefferson, NC: McFarland, 2003, pp. 269–283.

Seymour, Harold, and Dorothy Seymour. *Baseball: The Early Years*. New York: Oxford University Press, 1960.

_____, and _____. *Baseball: The Golden Age*. New York: Oxford University Press, 1971.

_____, and _____. *Baseball: The People's Game*. New York: Oxford University Press, 1990.

Shearon, Jim. *Over the Fence Is Out! The Larry Walker Story and More of Canada's Baseball Legends*. Kanata, Ontario: Malin Head, 2009.

Simon, William M. "From Exaltation to Historiography: A Celebration of 143 American Jews in America's Game 1871–2005." *The Cooperstown Symposium on Baseball and American Culture, 2005–2006*. Jefferson, NC: McFarland, 2007, pp. 179–197.

Smith, Ronald A. "The Lost Battle for Gentlemanly Sport, 1869–1909." *The Curse and the HUB: A Random History of Boston Sports*. Randy Roberts, ed. Cambridge: Harvard University Press, 2005.

Snyder, Brad. *A Well-Paid Slave: Curt Flood's Fight for Free Agency in Professional Sports*. New York: Viking, 2006.

Snyder, David L., and Michael K. Zietlli. "The Case for Curt Flood: Why He Should Be in Baseball's Hall of Fame." *Mound City Memories: Baseball in St. Louis*. Cleveland: SABR, 2007.

Springwood, Charles Fruehling. *Cooperstown to Dyersville: A Geography of Baseball Nostalgia*. Boulder, CO: Westview, 1996.

Stang, Mark. *Indians Illustrated: 100 Years of Cleveland Indians Photos*. Wilmington, OH: Orange Frazer, 2000.

Stebner, Eleanor J., and Tracy J. Trothen. "A Diamond Is Forever? Women, Baseball, and a Pitch for a Radically Inclusive Community." *The Faith of 50 Million: Baseball, Religion, and American Culture*. Christopher H. Evans and William R. Herzog II, eds. Louisville, KY: Westminster John Knox, 2002, pp. 167–184.

Stein, Andi. "When Baseball Players Wore Skirts: The Promotion of the All-American Girls Professional Baseball League." *The Cooperstown Symposium on Baseball and American Culture, 2002*. Jefferson, NC: McFarland, 2003.

Suggs, Welch. *A Place on the Team: The Triumph and Tragedy of Title IX*. Princeton, NJ: Princeton University Press, 2005.

Trombe, Carolyn M. *Dottie Wiltse Collins: Strikeout Queen of the All-American Girls Professional Baseball League*. Jefferson, NC: McFarland, 2005.

Weber, Bruce. *As They See 'Em; A Fan's Travels in the Land of Umpires*. New York: Scribner, 2009.

Wertheim, Margaret. *Pythagoras' Trousers: God, Physics, and the Gender Wars*. New York: W.W. Norton, 1997.

Wisnia, Saul, with Dan Schlossberg. *The Wit and Wisdom of Baseball*. Lincolnwood, IL: Publications International, 2007.

Wong, Stephen. *Smithsonian Baseball: Inside the World's Finest Private Collections*. New York: HarperCollins, 2005.

Youngen, Lois J. "A League of Our Own." *Baseball and the American Dream: Race, Class, Gender and the National Pastime*. Robert Elias, ed. Armonk, NY: M.E. Sharpe, 2001, pp. 248–254.

Zimbalist, Andrew. *Baseball and Billions: A Probing Look Inside the Business of Our National Pastime*. New York: Basic, 1992 and 1994.

Zumsteg, Derek. *The Cheater's Guide to Baseball*. Boston: Houghton Mifflin, 2007.

Articles in Scholarly Periodicals

Adams, Carly. "Leagues of Their Own? A Case Study of Women's Community Sport Participation, London, Ontario 1920–50." *North American Society for Sport History Proceedings* (2005): 144.

Altherr, Thomas. "Chucking the Old Apple: Recent Discoveries of Pre–1840 North American Ball Games." *Base Ball: A Journal of the Early Game* 2 (Spring 2008): 29–43.

Ardell, Jean Hastings. "Baseball Is a Man's Game: Or Is It?" *Elysian Fields Quarterly* 12 (Spring 1993): 8–10.

Ardolino, Frank. "Film Review: The Brooklyn Dodgers: The Ghosts of Flatbush, HBO Sports, 2007." *NINE: A Journal of Baseball History and Culture* 17 (Fall 2008): 158–60.

Aronson, Anne. "Leveling the Playing Field: Women's Baseball in Australia." *Elysian Fields Quarterly* 24 (Fall 2007): 22–33.

Bennett, Jay. "Did Shoeless Joe Jackson Throw the 1919 World Series?" *The American Statistician* 47 (1992): 241–250.

Bjarkman, Peter C. "Baseball Novels from Gil Gamesh to Babe Ragland to Sidd Finch: A Bibliographical Survey of Serious Adult Baseball Fiction Since 1973." *Minneapolis Review of Baseball* 9 (Spring 1990): 32–54.

_____. "Diamonds Are a Gal's Worst Friend: Women in Baseball History and Fiction." *Elysian Fields Quarterly* 12 (Spring 1993): 93–105.

Blaisdell, Lowell L. "The Cobb-Speaker Scandal: Exonerated but Probably Guilty." *NINE: A Journal of Baseball History and Culture* 13 (Spring 2005): 54–70.

Block, David. "The Story of William Bray's Diary." *Base Ball: A Journal of the Early Game* 1 (Fall 2007): 5–11.

Borst, William A. "Baseball for Credit." *Baseball Research Journal* 4 (1974). Seen at *http://brj.sabrwebs.com*

Briley, Ron. "Baseball and Dissent: The Vietnam Experience." *NINE: A Journal of Baseball History and Culture* 17 (Fall 2008): 54–69.

Carriere, Michael H. "'A Diamond Is a Boy's Best Friend'; The Rise of Little League Baseball, 1939–1964." *Journal of Sport History* 32 (Fall 2005): 51–37.

Chandler, Timothy. Review of William J. Baker, *Playing with God: Religion and Modern Sport* (Cambridge: Harvard University Press, 2007). *Journal of Sport History* 35 (Spring 2008): 161–163.

Christensen, Chris. "Merkle Haunts Moises, or Why the Cubs Will Never Win It All." *Elysian Fields Quarterly* 25 (Summer 2008): 13–18.

Crepeau, Richard. "Remembering Jules Tygiel." *Elysian Fields Quarterly* 25 (Spring 2008): 93–95.

Durrell, Mike. "The Scorebook: Letter to the Editor: Ballparks for Billionaires." *Elysian Fields Quarterly* 25 (Spring 2008): 79.

Frohlich, Cliff, and Gary R. Scott. "Where Spectators Sit to Catch Baseballs." *Baseball Research Journal* 11 (1982). Seen at *http://brj.sabrwebs.com*

Gabriel, Daniel. "One Part Baseball and One Part Brawl." Review of Bill Felber, *A Game of Brawl* (Lincoln: University of Nebraska Press, 2007). *Elysian Fields Quarterly* 25 (Spring 2008): 96–99.

Gmelch, George. "The Changing Culture of Professional Baseball." *Elysian Fields Quarterly* 25 (Spring 2008): 80–91.

Goldstein, Tom. "The Mitchell Apologia." *Elysian Fields Quarterly* 25 (Spring 2008): 2–4.

_____. "Why I Don't Go to the Ballpark." *Elysian Fields Quarterly* 25 (Fall 2008): 2–4.

Helmer, Diana. "You Hit Like My Mother! And I Mean That as a Compliment." *Elysian Fields Quarterly* 12 (Spring 1993): 22–23.

Hershberger, Richard. "A Reconstruction of Philadelphia Town Ball." *Base Ball: A Journal of the Early Game* 1 (Fall 2007): 28–43.

"In the Owner's Box." *Minneapolis Review of Baseball* 9 (Spring 1990): 1.

Jette, Shannon. "Little/Big Ball: The Vancouver Asahi Baseball Story." *North American Society for Sport History Proceedings, 2006* (34th Annual Conference, Glenwood Springs, CO): 35.

Kashatus, William C. "The Origins of Baseball Chapel and the Era of the Christian Athlete, 1973–1990." *NINE: A Journal of Baseball History and Social Policy Perspectives* 7 (Spring 1999): 75–90.

Keating, James. "Sportsmanship as a Moral Category." *Ethics* 75 (October 1964): 25–35.

Koppett, Leonard. Quoted in "Diamond Quotes." *NINE: A Journal of Baseball History and Culture* 17 (Fall 2008): vi.

Lamb, Chris. Review of Peter Morris, *Level Playing Fields: How the Groundskeeping Murphy Brothers Shaped Baseball* (Lincoln: University of Nebraska Press, 2007). *NINE: A Journal of Baseball History and Culture* 17 (Fall 2008): 141–142.

Lehman, Stephen. "They Played the Game." *Elysian Fields Quarterly* 12 (Summer 1993): 1.

Lowenfish, Lee. "He Still Has the Good Hands." *Minneapolis Review of Baseball* 9 (Spring 1990): 28–31.

Mandell, David. "Danny Gardella and the Reserve Clause." *The National Pastime: A Review of Baseball History* 26 (2006): 41–44.

Mars, Sally. "A Lens on Life." *Elysian Fields Quarterly* 24 (Summer 2007): 70.

Mills, Dorothy Jane. Review of Daniel A. Nathan, *Saying It's So: A Cultural History of the Black Sox Scandal* (Champaign: University of Illinois Press, 2003). *Sport in History* 23 (Summer 2003): 152–155.

Minichino, Camille. "Memoir: The Boston Braves." *Elysian Fields Quarterly* 12 (Summer 1993).

Nader, Ralph. "What Hath George Wrought? An Open Letter to Boss Steinbrenner." *Elysian Fields Quarterly* 23 (Fall 2006): 25–26.

Newman, Roberta. "The American Church of Baseball and the National Baseball Hall of Fame." *NINE: A Journal of Baseball History and Culture* 10 (Spring 2002). Excerpt in *Questia, www.questia.com*

Ogden, David C. "African-Americans and Pick-up Ball." *NINE: A Journal of Baseball History and Culture* 9 (Fall 2001): 201–207.

Paraschak, Victoria. "The Canadian Sport Policy: A Good Framework for Northwest Territories' Sport and Recreation?" *North American Society for Sport History Proceedings 2005*: 67–68.

Parks, Richard H. "Mass Deception." Review of Kevin Nelson, *Operation Bullpen: The Inside Story of the Biggest Forgery Scam in American History* (Benicia, CA: Southampton Books, 2006). *Elysian Fields Quarterly* 25 (Spring 2008): 104–106.

Percoco, James A. "Baseball and World War II: A Study of the Landis-Roosevelt Correspondence." *OAH Magazine of History* 7 (Summer 1992). Seen at *http://www.oah.org/pubs/magazine/sport/percoco.html*

Pietrusza, David. "Grace Coolidge — The First Lady of Baseball." *Elysian Fields Quarterly* 12 (Summer 1993): 36–39.

Reaves, Joseph A. "Silk Gowns and Gold Gloves: The Forgotten History of Chinese Bat Ball." *NINE: A Journal of Baseball History and Social Policy Perspectives* 7 (Spring 1999): 60–74.

Reis, Elizabeth. "The Devil, the Body, and the Feminine Soul in Puritan New England." *Journal of American History* 82 (June 1995): 15–36.

Reisler, Jim. "Jack Kerouac: The Beat of Fantasy Baseball." *The National Pastime* 28 (Fall 2008): 40–44.

Riess, Steven A. "The Lead-off Batter Who Slugged Home Runs: Harold Seymour and the Making of the History of Baseball." *Journal of Sport History* 29 (Spring 2002): 135–144.

Ring, Jennifer. "Still Second Class: USA Women Are World Cup Baseball Champions." *Elysian Fields Quarterly* 23 (Fall 2006): 34–39.

Rogers, Brad. "Win Your Fantasy League for Only $250 a Day!" Review of Sam Walker, *Fantasyland: A Season on Baseball's Lunatic Fringe* (New York: Viking, 2006). *Elysian Fields Quarterly* 24 (Spring 2007): 102–104.

Roseboro, John. Quoted in "Diamond Quotes." *NINE: A Journal of Baseball History and Social Policy Perspectives* 7 (Spring 1999): frontispiece.

Ruck, Robb. Review of Samuel O. Regalado, *Viva Baseball! Latin Major Leaguers and Their Special Hunger* (Champaign: University of Illinois Press, 1998). *NINE: A Journal of Baseball History and Social Policy Perspectives* 7 (Spring 1999): 132–134.

Rycenga, Jennifer. Review of Tara Magdalinski and Timothy J.L. Chandler, *With God on Their Side: Sport in the Service of Religion* (London: Routledge, 2002). *Journal of Religion and Popular Culture* (Fall 2002). Seen at *http://www.usask.ca/relst/irpc/br-gononside-print.html*

Shiner, David. "Revisiting the Clemente Myth." Review of David Maraniss, *Clemente: The Passion and Grace of Baseball's Last Hero* (New York: Simon & Schuster, 2006). *Elysian Fields Quarterly* 24 (Spring 2007): 94–99.

Shipley, Robert E. "The Great American Baseball Trivia Sting." *Baseball Research Journal* 8 (1989). Seen at *http://brj.sabrwebs.com*

Shymanik, Steve. "A Baseball Enlightenment?" *Elysian Fields Quarterly* 22 (Summer 2005): 80–86.

Stevens, William S. "The Common Law Origins of the Infield Fly Rule." *University of Pennsylvania Law Review*, June 1975.

Stolfa, Ellen. "Baseball 101: Souvenir of Chicago." *Elysian Fields Quarterly* 12 (Spring 1993): 45–48.

Stucker, Angela Welch. "How Baseball Breaks Your Heart." *Elysian Fields Quarterly* 25 (Spring 2008): 16–19.

Szymanski, Stefan. "The Theory of the Evolution of Modern Sport." *Journal of Sport History* 35 (Spring 2008): 1–32.

Thomsen, Melinda. "Naming Rights." *Elysian Fields Quarterly* 25 (Spring 2008): 66–67.

Waddle, Sarah. "Refuge." *Elysian Fields Quarterly* 24 (Summer 2007): 70.

Wolter, Tim. "National Amp Baseball." *Elysian Fields Quarterly* 25 (Summer 2008): 442–47.

Articles in Popular Periodicals

Angell, Roger. "An Editor's Note: The Fadeaway." *New Yorker*, February 9 and 16, 2009, p. 39.

Beinart, Peter. "The Devil in Every Fan." *Time Magazine*, September 20, 2007.

Coll, Steve. "Comment: The Get." *New Yorker*, September 22, 2008, pp. 31–32.

Deford, Frank. "Now Georgy-Porgy Runs Away." *Sports Illustrated*, April 22, 1974. Seen at *http://cnnsi.printthis.clickability.com*

Dolgoff, Stephanie. "The Best (and Worst) Moments in Women's Health." *Health*, September 2008, pp. 138–140.

Falk, William. "Editor's Letter." *The Week*, June 15, 2007.

_____. "Editor's Letter." *The Week*, October 12, 2007.

Fallows, James. "Throwing Like a Girl." *The Atlantic*, August 1996. Seen at *http://www.theatlantic.com/doc*

"FFRF Halts Praying Coach." *Freethought Today* (Madison, WI), January/February 2009.

"Findings." *Harpers Magazine*, December 2008.

Fitzgerald, Mark. "Study: Newspaper Sports Departments Mostly Male, White." *Editor and Publisher*, June 26, 2008. Seen at *http://www.editorandpublisher.com*

Fretts, Bruce. "Wild Things." *MLB Insiders Club Magazine* 2 (January 2008): 60–63.

"From Our Pages: Picked-Up Pieces, Moments from a Half-Century of Updike." *New Yorker*, February 9 and 16, 2009.

Ghosh, Bobby. "The Original Amazing Indian Reality Show." *Sports Illustrated*, March 9, 2009.

"Global: Short Takes; Cuba." *Ms. Magazine*, Winter 2009, p. 32.

Goldberger, Paul. "The Sky Line: Home; New Stadiums for the Yankees and the Mets." *New Yorker*, March 23, 2009, pp. 76–77.

"Good Week for: Die-Hard Fans." *The Week*, December 12, 2008.

"Harper's Index." *Harper's Magazine*, August 2008, p. 11.

Hawthorn, Tom. "Romancing the Diamond." *(Vancouver) B.C. Business*, September 1, 2004. Seen at *http://www.bcbusinessonline.ca/node/531*

Heilemann, John. "Let Juice Loose." *New York Magazine*, April 10, 2006. Seen at *http://ny mag.com/news/politics/powergrid*

Hitchens, Christopher. "Cruel and Unusual: V.S. Naipaul Has Produced Works of Extraordinary Skill — and Lived a Life of Equally Extraordinary Callousness." *The Atlantic*, November 2008, pp. 134–139.

Hohn, Donovan. "Through the Open Door: Searching for Deadly Toys in China's Pearl River Delta." *Harper's Magazine*, September 2008, pp. 47–58.

Holmes, Evelyn. "Baseball Fans Hoping, Praying for Wins." *Chicago News*, October 4, 2008. Seen at *http://abclocal.go.com/wls*

"How Fear Leads to Magical Thinking: Health and Science." *The Week*, October 14, 2008, p. 21.

"How We're Doing: Girls + Math = Smart!" *Ms. Magazine*, Fall 2008.

Hyman, Mark. "Take Me Out to the Museum." *Business Week*, April 11, 2005. Seen at *http://www.businessweek.com/magazine/content*

"It Wasn't All Bad." *The Week*, March 10, 2008.

Johnston, David Cay. "Fiscal Therapy." *Mother Jones*, January/February, 2009, pp. 28–34.

Klosterman, Chuck. "The Last Word: Why Barry Bonds Matters." *The Week*, May 12, 2006.

Krauthammer, Charles. "The Decline of Baseball Civilization: Our Pastime Isn't What It Used to Be, and Neither Are We." *The Weekly* Standard, April 13, 1998. Seen at *http://www.weeklystandardcom/Utilities/printer_preview.asp?idArticle=1570&R=13CIE*

Kurkjian, Tim. "The Closer: Nothing Better — Few Things in Life Can Match a Day at the Ballpark." *MLB Insiders Club Magazine* 2 (2009): 64.

McDonell, Terry. "Spinning Alex Rodriguez." *Sports Illustrated*, March 2, 2009.

"Media: Is a Sports Star's Infidelity News?" *The Week*, June 15, 2007.

"Milestones." *Ms. Magazine*, Winter 2009.

Morris, Jan. "My Kind of Town: Oxford England; Among the Spires." *Smithsonian*, January 2009, pp. 22–24.

Nightengale, Bob. "Baseball's Rockies Seek Revival on Two Levels." *USA Today*, June 1, 2008. Seen at *http://usatoday.printthis.clickability.com*.

"Noted." *The Week*, April 11, 2008.

"Noted." *The Week*, September 5, 2008.

Nowlin, Bill. "Night Games." *Boston Magazine*, October 2002.

Park, Ted. "Letters: Defining the Line." *Scientific American*, August 2008, p. 10.

Sapakoff, Gene. "Little League's Civil War." *Sports Illustrated*, October 20, 1995. Seen at *http://cnnsi.printthis.clickability.com*

Shermer, Michael. "Sports Psychology: The Doping Dilemma; Game Theory Helps to Explain the Pervasive Abuse of Drugs in Cycling, Baseball and Other Sports." *Scientific American*, April 2008, pp. 80–89.

Surwiecki, James. "The Buffet of Baseball." *New Yorker*, September 23, 2002, p. 37.

USA Philatelic: The Official Source for Stamp Enthusiasts 14 (Spring 2009).

"Win a Baseball Dream Room!" *MLB Insiders Club Magazine* 1 (2008): 8–9.

Wolff, Alexander. "Prima Donna." *Sports Illustrated*, December 17, 1990. Seen at *http://cnnsi.printthis.clickability.com*

Young, Peter A. "The Varieties of Ritual Experience." *Archaeology*, November/December 2008, p. 6.

Newspaper Articles

Ackman, Dan. "Bookshelf: Playing Hard, Feeling Pain." Review of Mark Hyman, *Until It Hurts* (Boston: Beacon, 2009). *Wall Street Journal*, March 30, 2009.

Albach, Banks. "That Was a Fine Double Play, Sir." *San Mateo (CA) Daily News*, December 19, 2006. Seen at *http://www.sanmateodailynews.com*

"All Together: Let's Go Jack! Let's Go Jill!" *New York Times*, January 19, 2007.

Anderson, Dave. "Sports of the Times: Dear Bud: It's Time to Forgive Pete Rose." *New York Times*, October 27, 2007.

Araton, Harvey. "Tear Down the Stadium and Build Up the Bronx." *New York Times*, January 25, 2009.

Associated Press. "Women in I.O.C. Pitch." *New York Times*, April 7, 2009.

Atoz, P. "Dear Diary: Metropolitan Diary." *New York Times*, December 1, 2008.

Babwin, Don. "Born a Cubs Fan, Die a Cubs Fan." *Naples* (FL) *Daily News*, July 12, 2008.

Baker, Kevin. "Decades before Bartman, There Was Merkle." *New York Times*, September 23, 2008.

Bannerjee, Neela. "Religion and Its Role Are in Dispute at the Service Academies." *New York Times*, June 25, 2008.

Barra, Allen. "Fists Raised, but Not in Anger." *New York Times*, August 23, 2008.

Barron, James. "Possession of a Ball Is Some Tenths of the Law." *New York Times*, September 24, 2008.

"Baseball: Roundup; Rose Admits to Betting on the Reds Every Night." *New York Times*, March 15, 2007.

"Baseball Stars a Big Hit." *Naples (FL) Daily News*, January 26, 2007.

Beane, Billy, Newt Gingrich, and John Kerry. "How to Take American Health Care from Worst to First." *New York Times*, October 24, 2008.

"Bernice Gera, Umpire, 61." *New York Times*, September 25, 1992.

Blumenfeld, Laura. "In Baseball Now, More Teams Pray Before They Play." *Washington Post*, September 18, 2005. Seen at *http://www.washingtonpost.com*

Blumner, Robyn. "Bush's Church-State Mess Takes Liberties with Ours." *St. Petersburg Times*, July 2, 2007.

Boswell, Thomas. "Recovered History: A Baseball Star to Admire." *Washington Post*, July 2007. Seen at *Undernews, http://prerev.com/2007/07/recovered-history-baseball-star-tc.htm*

Bouton, Jim. "Art/Architecture: Fantasy Baseball of Another Kind." *New York Times*, June 29, 2003.

Boyer, Mary Schmitt. "Teams Hit Marketing Home Run Mixing Faith, Sports." *Cleveland Plain Dealer*, October 11, 2006. Seen at *http://www.faithstreams.com*

Branch, John. "Want to Tread on Jeter's Turf? Yankees Grass Is Now a Brand." *New York Times*, March 22, 2009.

"Buy Me Some Sushi and Baby Back Ribs." *New York Times*, June 8, 2008. Seen at *http://www.nytimes.com/2008*

Carillo, Mary. "Aspiring to Tennis's Play-by-Play Seat." *New York Times,* September 5, 2008.

Chadwell, Katie. "'High Pockets' to Celebrate 90th Birthday; Negro Leaguer Played during Segregated Times." (Georgetown, OH) *News Democrat,* March 12, 2009. Seen at *http://newsdemocrat.com*

Chaker, Anne Marie. "Winner by a Hair: Collectors Wooed with a Bit of Abe Lincoln." *Wall Street Journal,* November 18, 2008. Seen at *http://www.careerjournal.com/article*

Chambers, Marcia. "Barred from Men's-Only Event, Woman Sues Public Golf Club." *New York Times*, February 19, 2008.

Chass, Murray. "Pete Rose's Lesson for Roger Clemens." *New York Times,* December 20, 2007.

Cho, Adrian. "Letters to the Editor: Where Have All the Heroes Gone?" *New York Times*, December 15, 2007.

"The City Life: There's No Short Selling in Baseball." *New York Times*, February 8, 2009.

Clifford, Stephanie. "Math Whiz Finds Fame by Calling It for Obama." *New York Times*, November 10, 2008.

Cocco, Marie, and Carol Jenkins. Quoted in "Quotable Items from the 2008 NOW Conference." *National NOW Times,* Fall 2008.

Collins, Glenn. "For Mets Fans, a Menu Beyond Peanuts and Cracker Jack." *New York Times*, March 25, 2009.

Connelly, Marjorie. "Poll Finds That Rodriguez Has Limited Fan Support." *New York Times*, February 26, 2009.

Consoli, John. "A Network Takes Us Out to a Ballgame." *New York Times,* March 24, 2009.

"Cuban Athlete Is Barred for Kicking Referee's Face." *New York Times*, August 24, 2008.

"Cuban Crisis." *Naples (FL) Daily News*, August 24, 2008.

"Cubs Fans May Soon Have Chance to be Buried in Wrigley-Like Field." *Chicago Tribune*, September 12, 2008. Seen at *http://www.chicagotribune.com*

Curry, Jack. "Another Clue That Baseball Auction Has Stolen Items." *New York Times*, July 5, 2009.

_____. "One Fan Makes His Point: Ruth Called That Shot." *New York Times,* August 31, 2008.

Curtis, Bryan. "The National Pastime(s)." *New York Times*, February 1, 2009.

Dao, James. "Cincinnati Journal: Reds Fans Stand by Their Hometown Rogue, Pete Rose." *New York Times*, January 23, 2004.

"Diamonds Are Forever." *Racine* (WI) *Journal Times*, July 3, 2008.

Durkin, Karen. "Letters: Hurt Girls." *New York Times Magazine,* May 25, 2008.

Elliott, Stuart. "Olympics Draw High Percentage of Women Viewers and Ads Intended for Them." *New York Times*, August 19, 2008.

Erardi, John. "Players Show Up to Honor 'A Good Woman.'" *Cincinnati Enquirer,* March 7, 2004. Seen at *http://www.enquirer.com*

Fabricant, Florence. "Yankee Stadium Has a Full Plate." *New York Times,* March 25, 2009.

Fatsis, Stefan. "Ideas and Trends: What Recession? We're Ballplayers." *New York Times*, December 7, 2008.

"Finishing Second with a Champion's Grace." *New York Times*, August 17, 2008.

Fox, Margalit. "Sheldon Meyer, Oxford Press Editor, Dies at 80." *New York Times,* October 18, 2006.

Frommer, Frederic J. "Baseball to Add Women to Olympic Bid." *Seattle Post-Intelligencer,* April 6, 2009.

Goldstein, Richard. "Mary Garber, 92, Sportswriting Pioneer." *New York Times,* September 23, 2008.

_____. "Preacher Roe, Brooklyn Dodgers Star Known for His Spitball, Dies at 92." *New York Times,* November 11, 2008.

_____. "Sal Yvars, 84; Revealed Baseball Scheme." *New York Times,* December 12, 2008.

González Echevarría, Roberto. "Castro at the Bat." *New York Times,* January 11, 2006.

Grimes, William. "William S. Stevens, 60, Dies; Wrote Infield Fly Note." *New York Times,* December 12, 2008.

"A Hall of Fame for Great Stories." *New York Times,* March 1, 2007.

Herring, Chris. "Field Study: Convention Greets Devoted Baseball Fans." *Cleveland Plain Dealer,* June 28, 2008.

Hyman, Mark. "Challenges for Girls Playing High School Baseball." *New York Times,* March 1, 2009.

Isherwood, Charles. "Theater Review: Peanuts, Cracker Jack and Some Illegal Juice." *New York Times,* November 19, 2008.

Jones, Justin. "Building a Young Audience at Ballparks." *New York Times,* August 30, 2008.

"Just a Few More Questions, Ms. Thomas." Review of *Thank You, Mr. President: Helen Thomas at the White House,* a film for HBO. *New York Times,* August 18, 2008.

Kastner, Jeffrey. "Out of Tiffany's Shadow, a Woman of Light." *New York Times,* February 26, 2007.

Kepner, Tyler. "As Team Looks On, Rodriguez Details His Use of Steroids." *New York Times,* February 18, 2009.

_____. "Dugout Drafters: On Sundays in the Fall, Baseball Players Live Out Their Fantasies as Owners." *New York Times,* August 31, 2008.

_____. "Rodriguez Takes the Field, and Few Seem to Notice." *New York Times,* February 25, 2009.

Klinkenborg, Verlyn. "Politeness and Authority at a Hilltop College in Minnesota." *New York Times,* October 15, 2007.

Lacy, Marc. "Revered by the Castros and Their Opponents." *New York Times,* July 28, 2008.

Lewin, Tamar. "Many Specialists at Private Universities Earn More Than Presidents." *New York Times,* February 23, 2009.

_____. "Math Scores Show No Gap for Girls, Study Finds." *New York Times,* July 25, 2008.

"Like Messages from the Departed." *New York Times,* September 8, 2008.

Lindgren, Hugo. "I'll Manage." Review of Scott Gray, *The Mind of Bill James* (New York: Doubleday, 2006), and Sam Walker, *Fantasyland: A Season on Baseball's Lunatic Fringe* (New York: Viking, 2006). *New York Times Book Review,* June 4, 2006.

Longman, Jere. "Omega and Phelps: The Timekeeper and the Gold Medalist." *New York Times,* August 31, 2008.

Macur, Juliet. "Teaching Baseball as Second Language in China." *New York Times,* July 5, 2008.

Malozzi, Vincent M. "At Rutgers, Yankee Stadium 101." *New York Times,* October 26, 2008.

Marchiano, Sal. "The Shot Seen Round the World." *New York Times,* October 22, 2008.

McCauley, Janie. "South Korea Beats Cuba for Gold; United States Takes Bronze in Baseball's Olympic Swan Song." *Naples* (FL) *Daily News,* August 24, 2008.

"Memorabilia Will Go, Memories Will Linger." *Cleveland Plain Dealer,* July 11, 2008.

"Metropolitan Diary." *New York Times,* September 22, 2008.

Miller, Jen A. "City Stops to Enjoy Parade as Phillies Fans Flood Broad Street." *New York Times*, November 1, 2008.

Mizell, Hubert. "Baseball's Decline Is Traced to Youngsters." *St. Petersburg Times*, April 6, 2003. Seen at *http://www.sptimes.com/2003/04/06/news*

Moulton, Donald. "It's Sad to Say: Olympics Are Out of Control." *Naples* (FL) *Daily News*, September 17, 2008.

"A Network to Satisfy the Appetite of Baseball-Hungry Fans." *New York Times*, October 3, 2008.

"#1 Vegetarian Ballpark." *Cool Cleveland*, April 2004.

"Obama Seeks Bigger Role for Religious Groups." *New York Times*, July 2, 2008.

Oberhaus, Linda A. "Why Does She Stay? Sometimes, It's Society's Fault." *Naples* (FL) *Daily News*, October 7, 2007.

O'Keefe, Michael, and Bill Madden. "Cooperstown Haul of Fame; Thieves Steal Millions in Baseball Treasures." *New York Daily News*, August 20, 2000.

Olney, Buster. "An Outside-the-Park Investigation." *New York Times*, April 1, 2006.

Powelson, Richard. *Pittsburgh Post-Gazette*, December 31, 2003.

Read, Madlen. "The Name Game: Naming a Stadium, Frivolous or Good Marketing?" *New York Times*, February 5, 2009.

Rhoden, William C. "Concerned Coaches Are Wondering, Why So Few Blacks?" *New York Times*, June 11, 1990.

_____. "Recession Is a Relative Term in Baseball." *New York Times*, November 17, 2009.

Robinson, Joshua. "Opening Up to the World: Collectors Reveal Their New Cards on Internet." *New York Times*, April 4, 2009.

"Rooting for the Home Team, Hot Dog in Hand." Letters to the Editor, *New York Times*, July 20, 2008.

Rossetti, Diana. "Largest Baseball Exhibit Opens in Pennsylvania." *Canton* (OH) *Repository*, July 6, 2008.

Ruger, Todd. "Deputy Accepts $370,000 in Gender Bias Lawsuit." *Sarasota (FL) Herald Tribune*, February 20, 2009. Courtesy of Debbie Delahanty of NOW, February 22, 2009.

Sandomir, Richard. "Naming Rights Called 'Ego Boost.'" *New York Times*, February 26, 2009.

_____. "Sports Museum Having Problems." *New York Times*, December 10, 2008.

_____. "Tickets for New Stadiums: Prices, and Outrage, Escalate." *New York Times*, August 26, 2008.

_____. "TV Sports: Baseball Ratings Don't Trump King Football." *New York Times*, October 8, 2008.

Santini, Simone. Letter to the Editor. *New York Times*, August 23, 2008.

Santos, Fernanda. "City Gives Up Suite at Yankee Stadium in Exchange for Cash." *New York Times*, January 7, 2009.

Savage, David D. "Fantasy Baseball Leagues Can Use Real Players' Names, Supreme Court Agrees." *Los Angeles Times*, June 3, 2008.

Schiesel, Seth. "Root, Root, Root for the Home Team ... Wait, I Am the Home Team." *New York Times*, April 16, 2009.

___. "Supreme Court Backs U.S.O.C. in Discrimination Case." *New York Times*, October 7, 2008.

Schmidt, Michael S. "The Mitchell Report: 11 Months Later, Baseball Is Praised." *New York Times*, November 26, 2008.

_____. "Yankees Defend Spending As Almost a Public Service." *New York Times*, December 25, 2008.

Schwarz, Alan. "As Paralympics Begin, U.S. Athletes Add Equality to Their Goals." *New York Times*, September 6, 2008.

_____. "Numbers Are Cast in Bronze, But Are Not Set in Stone." *New York Times*, July 21, 2005.

Solomon, Deborah. "Anger Management." *New York Times*, June 17, 2007.

Spanberg, Erik. "An Industry Reshuffles to Recapture Its Youth." *Christian Science Monitor*, August 1, 2004. Seen at *http://www.csmonitor.com/2005l*

Spinski, Tristan. "Our World: The 10th Man." *Naples* (FL) *Daily News*, March 13, 2006.

Spitz, Bob. "No Asterisk." Review of Leigh Montville, *The Big Bam: The Life and Times of Babe Ruth* (New York: Doubleday, 2006). *New York Times Book Review,* June 4, 2006, p. 13.

"Steiner Sports Live at the Times Center; The New York Times Store Event." *New York Times*, September 28, 2008.

Steinhauer, Jennifer. "A Cozy Spot to Eat After Golf, but Women Are Out of Bounds." *New York Times*, June 28, 2008.

"Steroids in Sports: Better Baseball through Chemistry." *Naples* (FL) *Daily News*, December 15, 2007.

Strand, Charles. "Girls Baseball Moguls Smoke Pipe of Peace." *New York Post Home News*, June 18, 1948. Copy courtesy of Merrie Fidler.

Sulzberger, A.G. "Yankees in a Bubble: New Stadium's Design Keeps Autograph Seekers at Bay." *New York Times*, June 3, 2009.

Taub, Eric A. "Webcam Brings 3-D to Topps Sports Cards." *New York Times,* March 9, 2009.

Thomas, Katie. "In Cape Cod League, Tradition vs. Trademark." *New York Times*, October 24, 2008.

_____. "The United States Archery Coach Fastens Religion to His Sport." *New York Times*, August 19, 2008.

Thomas, Pam. "Columnist Moulton Strikes Out in His Tribute to Moms." *Naples* (FL) *Daily News*, May 21, 2008.

Thorn, John. "Play's the Thing." *Woodstock* (NY) *Times*, November 15, 2007.

Tierney, John. "A New Frontier for Title IX: Science." *New York Times,* July 15, 1008.

Traub, James. "Designated Villain." *New York Times Magazine*, August 19, 2007.

Vecsey, George. "Feeling Connected to Gehrig, a Fan Fights On." *New York Times,* November 8, 2008.

_____. "Mom, Apple Pie, and Baseball Cards." *New York Times,* January 16, 2009.

_____. "Sports of the Times: Bonds Will Pass 714, but Not the Legend." *New York Times*, May 2, 2006.

_____. "Sports of the Times: Giving the Mets' New Ballpark a Bad Name." *New York Times*, December 2, 2008.

_____. "Sports of the Times: Parents Feel Betrayed by Millionaire Role Models." *New York Times*, February 10, 2008.

_____. "Sports Thursday: Torre Hovers Over Razing of Yankee Stadium." *New York Times*, September 18, 2008.

_____. "Years of Suffering Fuel Fans' Devotion." *New York Times*, October 27, 2008.

Vincent, Fay. "Union-Busting at the Hall of Fame." *New York Times,* December 8, 2007.

Walker, Rob. "Crown Jewelry: A Cap Manufacturer's Evolution into a Fashionable Brand." *New York Times Magazine*, June 4, 2006.

Weber, Bruce. "Cheating Matters (Sometimes)." *New York Times*, December 16, 2007.

_____. "Instant Replay May Be Moving into Foul Territory." *New York Times*, August 31, 2008.

Will, George F. "Fielder of Dreams." Review of David Maraniss, *Clemente: The Passion and Grace of Baseball's Last Hero* (New York : Simon & Schuster, 2006). *New York Times Book Review*, May 7, 2006.

Williams, Michael G. "The Real House that Babe Ruth Built." *The Erickson Tribune* (Baltimore, MD), November 2008.

Wilson, Duff. "Friendlier Tone, but Plenty of Tough Talk." *New York Times,* January 16, 2008.

_____, and Michael S. Schmidt. "Report Ties Star Players to Baseball's 'Steroids Era.'" *New York Times*, December 14, 2007.

"Women Gain in Education but Not Power, Study Finds." *New York Times*, November 23, 2008.

"Women's Baseball Celebrated." *Kenosha* (WI) *News*, June 24, July 4, 5, 6, 7, 2008.

Zak, Dan. "The Girls of Summer: This Women's Baseball League Is the Real Deal — Now All It Needs Are Fans." *Washington Post*, May 27, 2007. Seen at *http://www.washington post.com.*

Zinser, Lynn. "Baseball and Softball Lobby for Return to Olympics." *New York Times*, November 15, 2008.

Zoll, Rachel. "Study: More Americans Say They Have No Religion." *Naples* (FL) *Daily News*, March 9, 2009.

Emails, Interviews, and Phone Calls

Ackmann, Martha. Personal email to the author, March 29, 2009.

Adler, Adriane. Personal email to the author, March 12, 2009.

Anonymous respondent from the AAUW Action Network. Personal email to the author, February 13, 2007.

Anonymous respondent from the Arizona Diamondbacks. Personal email to the author, September 11, 2008.

Arbuthnot, Cynthia. Personal email to the author, May 18, 2000.

Ardell, Jean Hastings. Personal email to the author, November 18, 2008.

Aronson, Anne. Personal emails to the author, January 3, 2008, March 3, 2009.

Bettencourt, Deb. Personal email to the author, March 1, 2009.

Bogard, Dick. Interview in Naples, Florida, March 7, 2009.

Bookhardt, Eric. Personal email to the author, May 18, 2000.

Buczynski, Katherine. Interview in Naples, Florida, September 10, 2008.

Carney, Gene. Personal emails to the author, November 4, 6, 7, 2008.

Cobb, Ron. Personal email to the author, July 7, 2008.

Everett, Michael. Personal email to the author, September 9, 2008.

Falk, William. Personal email to the author, July 24, 2008.

Garry, Ronald T. Interview in Naples, Florida, October 2, 2008.

Giffen, Tom. Personal emails to the author, February 24, 25, 27, 2009.

Glennie, Jim. Personal email to the author, December 4, 2007.

Higham, Harry. Interview in Cleveland, Ohio, June 28, 2008, and personal emails to the author August 28, 29, 30, 2008.

Howley, Brandan. Personal email to the author, May 19, 2000.

Igatlin, Laurie. Personal email to the author, May 17, 2000.

Kaplan, Ron. Personal email to the author, September 25, 2006.

Kates, Maxwell. Personal conversation, Toronto, August 7, 2005.

Kittel, Pat. Personal emails to the author, June 12, 2008.

Kovach, John M. Personal emails to the author, November 19, 20, 2008.

Marshall, Bill. Interview in Cleveland, Ohio, August 2009.

McCarthy, Tina and David. Personal emails to the author, September 1, 2008.

McCroskey, Dennis. Personal emails to the author, October 11, November 5, 6, 7, 2008.

Milliken, Jo Ann. Personal emails to the author, February 24, March 1, 2008.

Mitchem, Gary. Personal email to the author, September 25, 2008.
Motley, Byron. Personal email to the author, September 9, 2008.
Nemerovski, Jim. Personal emails to the author, October 11, 12, 13, 15, 30, December 19, 2008; January 1, 2, 2009.
Nola, Mike. Personal emails to the author, September 9, 10, 2008.
Ogurcak, Janice. Personal emails to the author, August 26, 31, November 1, 2008.
Oliver, Kent. Personal email to the author, March 5, 2008.
Petroski, Catherine. Personal email to the author, August 11, 2008.
Poplock, Mel. Personal emails to the author, August 27, 2008.
Rhoades, Nancy. Personal email to the author, March 19, 2009.
Rice, Mike. Personal email to the author, May 19, 2000.
Rinaldi, Marc A. Personal emails to the author, November 20, 2008, March 23, 2009.
Rodgers, Anne. Personal email to the author, April 22, 2009.
Sagert, Kelly Boyer. Personal email to the author, March 28, 2009.
Schecter, Brian, Personal email to the author, September 8, 2008.
_____. Personal phone call, September 10, 2008.
Shuman, Ed. Personal emails to the author, September 29, October 10, November 19, December 15, 2008.
Siegal, Justine. Personal emails to the author, March 7, April 30, May 6, 2009.
Sikorski, Sheila. Personal email to the author, April 7, 2009.
Snyder, Marjorie. Personal email to the author, March 20, 2009.
Soule, Oscar. Personal email to the author, September 17, 2008.
Tash, Max. Personal emails to the author, March 21, April 2, 2009.
Thomas, Joan. Personal email to the author, March 28, 2009.
Thomson, Cindy. Personal emails to the author, March 27, 2009.
Trimble, Joe. Personal interview with the author, Lakewood, Ohio, Summer 1956.
Van Sickle, Alexa. Personal email to the author, September 9, 2008.
Weaver, Ken and Paula. Personal email to the author, March 14, 2009.
Weinstein, Bob. Personal email. September 8, 2008.

Films, Dramas, Screenplays, Documentaries

Burns, Ken, with Lynn Novick. *Baseball.* Walpole, NH: Florentine Films, 1994.
_____, and Lynn Novick. "When Things Get Tough." Episode 2 of *The War: A Ken Burns Film.* Walpole, NH: Florentine Films, 2006.
Carney, Gene "Two Finger." *Mornings After.* A drama, with music by Lowell Kammer, presented live at the Society for American Baseball Research Convention, Toronto, August 6, 2005.
A City on Fire: The Story of the '68 Detroit Tigers. A film made for television, HBO Studio Productions, July 29, 2008.
The Life and Times of Hank Greenberg, a film directed by Aviva Kempner. 20th Century–Fox, 1999.
Marchiano, Sam, producer. *Baseball Discovered.* Documentary film by MLB, 2008.
"Mr. Monk Goes to the Ballgame." Film episode of *Monk* on DVD, Season 2, Episode 3, screened June 27, 2003.
The National Press Club: A Century of Headlines; A Documentary on the World's Largest and Most Prestigious Press Club and Its Impact on the History and Future of American and International Journalism. National Press Club, Washington, D.C., 100th Anniversary DVD, 2008.
"Reel Baseball 1899–1925: Baseball Films from the Silent Era." Collection of early films on DVD, produced in New York by Kino, 2008.

Siegel, Lois. Author/director. *Baseball Girls.* A film produced by Silva Basmajian. National Film Board of Canada, 1995. Available on DVD.

Signs of the Times: The Myth, The Mystery, The Legend of Baseball's Greatest Innovation. Don Casper and Jim Hughes, producers. Film documentary by Crystal Pix, Fairport, NY, 2008.

Tash, Max., director and filmmaker. *Girls of Summer.* Produced by IMDb Video. Shot in Cooperstown, New York, 2008.

Women Who Dare: Library of Congress 2009 Engagement Calendar. San Francisco: Pomegranate Communications, 2008.

Newsletters

AWSM: The Association for Women in Sports Media. *Newsletter,* Fall/Winter 2008; Spring 2009.

Bailey, Bob. "Grave Photos." *Nineteenth Century Notes,* a newsletter available to members via email. SABR: Fall 2008, 11.

Carson, Bob. *Minor Trips Newsletter.* Strongsville, Ohio, January 2006.

Foster, George G. *Fifteen Minutes Around New York,* 1854. Quoted in "A Glimpse of Elysian Fields, Hoboken, New Jersey." *Nineteenth Century Notes,* a SABR newsletter. Fall 2008: 7.

Heaphy, Leslie; Claudia Perry; and Justine Siegal. *Women's Baseball League,* a series of newsletters, 2005–2008.

Idelson, Jeff. "Growing Experience in Cooperstown (1980–2000)." *National Baseball Hall of Fame and Museum News,* 2007. A newsletter published in Cooperstown, New York.

Macht, Norman L. "Connie Mack and the Early Years of Baseball." Lincoln, NE, 2007. Quoted in *Nineteenth Century News,* a SABR newsletter. Fall 2008:4.

Mills, Dorothy Jane. *The HSC Baseball History Newsletter.* An emailed newsletter published to a list of subscribers 1998–2008.

Oral Presentations and Manuscripts

Bouton, Jim. Oral presentation at the SABR 36 Awards Luncheon, June 30, 2006, Courtyard Hotel, Seattle, Washington.

Bustad, Jacob. "'One-Hundred Per Cent American'; Nationalism, Masculinity, and American Legion Baseball in the 1920s." Paper read at the Fifteenth Annual *NINE* Spring Training Conference, March 2008. Conference Schedule, February 12, 2008.

Dellinger, Susan. Oral presentation on her book, *Red Legs and Black Sox* (Cincinnati: Ennis Books, 2008) at a SABR chapter meeting, Naples, Florida, March 6, 2009.

Johnson, Pamela. "The NAWBL: A League of Our Own." Manuscript dated September 28, 2007, received from Robin Wallace, March 5, 2009.

McPherson, Emily. "The Hard Way Home." Essay published with permission of the author. Courtesy of Adriane J. Adler of the East Coast Women's Baseball League via a personal email March 4, 2009.

Meyer, Sheldon. Personal correspondence with the author, on file in the Seymour Collection of the archives at the Krock Library, Cornell University.

Siegal, Justine. "A High School Female Baseball Player: A Case Study." Presentation at Women's Baseball Committee Meeting, SABR Convention, Cleveland, Ohio, August 2008.

Art and Music

Brodner, Steve. Cartoon for his blog reprinted in *Mother Jones,* March 2, 2007, and in the January/February issue, 2008.

Kelley, Steve. Cartoon for *New Orleans Times-Picayune* reprinted in *New York Times*, December 16, 2007.

Neville, Walter, of the Olympic B.B. Club of New York. *Hurrah for Our National Game.* (1869). Silverman, Jerry. *The Baseball Songbook.* Van Nuys, CA: Alfred Publishing, 2008: 18–21.

"Photo Finish," a display of photos of American Presidents. *Smithsonian,* April 2004, p. 124.

Photos of the Kenosha Event, a women's baseball weekend (Kenosha, Wisconsin, 2008), sent via email by Merrie Fidler, July 5, 2008.

Pamphlets, Press Releases, Handouts, Programs, Ads

American Sports University, Dan Bernardino, California. An undated pamphlet mailed in 2008.

Annual Convention Program, SABR 38, June 25–June 29, 2008. SABR, 2008, pp. 80–86.

Baseball Books. A pamphlet produced in Jefferson, NC: McFarland, 2005–2006.

Candy-Coated Popcorn, Peanuts, and a Prize. Handout at exhibit on Culinary Baseball by the Baseball Reliquary, Pomona Public Library, Pomona, California, 2003.

"Florida International Museum." *Baseball as America.* Press Release, October 16, 2001. *http://www.baseballasamerica.org/pr2003.*

"Genuine Big League Baseball Mud." Advertisement in *Elysian Fields Quarterly.* 25 (Spring 2008): 55.

The Graney Generation; A Celebration of the Life and Careers of Jack Graney, The First Player-Turned-Broadcaster. Morris Eckhouse, Editor. A Pamphlet dated September 28, 2003.

"It's Harder to Catch Up when You Start from Behind." Ad for the AAUW in *National NOW Times,* Fall 2008.

Join the Greatest Team Ever! Membership leaflet from the Baseball Hall of Fame and Museum, Cooperstown, New York, 2008.

MLB Insiders Club Fan Guide: Your Major League Baseball Travel Resource. Minnetonka, MN: 2009, MLB Insiders Club.

Shrine of the Eternals: 2008 Induction Day. Release from The Baseball Reliquary, July 9, 2008.

Siegal, Justine. *Women's College Friendship Game.* Program for game, Springfield, MA, May 3, 2009.

Where Baseball's Past and Present Unite. Brochure for visitors to the Cooperstown Baseball Hall of Fame and Library, 2007.

Wiley, Kate. "All-American Girls Professional Baseball League Slides into Smithsonian's National Museum of American History." *NMAH,* March 29, 2007. Press Release. *http://americanhistory.si.edu/news/*

Poems

Bronson, Daniel. "Oscar Charleston's Lament." *Elysian Fields Quarterly.* 24 (Fall 2007): 10.

Eisner, Keith. "Shall I Compare Thee to a Triple Play?" *The Minneapolis Review of Baseball.* 9 (Spring, 1990): 10.

Index

Numbers in **_bold italics_** indicate pages with illustrations.

Mechanics' Institute Library
3 1750 03371 9207